Praise for
Wayward

"Alice Greczyn's carefully detailed account of religious fundamentalism is a necessary addition to the literature surrounding spiritual abuse. As she charts her transition from a harmful framework to a more loving one, Greczyn honors the survivors of such trauma and provides a pathway for others to follow. I saw myself in many of these pages, and I'm grateful to see her continuing the important work of offering a safe space for those who have crossed the borders of faith and doubt."

—**Garrard Conley,** author of the *New York Times* best-selling memoir *Boy Erased*

"By turns soberly reflective and laugh-out-loud funny, Alice Greczyn's *Wayward* provides a refreshingly honest look at the psychologically abusive nature of evangelicalism in crisp, engaging prose. Greczyn writes with admirable self-awareness, and her memories of discomfort with the things evangelical ideology and leaders demanded of her, such as apologizing to all the boys on her Youth With a Mission team for 'accidentally flirting' and 'tempting' them, are deeply relatable to me as a survivor of the same toxic, purity-obsessed, authoritarian Christianity. Episodes like this may be shocking to readers unfamiliar with evangelical subculture. If so, I hope they will take what they learn and demand that the American public sphere at long last take the voices of ex-evangelicals and other former fundamentalists seriously."

—**Chrissy Stroop,** PhD, co-editor of the award-winning anthology *Empty the Pews*

"In secular circles, much of our discourse tends to be cerebral, promoting arguments for reason and rationality. In *Wayward*, Alice Greczyn brings another invaluable element to the conversation: the art of telling a deeply human story. As Alice draws you into her life and her world, you will smile, you will cry, and you will be riveted by her intelligence, her insight, and her courage. And if you are young and struggling with issues of faith, belief, and identity, you will know that you are not alone. *Wayward* isn't just a book you read. It is a book you *feel*—with every beautifully written page. A truly towering achievement."

—**Ali A. Rizvi,** author of *The Atheist Muslim: A Journey from Religion to Reason*

"Alice Greczyn's stirring memoir *Wayward* vividly illustrates the experience of growing up in the frenzied fold of Charismatic Christianity. From her childhood in the rural plains of the Midwest, where a life ruled by God was all she knew, to the red carpets of Hollywood, where she found herself calling into question everything she once believed to be true, Greczyn shares her story with brave vulnerability. Her journey will become required reading for those seeking to heal from religious trauma, recover a sense of purpose, and rebuild a life worth living."

—**Jessica Wilbanks,** author of *When I Spoke in Tongues: A Story of Faith and Its Loss*

"*Wayward* is a deeply compelling coming-of-age story about a young woman groomed to passively follow men's directions (directions they swear God gave to them for her) as she journeys from faith in a patriarchal religion to doubt, and from doubt in herself to faith."

—**Linda Kay Klein,** author of *Pure: Inside the Evangelical Movement That Shamed a Generation of Young Women and How I Broke Free*

"Religions may disagree on a lot, but one thing they agree on is how essential it is that a woman remain pure and chaste until it's time to be subservient to her husband. In Alice Greczyn's beautifully written memoir, she describes how dehumanizing it is to be viewed as—and to view ourselves as—an object precariously perched atop a 'pedestal of purity.' Alice's story of how, with the help of a jar of cinnamon, she stood up and walked her own path is both heartbreaking and inspiring. I'm sure her brave example will console others who dare to doubt."

—Yasmine Mohammed, author of
Unveiled: How Western Liberals Empower Radical Islam

"Alice Greczyn's vivid memoir is a personal and engaging story of one woman's struggle to escape and heal from the Christianity of her youth, while at the same time providing intelligent insights into the scientific analysis of her experience. I was moved by her description of intense efforts as a child to have charismatic experiences and then impressed by her grasp of the neuropsychology involved."

—Marlene Winell, PhD, psychologist, and author of
*Leaving the Fold: A Guide for Former Fundamentalists
and Others Leaving Their Religion*

a memoir of

Wayward

spiritual warfare & sexual purity

alice greczyn

RIVER GROVE
BOOKS

This book is a memoir reflecting the author's present recollections of experiences over time. Its story and its words are the author's alone. Some details and characteristics may be changed, some events may be compressed, and some dialogue may be recreated.

Published by River Grove Books
Austin, TX
www.rivergrovebooks.com

Distributed by River Grove Books

Design and composition by Greenleaf Book Group
Cover design by Greenleaf Book Group
Cover Images from The National Agricultural Library, The Beinecke Rare Book & Manuscript Library, Biodiversity Heritage Library courtesy of The Public Domain Review

Publisher's Cataloging-in-Publication data is available.

Print ISBN: 978-1-63299-354-0

eBook ISBN: 978-1-63299-355-7

First Edition

*To anyone who has ever dared to doubt
their belief system, this book is for you.*

Contents

Author's Note

The tricky thing about memory is that it is subjective, malleable. Some neuroscientists used to suspect that once a memory is constructed, it isn't easily changed. Newer data reveals the opposite: that our memories change as we need them to, as others influence them, and even as they are formed. Stress and trauma can distort how our brains record and store memory. This makes the writing of a memoir a brave and foolish undertaking; a work of art as raw and authentic as it is fallible and fragmentary.

Memoir rides the line between fact and fiction, account and story, autobiography and revealing tale. A memoir is one person's narrative of what happened. As most people can attest, individuals sharing the same experience can come away with extraordinarily different understandings. I've done my best to stay as true to verifiable facts as I can. Journal entries, letters, and internet searches affirm much of what I retained and share in the following pages. Non-verifiable impressions, including the recreation of dialogue and the perceived emotions of characters, are subjective truths. They are my truths, forged under my perceptions, as everyone's memories are. Certain names and identifying details have been changed to protect others' privacy. Everything else is my sincerest recollection.

Prologue

I banged my head against the concrete wall. My panic subsided with every dull thud, replaced by a numbness that felt like mercy. *Thud. Thud.* The back of my scalp was bleeding a little, but I knew my hair would cover it. That was why I didn't cut myself. I was a TV and film actress, and I never knew when a job might require me to be in a swimsuit. The knives in my kitchen tempted me, just as my parents' knives had tempted me to slit my wrists when I was thirteen, but the thickness of my dark hair covered my self-inflicted wounds less conspicuously than bandages. I touched the back of my head with my fingertips. Blood was a comforting reminder of my mortality. *Life will all be over one day*, the red droplets whispered.

I was twenty-one years old in the fall of 2007. My panic attacks had been a nightly occurrence for nearly two weeks. I didn't know then what a panic attack was, or why I felt too afraid of the world to leave my home, even to get food. I didn't connect the dots of the terror I was experiencing to my Christian upbringing.

My skull buzzed from the slamming. My heart rate slowed. I felt dizzy, peaceful. A dreamlike high of endorphins swept over me, lulling my aching body into the limpness of relief. For a moment, I felt like laughing. A giggle escaped my mouth, followed by a fearful whimper. My sliver of tranquility faded with panic's return. It slithered from my gut to my neck, crushing my lungs and making them beg for air. Panic bore its way through the haze of my body's natural painkillers, and I tried to fight it, but panic won, forcing me to my feet. I paced my loft in circles. Time didn't exist those nights. When I needed a break from my relentless walk, I slapped myself as hard as I could until my face tingled with shock. For a moment, I could hold still. My lungs drained empty. My heart pounded between my ears. Peace lasted only a few seconds before panic forced me to pace again, wringing my arms and contorting them into twisted shapes. When I wanted them to stop, I threw my hand into my mouth and bit down as hard as I could, my knuckles raw from where I chewed them earlier. I kept chewing until I tasted the rusty tang of broken scabs.

Sometimes I felt like there were two of me: the girl going insane and the observer who watched her, helpless, yet indifferent. Without God, there was no longer a point to life.

PART I

For though we live in the world,
we do not wage war as the world does.
2 Corinthians 10:3

Do not get drunk on wine . . .
Instead, be filled with the Spirit.
Ephesians 5:18

1

The Lord's Army

"Attennnnntion!" hollered the children's pastor, a smiling young woman we called Miss Valerie. I joined the clamor of a dozen or so kindergartners lining up in even rows to face her. "Knock your feet together," she said. The rubber of tennis shoes squeaked into place. "Right hands to your eyebrows." Everyone mirrored her military salute. "And march!" We stomped our feet while our young voices belted the stirring tune.

> *I may never march in the infantry*
> *Ride in the cavalry*
> *Shoot the artillery*
> *I may never fly o'er the enemy*
> *But I'm in the Lord's army*
> *Yes, sir!*

It was my favorite song. Every time I sang it, I fantasized about riding a penny-colored horse into battle amid cannon blasts, like a soldier in the movie *Glory* that Mom and Dad liked to watch. My siblings and I weren't allowed to see the Civil War film, but one time I claimed to have accidentally forgotten a toy in the living room so I could sneak a peek at the TV screen. The guilt of lying made my ears prickle, but the combat scenes accompanied by sweeping music mesmerized me. I didn't know the gruesome effects of real warfare. I just thought Denzel Washington and Matthew Broderick looked handsome with their navy uniforms and bayonetted rifles, their brows furrowed and voices tense with a sense of mission. I wanted to be part of a mission. Singing "I'm in the Lord's Army" was as close as I could get.

After my peers and I finished the song and took our seats on the worn carpet, Miss Valerie explained the deeper meaning behind the lyrics. They gave me my life's purpose.

"There's a war going on between God and Satan," Miss Valerie said. "Satan wants to hurt you. He wants to steal your souls away from God. But God's on *your* side. He wants you to join His army and help Him beat Satan and his bad guys, the demons. Does anyone know how we do this?"

Miss Valerie's ominous expression made me squirm on my heels. I shook my head, eager and a little scared to learn how I could help God fight Satan. A girl raised her hand.

"What are the demons?" she asked.

"Demons," Miss Valerie said, "are the angels God banished from heaven when he sent Satan to hell. They're the bad angels. We have the good angels on our team. Does anyone know how we can help God's angels by being good teammates? No?"

She opened her Bible and read from the book of Ephesians. "'Put on the full armor of God so that when the day of evil comes—'" She paused to look up at us. "That means when Satan and his demons come. 'You may be able to stand your ground. Stand firm with the belt of truth buckled around your waist, with the breastplate of righteousness in place, and with your feet fitted with the readiness that comes from the gospel of peace. Take up the shield of faith, with which you can extinguish all the flaming arrows of the evil one. Take the helmet of salvation and the sword of the Spirit, which is the word of God.'"

Most of the verse went over our heads, but Miss Valerie was a creative teacher. She set down her Bible and grinned at us. "I brought toys."

We all cheered. From a box, Miss Valerie pulled out several kid-sized medieval armor pieces. "First," she said, holding up a plastic silver belt. "We have the belt of truth. It's very important to always tell the truth. When we tell lies, we give Satan power, and his army advances. But when we tell the truth, God's army advances."

Miss Valerie handed the christened belt of truth to a boy sitting in the front row, telling him to pass it around.

We took turns trying on the props as Miss Valerie described what they symbolized. "The breastplate of righteousness," she said, "means that we always need to do what is right. You know the bad feeling you get when you know you're doing something wrong? That's God reminding you that you're letting Satan get closer. God gave us feelings so we can understand what the Holy Spirit is trying to tell us, so we stay fighting on God's side."

I knew the bad feeling she was talking about. I didn't like it, especially now that I knew the feeling meant Satan was getting closer. I imagined a hideous monkey with horns, decaying flesh, and red eyes creeping up behind me. I wouldn't be sneaking peeks at *Glory* anymore. Not if my prickly feeling of guilt meant I was letting Satan's army advance.

"The shoes on your feet should always lead you to walk in peace," Miss Valerie continued. "God doesn't like fighting. He doesn't like when you argue with your parents. He doesn't like when you're mean to other kids. Jesus said, 'Blessed are the peacemakers.' Do you want to be peacemakers?"

I nodded with everyone else, but something didn't sound right. If God wanted us to be peacemakers, why was He calling us into His army to fight?

Miss Valerie held up a plastic shield with a coat of arms stamped on its front. "The shield of faith is one of your most important tools in God's army," she said. "There are people out there who don't believe in Jesus, and Satan's going to use them to try and get you. If you ever doubt God's love, you let Satan win. Faith is the weapon you need to block out his evil arrows."

I promised myself I would never doubt God's love.

Miss Valerie explained that the helmet of salvation was our belief that Jesus died on the cross for our sins. "You don't want to sin, do you?"

We shook our heads.

"Good. And last, we have the sword of the Spirit."

Several kids ooh-ed and aah-ed over the grand finale of armor, clamoring to be the first to hold the plastic weapon.

"The sword of the Spirit is God's word," Miss Valerie said. "How many of you have your own Bible?"

My hand rose, along with several others.

"Very good," said Miss Valerie. "The Bible is your sword, and with it, you can kill thousands of demons. Satan's afraid of God's word, because he knows it contains the truth. So whenever you're feeling scared, you just read your Bible and Satan will run away."

I imagined flinging open my illustrated children's Bible at the horned monkey and watching him scuttle into the shadows.

"And remember," Miss Valerie continued. "There are people out there who don't believe in God, and they're going to try to destroy you with doubt. Satan appears as an angel of light, a good angel, so even if they're saying things that sound true or feel good, you need to turn away from them. Memorize Scripture so you can be prepared to defend your faith. You have the truth. This is your sword, and with it, you can help God's army grow and beat Satan and his evil bad guys!"

I wasn't much of a cheerer, but even I was swept into the victorious whooping.

On our way out the door when children's ministry ended, Miss Valerie handed us each a sheet of paper with a picture of a medieval soldier printed on it. She'd written down what each piece of his armor symbolized according to her Bible lesson. "This is to remind you to suit up in your armor every day," she said. "Truth, righteousness, peace, faith, salvation, and the Bible."

I committed the picture to memory. I would be a good soldier in the Lord's army.

~

People would always say I took things too seriously. My faith in partic-ular left no room for mistakes, not when the consequences were heaven or hell. That night in my children's ministry class was the first time I can remember being taught how to wage spiritual warfare. From a young age, I understood being a Christian was a grave matter.

I was seven years old the first time I questioned God's goodness. My family had gone to visit a Baptist church no one can remember the name of. There was no Sunday school for children, so I was sitting in the pew when the pastor opened his sermon with the story of how his two-year-old daughter had accidentally suffocated to death in a dry-cleaning bag.

"I didn't understand how God could let something like this happen," the man said, tears pouring from his eyes. "But the Lord asked me to have the faith of Job."

Job, I learned, was a man in the Bible whom God allowed Satan to torment by killing Job's family, among other tribulations. God wanted to prove to Satan that Job's faith would remain solid no matter what. Seeing the pastor cry made me cry, and back at home, my mind refused to let go of the image of a toddler gasping for air in a clear dry-cleaning bag. It could have been one of my brothers or sisters. My belief in God's omnipotence and my horror at the things He allowed collided for the first time. I found Dad in the dining room, his lanky frame bent over the table as he read his Bible.

"Dad," I said. "Why did God kill the little girl?"

"Oh, he didn't kill her, honey," Dad said. "He allowed her to die."

"But why didn't he save her?"

Dad cleared his throat. "Well," he said. "Sometimes God does things we don't understand."

"But he can do anything," I said.

"Yes, He's all-powerful. There's nothing in the world God can't do."

"Then why didn't He stop her from suffocating?"

Dad explained that sometimes God challenged us by allowing bad things to happen, and we wouldn't always get to understand His ways.

Outrage surged through me at this perceived injustice. I didn't have the vocabulary to share my feelings with Dad.

"But God loves us," Dad continued. "And everything He allows in our lives is to bring us closer to Him."

It occurred to me that maybe Dad wasn't being truthful. Maybe he knew the real reason God allowed bad things to happen and he just didn't want to tell me. Maybe he thought I was too young. Troubled and unconvinced, I gave up asking why God had allowed the little girl to suffocate. It didn't make sense to me that God would let such a thing happen and then not even comfort her parents by telling them why. Either Dad was lying to me or God wasn't as loving as he thought.

~

My family of seven lived in Rockford, Illinois, a once-thriving industrial city that had lost its sense of purpose. Our house was a shabby but striking Victorian peeling with paint and surrounded by tall oak trees. I loved it from the moment I saw its gingerbread trim. A turret curved along one corner, where floor-to-ceiling windows spilled sunlight over the designs of a parquet floor. Three slate fireplaces, crown molding around every window, and a spiral staircase that wound four stories high made me feel like I lived in a castle. The Victorian would be the only place that ever truly felt like home to me.

The church my family attended was called Vine City Fellowship. Vine City wasn't an average church with two services on a Sunday morning. Neither did its members like referring to their gatherings as church, opting for the less formal term "fellowship" to describe their Saturday night assemblies in the basketball gym of a local school. Potlucks were called "common meals," Sunday school was called "children's ministry," and the people of Vine City thought of Jesus as a salt of the earth dude who didn't need His followers to dress up for Him. They encouraged a come-as-you-are environment emphasizing Jesus' love for the downtrodden and outcast.

My parents, who had been missionaries and pastors in the Foursquare Gospel Church, liked that Vine City was nondenominational. Though the fellowship had roots in the Vineyard denomination, which had further roots in Pentecostalism, my parents and the people of Vine City felt God could move more freely when we didn't limit Him with branch doctrine.

For all of their emphasis on being nondenominational, Vine City's members seemed to like thinking of themselves as a Messianic Jewish congregation with Pentecostal leanings. Like Messianic Jews, we practiced certain traditions of Judaism while believing Jesus to be the Messiah. Like Pentecostals, we let our services be guided by the spontaneity of the Holy Spirit. Ours was the kind of church where people danced and waved streamers during worship, where young and old alike skipped down the aisles carrying homemade banners emblazoned with the Lion of Judah. We celebrated Christian holidays, like Easter and Christmas, and Jewish holy days, like Passover and Rosh Hashanah. I went to Jewish dance classes and Hebrew summer camp. Dad said it was important for Christians to stay close to their Jewish roots. After all, Jesus had been a Jew.

People would always ask why my parents decided to homeschool my siblings and me. Was it for religious reasons, they wondered? Did my parents not trust the government? The truth was that Mom simply enjoyed teaching. My college-educated mother happened to be a good teacher. I wouldn't be able to appreciate until I was an adult how well rounded her homeschool regimen was compared to others. In some circles in the early '90s, teaching one's children at home bordered on child neglect. Mom's diligence kept us prepared in case a social worker ever came knocking. When I picture a typical homeschool day, I see Mom cooking at the kitchen stovetop with a wooden spoon in hand and a teacher's curriculum on the counter, my siblings and me gathered around the yellowed oak table. Mom's faded linen apron over navy blue sweatpants is the uniform she wears in my memory; her cola-colored hair scrunchied into a bun with a cowlick of bangs arching above her freckles. Dad called the arch her "quail tail." His brown eyes always twinkled when he bopped it.

I never stopped wondering what it would have been like to go to school. As the eldest of five, my two brothers and two sisters gave me constant playmates, so I rarely felt deprived of social interaction. When we went to Vine City on Saturday nights, I felt the sting of how sheltered I was. The jokes I didn't get and school gossip I couldn't follow excluded me from most conversations. My parents forbade me from most of pop culture, so whenever my peers debated *FernGully, Home Alone,* and *Jumanji,* I had two choices: pretend to know what they were talking about and risk being exposed as a dweeb, or remain in the background. I usually opted to remain in the background.

On the ice was the only place I ever felt cool; the only place I felt I stood out among my peers in a good way. I'd been taking figure skating lessons since I was four. Whenever school kids came to the rink for field trips, their mouths dropped when they saw me land a sequence of jumps or when they admired my ice-scarring spins. Sometimes a few kids even asked for my autograph, thinking I might be the next Oksana Baiul. I secretly hoped so. I loved skating. The cold rush of wind in my hair and the sparkly costumes I wore in competitions made me dream of being an Olympic gold medalist, like Kristi Yamaguchi. The trophies on my dresser told me I might have a shot if I worked hard enough.

My two best friends were Danika Muller and Bethany Andersen. Their families also went to Vine City, and while Danika wasn't always there and Bethany was a year younger than me, we played a lot because our parents were good friends. Every weekend seemed to include a sleepover at someone's house. I liked going to Danika's because she made me laugh until I cried, and her mom made the best sunny-side-up eggs. I liked going to Bethany's because she enjoyed inventing businesses with me, from lemonade stands to church newspapers, and her mom always had chocolate chip cookies.

My mom was what she proudly called "a homemaker." My dad, a former police officer and pastor, operated a self-owned snack vending business. My parents loved the freedom self-employment offered. There was nowhere they would rather be than in the great outdoors, and on weekdays with good weather, the seven of us enjoyed the emptiness of state parks and visitor's center museums. Sometimes Mom brought our schoolbooks with us, so she could instruct us on picnic blankets while we took turns fishing, or drill us with spelling bees before treating us to cider doughnuts at a local orchard. Mom never failed to turn an outing into a fun learning event.

By the time I was eight, I had grown comfortable with the routine that shaped the elementary years of my childhood. I homeschooled and ice-skated Monday through Friday, went to Vine City Fellowship on Saturdays, and usually did something outdoorsy with my family on Sundays. I didn't know it then, but these were the years I would one day yearn for, the memories of stability I would cling to as God started asking my parents to do unstable things.

2

Signs and Wonders

I n January of 1994, on the snow-covered plains of Ontario, Canada, a spiritual revival was birthed that would change my family forever. It would come to be known as the Toronto Blessing. Some say it began when a pastor named Randy Clark prayed over a small congregation in the outskirts of Toronto. The Holy Spirit fell upon them, and just like the first Pentecost in the book of Acts, the worshippers were bathed in laughter and weeping. The professed anointing spread to other local churches, and then to churches farther still. By the time the Toronto Blessing reached my fellowship in Rockford, the movement was fast on its way to becoming a worldwide phenomenon. It changed Vine City in a matter of weeks. We had always been a tongues-speaking church, but the Toronto Blessing allowed the power of God's Spirit to fully unleash in ways that reminded me of the Great Awakenings in my homeschool history books. The first time I watched grown-ups seize and fall to the floor frightened me. Soon, the symptoms of God's touch became just another Saturday night.

Adults called it being slain by the Spirit. They likened being slain to being drunk, and the manifestations of the Spirit did indeed mimic symptoms of alcohol intoxication, with raucous laughter and uncontrollable weeping accompanying the slurred words and staggered gaits of those affected. "Get drunk in the Spirit!" became a popular catchphrase, not unlike the "Get high on Jesus!" slogan from the revivals of the '60s and '70s.

I never got slain by the Spirit. I desperately wanted to be.

Perhaps no one was more famous for pouring out the wine of the Spirit than evangelist Rodney Howard-Browne. I was ten when my parents took me to see the self-proclaimed Holy Ghost bartender. Rodney Howard-Browne was known for his ability to channel God's sense of humor, and Spirit-led fits of the giggles interrupted the schedule of many a conference where he was present. These mass giggle fits were called Holy Laughter. When Dad encouraged me to receive prayer from the man who could send people howling to the floor with the point of his finger, I knew that if the Holy Spirit would slay me through anyone, it would be him.

Mr. Howard-Brown was puffy-chested and red-faced with a thick neck constrained by a tie. He doled out Holy Laughter from the stage as I made my way toward him, watching with nervousness as people were yanked backward by an invisible force. They landed on the floor in breathless states of delirium. I worried being slain might hurt, but Mom told me it didn't because God cushioned people's bodies supernaturally when they fell. I reached an opening that allowed Mr. Howard-Browne to see me. He seemed excited to spot a child among the throng of adults, motioning me up the center stairs leading to the stage he stood on. I was almost to the top when his meaty hand fell on my head and stopped me. I stood with my arms limp at my side, focusing on Mr. Howard-Browne's belt buckle. It felt like everyone's eyes were on me.

"Bless your little one, Lord," Mr. Howard-Browne said into the mic. Then he launched into a repetition of words inviting the Spirit to slay me. "More new wine, yes Lord. The power of God, the fire of the Holy Ghost. Yes Lord, yes Lord, yes Lord."

I waited for the rush of the Holy Spirit that I was sure would hit me at any second. It felt like minutes passed, and I knew I was taking longer than anyone else had to fall. Mr. Howard-Browne's voice grew louder, as though he commanded the Spirit to hurry up. The weight of his hand forced my head into an awkward angle and my neck muscles started to ache. I scrunched up my shoulders to relieve the pain, but it wasn't enough. I stepped down one stair. Mr. Howard-Browne's hand moved with me. Then I realized his pressure was deliberate.

I barely finished the thought when my neck gave way under his sudden force. Mr. Howard-Browne's fingers pressed into my temples as he crushed me like a soda can, causing purple stars to blind me and a searing pain to shoot from the base of my skull through my neck. I crumpled on the stairs, my hands and knees landing on different steps. My vision came back in pulses. Humiliation coursed through my body in hot waves. Or was it anger?

I strained to look up at Mr. Howard-Browne, desperate to hope that maybe it had been an accident and he'd apologize for hurting me. He was in the middle of celebrating God's power.

"Hallelujah," he said. "Glory to God. Thank you, Jesus."

Then he looked down at me. His eyes seemed to glare with a warning, as if to say, "Make me look good."

Maybe I imagined it. Maybe I misread the slight rise of his eyebrows or mistook the snarl in his lip for a threat. Whatever I saw, it compelled my body to respond with automatic obedience. I quickly lay myself on the steps, closing my eyes as I had seen all of the others do before me. I did not laugh. When it felt like enough time had passed, I quietly made my way back to my chair and decided never to tell my parents what happened. Who would believe that a famous pastor had pushed a little girl down a flight of stairs?

There was another reason I didn't want to say anything: If anyone knew the Holy Spirit hadn't been the one to push me over, they'd know there was something wrong with me. There must be something wrong with me. Everyone else had been slain in less than a minute.

~

My parents hadn't always been Christians.

My dad, Ted, grew up in a woodsy part of central New Jersey where people's accents sounded more Philly than New York. Monday was "Mondee," Tuesday was "Tchewsdee." My siblings and I still poke fun at the way Dad says "orange" with a soft-vowel "o" that makes him sound like a pirate. Although Dad dutifully attended Sunday services with his family growing up, he wouldn't consider himself a Christian until he developed his own relationship with God at the age of twenty-seven, when Jesus healed his shattered leg from a motorcycle accident. The accident occurred when Dad got off his night shift as a police officer in Berkeley, California. I heard the story of Dad's accident so many times that I could almost recite it by heart.

"It was the Ides of March," Dad always began. He relished any chance to lace symbolism and metaphor into his speech. "I'd just gotten off my graveyard shift, and it was a beautiful Northern California morning, poppies blooming everywhere. All of a sudden, a jackrabbit ran across the road and startled me. My bike started to skid, so I put my left foot out, and I didn't see the pothole coming up. My foot got caught in it and just snapped."

The spinning of Dad's tires sent him flying through the air, landing him in a patch of stinging nettle that felt like fire on his cuts. He tried to stand up but couldn't. He felt a burst of anger at God.

"Come down!" he shouted at the sky. "What am I supposed to learn from this?"

Dad hadn't given God much thought. Now that he was badly injured and stranded in a ditch, God was all he could think about.

Another motorcyclist spotted Dad's fallen bike. The grizzled biker found an ambulance less than a mile away, a fluke Dad thought was more than just coincidence, and it took him to the hospital where doctors operated on his broken leg. Steel screws were inserted to hold Dad's bones together, but weeks after the surgery, there was still no callus buildup around the fracture, which was necessary for Dad's leg to heal. He began to worry he'd lose his job. He couldn't be a police officer if he walked with a limp. Dad showed up to work anyway, propping his throbbing leg on a chair as he typed a morning report. Then he felt Jesus speak to him.

"Ted, what did you learn from all this?"

The question reverberated through his soul. Dad had been reading Merlin R. Carothers's *Power in Praise* ever since his accident. He wanted to make sense of why God had allowed his leg to be broken, and *Power in Praise* offered an explanation. The Christian book described how God could change our lives for the better when we praised Him for the challenges He brought. Dad concluded the motorcycle accident was his challenge, and that God was using his broken leg to get his attention.

Sitting at his desk in the police station, Dad asked Jesus to come into his heart. "Right away," Dad always said, "I felt this tingling in my leg, like an arm waking up from being asleep. The next time I had an x-ray, the doctors couldn't believe it. There wasn't even a fracture line where my break had been."

Dad was able to keep his job after his leg healed. He never walked with a limp.

My mom, Jane, rarely spoke about her past with me, or about how and why she came to Christianity. She maintains a very private life and out of respect for her wishes, I will not share more about her in these pages than I find necessary. Mom found love in what she once described as God. The God she came to know as an adult was and is different from the God I knew as a child. We didn't talk much about these differences while I was growing up. I assumed the God my mother worshipped was the same every other adult around me seemed to worship. Only in adulthood would I learn that Mom's relationship with God was as unique to her as everything else about the woman who raised me. Ever-seclusive, Mom never felt the need to explain her beliefs or justify her decisions to anyone.

My parents met in the early 1980s. My twenty-one-year-old mother was a student in her senior year, and my father, twenty-eight, patrolled the UC Berkeley campus. Since Mom was a police aide, a job that involved escorting students back to their dorms from classes in the evenings, she knew of the police officer named Ted Greczyn who all her female coworkers fawned over. Mom thought he was the most handsome man she'd ever seen. She never thought he'd be interested in her, but my father had noticed the half-Asian brunette with freckles.

One afternoon at a street stoplight, Dad pulled his policeman's motorcycle alongside Mom's brand-new Yamaha 750. She bought the bike as a graduation present for herself, even though she could barely work its clutch.

"Where do you think you're going on that thing?" Dad asked her with a teasing smile.

"All over America," Mom shot back.

Dad loved her feisty spirit, and as a matter of fact, he wanted to road trip all over America, too.

"If you wanna learn how to ride," Dad said, "give me call."

I always imagine my father writing his number on a blank traffic ticket. Mom called him a few days later. She discovered riding on the back of Dad's motorcycle was preferable to operating one herself. Dad didn't mind when she wrapped her arms around him on their weekend trips up the Pacific Coast Highway.

Five years after they married, with their growing family in tow, they quit their jobs to be missionaries in Thailand and Nepal. When the funds supporting us ran dry nine months later, Dad accepted a pastorship position at a small Foursquare Gospel church in Rockford, Illinois. We didn't know anyone there, but my parents viewed the opportunity as a door God was opening. He would always be doing that, opening and closing doors. God never wanted my family in one place for long before He uprooted us to go somewhere else.

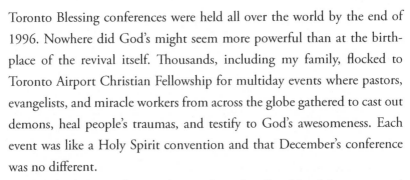

Toronto Blessing conferences were held all over the world by the end of
1996. Nowhere did God's might seem more powerful than at the birth-
place of the revival itself. Thousands, including my family, flocked to
Toronto Airport Christian Fellowship for multiday events where pastors,
evangelists, and miracle workers from across the globe gathered to cast out
demons, heal people's traumas, and testify to God's awesomeness. Each
event was like a Holy Spirit convention and that December's conference
was no different.

The day began with an explosion of worship. Bass blared from surround
sound speakers, and the crowd jumped in unison as people lifted their light-
ers like they were at a rock concert. Testimonies usually came after worship,
when speakers from around the world shared the challenges and miracles
they faced as missionaries and pastors. I half-listened as they testified to how
God overcame their obstacles, from setting up orphanages in Mozambique
to converting entire villages to Christianity. Winter's darkness had fallen by
the time they finished. I was absorbed in a game of tic-tac-toe with my sister Madeleine when I realized a worship team was climbing back on stage.
Dread clutched my stomach. It was time to get slain.

The keyboardist let out a long, synthesized note. The drummer tinkled
the chimes hanging above his snare. A female backup singer moaned into
her microphone and the eerie tone was set. John Arnott, the fellowship's
senior pastor, walked to the side of the stage with a mic in hand. I knew
he was about to announce the call-to-prayer. The call-to-prayer was what
I called the last act of a conference, when the pastor or speaker invited the
congregation to receive the Holy Spirit. Sure enough, Mr. Arnott faced
the crowd.

"If you'd like to receive the anointing of the Spirit," he said, "a vision
from God, or a healing, please make your way to the back of the auditorium where our elders will pray for you."

I had attended countless Toronto Blessing conferences by the time I was nearly eleven. The Holy Spirit still refused to slay me. I could usually sense when the call-to-prayer was coming, and ever since Rodney Howard-Browne had pushed me on the stairs, I pretended to have fallen asleep to avoid having to participate. I was too late this time. Dad saw me, wide awake.

"Why don't you go up for prayer, moppet?"

"I'm in the middle of my game," I said.

"Oh, c'mon," Dad said. "God might have something for you."

Sighing, I threw down my pen and huffed past him. Dad never urged the other kids to go up for prayer and I figured it was because I was the oldest. I tried to lose him in the shuffling crowd making its way to where the elders awaited us. Elders were like sub-pastors, standing beside long rows of tape stuck to the floor for people to stand on when they received prayer. The rows were spaced about six feet apart so that people wouldn't fall on each other when they got slain. I found a row where Dad wouldn't fit, lining up my toes evenly on the green stripe and eyeing the assortment of socks around me. All were encouraged to take off their shoes if they received prayer, since people often kicked when slain and this would help minimize bodily damage. I closed my eyes and assumed the position, extending my hands out in front of me, palms up. I rocked gently from side to side, hoping I looked deep in intercession with God as I listened to the elders make their way down the rows, person by fallen person. The music coming from the stage was a slow song pulsed by a heavy drumbeat. It matched the spooky atmosphere.

My heart skipped anxiously when I sensed an elder get to the man on my right. He wore silky-looking gray socks. That meant I was next. I couldn't help listening as the elder, a menopausal woman with a raspy voice, threw all sorts of prayer at the man beside me.

"You're very sick," she yelled, even though he was right there. "You've been sick a long time and God wants to heal you! Do you want to be healed? Are you ready for a healing!?"

She sounded like a chain-smoking cheerleader. I cracked my eyes open and peered as inconspicuously as I dared. The man shook with his eyes closed as the elder clutched his hands. Her eyes were closed as well, and I thought about how she had taken the time to apply makeup and curl her rusty-blond hair that morning. Another elder, a sturdy-looking fellow, stood behind the gray-socked man, ready to catch him when he got slain. It was quite a system they had, those elders. They must have partnered up in pairs beforehand. The elder in front of the prayer receiver was the prophet, while the elder who followed behind was the catcher.

The gray-socked man finally went down. He didn't seize backwards, like some of the people around me were doing. He just tipped back and the catcher slid him to the floor, calm and sleepy. He lay limp at my side while the prophet lady smiled with satisfaction and murmured approval. Then it was my turn.

I shut my eyes again and concentrated on looking Spirit-filled. The prophet lady's cold, knobby hands touched mine. She prayed in tongues for a minute. "Clambio skipee dee dee dee," she said. "Mosquavedo clee dee dee dee."

I waited to hear what else she would have to say to me, what God would have to say to me through her. I reminded myself not to expect anything, but I prayed in earnest. *Slay me, God. I'm ready and waiting. Welcome, Holy Spirit.*

The spittle flying out of the prophet lady's mouth distracted me, landing on exposed parts of my skin. Her breath smelled like mothballs. When she switched from tongues to English, she didn't yell at me like she did to the gray-socked man. "You're a very sad girl," she said. "God wants you to give Him all your cares and loneliness, all your fears and suffering. He has a vision for you, but you have to be ready to receive it. Are you ready?"

A thrill ran through me. I nodded.

The prophet elder went back to speaking in tongues as I wondered what my vision would be. From what I knew, visions were like daydreams that didn't come from one's own imagination, but from God. The prophet lady prayed over me for a long time. No visions came to mind unsummoned.

My excitement turned to disappointment when I realized a full song had played. I tried to sense God's presence, but I felt nothing but the prophet lady's hands on mine, and the fingertips of the catcher poking into the back of my ribs. When another song finished, I finally admitted that God wasn't going to give me a vision. Maybe He changed His mind. Maybe He never had a vision for me at all. I'd been a fool to think this call-to-prayer would be any different.

An angry restlessness surged through me at the understanding that I was refused by God and sandwiched by the elders. I felt trapped. The prophet lady yelled in my face, gripping my wrists so hard I knew marks would be left by her fingernails. The catcher's potbelly bumped into my back from behind. My heart raced as I tried to figure how to get out of their snare, for I knew they wouldn't leave me alone until the Holy Spirit visibly slayed me. The thought made me want to groan. Then, one of the prophet lady's hands moved from my wrist to my forehead. My eyes sprang open in panic as her entire palm pressed against my head so that my neck wanted to buckle. Instantly, my body remembered Rodney Howard-Browne doing the same thing. Never again. If God wanted to slay me, He would have, and since that wasn't happening, there was only one thing left to do. I had to fake it.

I let my panic wash over me, causing my whole body to shiver.

"Yes!" the prophet lady shouted. "Here it comes!"

I quivered my hands and made exaggerated jerking movements, hoping they passed for the touch of the Holy Spirit.

"Yes!" she shouted.

I threw in a violent body shudder.

"Let the waves wash over her, almighty Jesus!"

The prophet lady's voice rose even higher, so I figured I was doing a convincing job. I shook my head like it was vibrating and made grunting sounds as though someone were punching me in the gut. My anxiety had turned to fuel. I didn't feel afraid or trapped anymore. I felt vengeful.

"Yes!" the prophet lady shouted again. "Lord, get her! Get her!"

I convulsed mightily and let out a cry. The catcher moved his body with mine, thoroughly ready and prepared for me to fall at any angle I chose. I decided now was as good a time as any and threw myself backwards into his waiting arms. He slid me gently to the carpet.

I twitched and whimpered until the prophet lady's spindly hands came off my body. Squinting through my eyelashes, I saw her hovering over me, her hands making sweeping motions as she murmured more prayer. I felt impatient for the elders to move on to their next victim, an African woman to my left wearing an orange and yellow patterned dress with a matching turban. I wondered if it would roll off when she fell. Then I realized she was smiling down at me and shut my eyes.

When the African woman fell beside me, I made whimpering moans until I was sure the elders had moved further down the line. Hoping I looked like I was in a trance, I gradually allowed myself to stop twitching. No one would bother me as long as I looked slain. Guilt seeped in now that I was alone with my thoughts. I had lied to the elders. By lying to them, I'd lied to God. Maybe I had even committed what the Bible called the most unpardonable sin: blasphemy of the Holy Spirit. Surely my mockery of His manifestations was nothing less. Jesus said that all sins could be forgiven but this one, and the punishment for blasphemy was eternal damnation. Was I going to hell now? The thought filled me with terror. I hoped God was listening as I silently begged Him for mercy. He had to know why I faked my slaying. He had to remember how painful it had been when Rodney Howard-Browne hurt my neck, and He had to understand why I couldn't let that happen again. Only God knew why the Holy Spirit kept ignoring me in the first place and I shouldn't have to be punished for His oversight.

The shame of God's rejection brought tears to my eyes. There must be a reason the Holy Spirit refused to slay me. Maybe there was some sin in my life, a broken commandment that kept the Spirit at bay. I knew I was born with a sinful heart, because the Bible said everyone was, but I must be sinning in an active way, too. I once heard a pastor say that God ignored us sometimes to get our attention.

"If you're not hearing from God, or God's not moving in your life," I remembered him saying, "then there's a sin you haven't let go of that's blocking you from your heavenly father. God's silence is His way of getting your attention."

I couldn't remember which pastor said this or at what church, but the words came reverberating through my head. If I hadn't sinned before, I'd surely sinned now, having lied to everyone who watched me fake my Spirit slaying.

When I made my way back to my family's row of chairs, I found all of my siblings sleeping beneath them. Mom and Dad stopped talking when they saw me. Dad smiled.

"So, what did God do in your heart?" he asked. I froze. "I saw you lying on the floor when I passed. It looked like God was working on you."

I didn't want him or Mom to know I'd faked it. It would mean acknowledging that God had ignored me and I was a liar. Remembering the prophet lady said God had a vision for me, I decided to make one up.

"I was standing on top of a mountain," I said. "And then a huge eagle came flying toward me. I saw Jesus was riding the eagle. His hair was flowing and He had a gold crown with rubies in it. He invited me to join Him, so I did, and then He flew me all over the world. He showed me all the poor kids everywhere and said He would use me to help take care of them."

I was astonished at how easily the lie came out of me.

~

Dad took us kids to the hotel swimming pool the next morning. That was the best part of those Toronto trips, for the Regal Constellation Hotel had the most beautiful swimming pool I'd ever seen with a lush, tree-studded island in its center. My brothers and sisters jumped in the water to play a pool game called Shark, but I sat on one of the lounge chairs and contemplated why the Holy Spirit refused to slay me. It occurred to me that maybe God wasn't leaving me out because there was sin in my life. Maybe He wasn't slaying me because I didn't have enough faith.

I thought of the Bible story where Jesus walked on water. His disciples were boating on a lake during a bad storm when Jesus appeared like a ghost in the distance, walking on the water's surface. Peter, one of Jesus' disciples, climbed out of the boat and started walking on water himself. Then the wind scared him and he began to sink. Jesus didn't let him drown, but He did tell Peter that it was his fault he sank, because his doubt got in the way. I couldn't remember the whole verse, but I knew at one point, Jesus told Peter, "Oh ye of little faith."

Was I of little faith?

The possibility of genuinely getting slain was worth it for me to try and find out. It was the only way I could validate myself as someone worthy of God's love and attention.

My eyes fixated on the island in the center of the pool. If Peter could walk on water, even if only for a few steps, surely it was possible that I could walk on water, too. I stood. *God*, I silently prayed, *I believe in you. I have faith that I'll walk right over to that island.* The sounds of laughter faded. My heart pounded in my ears as my toes wrapped around the curved rim of the pool. I locked my eyes on one of the island's trees and took a breath, then I stepped off the edge.

Water plunged up my nose. My foot scraped the roughness of cement. Shame flooded my soul. I hung in the azure blue of silence, drawing my knees in to hug myself. I wanted to cry. No wonder the Holy Spirit didn't see me fit to slay. I didn't have the faith. I was a poser. A faithless, lying poser.

3

Birds of the Air

The seeds planted by the Toronto Blessing began to bloom in the spring of 1997. The changes crept into my life so calmly that I was barely conscious of their ramifications at the time, the way a bird is naive to the calculated nonchalance of a cat. It started at the kitchen table one evening as my family ate dinner. A balmy breeze drifted through the screen windows as we devoured Mom's brown rice quiche.

"What's for dessert?" Teddy asked.

"We don't have any dessert," Mom said.

"Can I have an Oatmeal Cream Pie?"

"If you find one in the pantry, you can all share it, but I think we're out."

My brother slumped in his chair. "Dad, can I go on the route with you tomorrow?"

"The route" was what we called Dad's job. Sometimes he let us take turns riding with him to businesses in the Rockford area to restock his vending boxes with snack foods. From banks in Freeport to mechanic shops in Belvidere, we helped Dad refill his cardboard trays with Fritos, Zebra Cakes, and other junk food goodies. We were allowed to keep any snacks that had expired, so our pantry always had a Little Debbie box full of treats. No doubt Teddy wanted to go on Dad's route with him the next day to restock our supply.

Dad finished his mouthful, then he answered Teddy's question. "We're not going on the route anymore." He looked up at us. "God asked me to give the route to Danny Cowell."

Danny Cowell was a seventeen-year-old from the youth group my parents pastored at Vine City. I knew Danny had been helping Dad with the route, but I didn't know it was to prepare him for taking it over entirely.

"Why?" I asked.

"God put it on my heart."

"So we don't get to have any more Oatmeal Cream Pies?" Teddy asked.

"What's your job now?" I asked.

"My job," Dad said, taking a second to look us all square in the eye, "is to learn how to be a son of God. That's the only job my Daddy in heaven wants me to do right now."

"But . . ." I hesitated. "What about money?"

"God will provide for us," Mom said.

I struggled to understand what was happening. "But how will God—"

"You'll just have to wait and see."

Mom's brusque tone warned me not to ask any further questions.

A few days later, I overheard Dad telling his friend Bruce Graham about how the Toronto Blessing had taken his faith to new heights.

"I was reading Matthew, chapter six," Dad said. "And I felt like God was speaking to me. 'Don't worry about how you will eat, drink, and clothe yourselves, for your heavenly Father knows you need these things. Seek first His kingdom, and all these will be given to you.'"

"Hmm," said Mr. Graham. I crept closer to the kitchen door. "So, you feel like God wants you to trust in Him to provide?"

"Yes!" Dad said, excited that Mr. Graham seemed to understand. "For years, I was consumed with learning how to live up to worldly titles—the title of being my parents' son, of being a police officer, a missionary, a pastor, a vendor. I thought I had to provide. I wasn't trusting my heavenly father. He wants me to learn how to trust Him, to let Him take care of me and not worry about tomorrow." Dad quoted another Bible verse. "'Look at the birds of the air, they don't stow away in barns, yet your heavenly Father feeds them.'"

Mr. Graham's response was too quiet for me to hear, but I made out the word "family."

"That's just it," Dad said. "I always thought I was providing for my family. I wasn't. He was providing for us the whole time. He just let me think I was providing until He opened my eyes, then it hit me like a ton of bricks. My job is to learn how to be God's son, not just in word, but in action. By faith."

I crept away from the door. Part of me felt grateful to have a fuller explanation of why Dad had quit his job. Another part of me felt alarmed by what I'd learned. Like Mr. Graham was probably thinking, I wondered how God would realistically provide for my family. I knew we were poor, because we did our grocery shopping at Cub Foods, a musty warehouse stocked with knock-off brands. My friends' families went to Logli's. Maybe Dad surrendering the route would be a good thing. Maybe we wouldn't have to eat knock-off brands or expired foods anymore. Maybe we'd somehow end up with more money than when Dad thought he was providing for us instead of God.

I wondered if God would provide me with a cat. My siblings and I had always wanted a cat, and one night, when all of us were snuggling in Mom and Dad's bed, I brought up the possibility of getting one.

"No," Mom said, without hesitation.

"What about a dog?" Madeleine asked.

"Definitely not a dog," Mom declared with disgust.

Dad agreed with her, saying a dog would tear up the lawn.

"Then why not a cat?" I asked.

Mom lectured the five of us kids on how much responsibility an animal was, and how we didn't even finish our chores before going outside to play. "If God brings a cat to our door," Mom said, rolling her eyes at the improbability, "you can keep it."

"Really?" Teddy asked.

"It would have to be the perfect cat," she said. "I mean *the* perfect cat. It would have to let you pick it up, hold it upside down, pull its tail—"

"We can find one!" Madeleine said.

"No," said Mom. "You may not find one. This cat would have to come from nowhere. I mean it. Don't you kids go looking around. It would have to show up. On our doorstep."

So we prayed. Every day, I asked God to please let there be a cat waiting for me when I looked out the back door. My brothers and sisters prayed, too. We never prayed so hard for anything or anyone in our lives, obsessed about having a cat of our own for reasons none of us remember. Then one morning, there she was. A young cat showed up on our back porch not even a week after Mom's stipulation. Small and black, speckled with orange markings, she came hungry and collarless. My siblings and I could hardly believe it. Had God really answered our prayer? The cat let us hold her and showed no signs of scratching or hissing, even when Teddy tipped her upside down. In fact, she purred. Mom was flabbergasted, but she kept her promise and let us keep her. We named her Mila.

Another surprise came to my siblings and me a week later. We were all slurping Dad's spaghetti when my parents made another announcement.

"You know how you guys have always wanted to go to California?" Mom asked.

We nodded, our mouths full.

"Well," she continued. "God might have opened a door. How would you guys like to take a road trip out there?"

I stopped mid-chew. Something felt off. I wanted to go to California, but I had a nagging suspicion about the way my parents were presenting the whole idea. Usually they just stated we were going camping somewhere. They never asked us what we thought about it.

My siblings were already cheering.

"How long of a road trip?" I asked.

"We're not sure," Mom said. "We're just going to go where the wind takes us. Maybe a month, maybe more."

"A month?" I squawked. We'd never been away from home for more than a couple of weeks.

"Yeah," Mom said. "Maybe less. Maybe more. We don't know."

I could tell she was being deliberately vague with me. Mom's tone always grew aloof and slightly sarcastic when she dodged questions she didn't want to answer.

My parents said friends would house-sit for us while we were gone.

"But we're taking Mila with us, right?" Madeleine asked.

Mom and Dad exchanged a look.

"We have to!" Teddy cried out.

"Yeah, Mom, you *said*," Madeleine told her, about to burst into tears.

Mom sighed. "Alright, I guess we can bring the cat with us."

Mom rarely called Mila by her name. She always called her "the cat," or, even more slighting, "that cat."

I was quiet the rest of the night. Despite my desire to see the West Coast, I had a bad feeling about our upcoming trip.

~

My family set off for California the day after the 4th of July. Our navy blue '93 Suburban took us across the rugged beauty of the American northwest over the next two weeks, and Mom made our journey as much of a homeschooling field trip as possible. We stopped at nearly every historical or scenic site along our route, from South Dakota's Mount Rushmore to Oregon's Crater Lake. My siblings and I participated in every Junior Ranger program a national park offered, making us avowed guardians of God's creation with the ability to identify various animal tracks, poop, and vegetation. Mom also gave us each a binder of assignments. By the end of our trip, I had memorized every state's capital, bird, and flower.

Everyone cheered as we crossed the last state line on our journey, but it didn't feel like I was truly in California until I saw palm trees. The green fronds splaying from their tops symbolized everything I fantasized about the state: warm sunshine, beaches, and the carefree spirit the Beach Boys sang of. I had no memory of when I'd lived in the Bay Area before my parents moved overseas to be missionaries. My family hadn't been back since.

"A lot of memories coming back, huh, Janey?" Dad said to Mom as we rounded the curve that was the exit for Concord. Dad called Mom Janey whenever he was feeling especially affectionate. I could tell that being back in the place where they'd fallen in love was making Dad nostalgic. Mom, not inclined to be sentimental, indulged him with a brief smile.

My parents didn't tell me until years later that the real reason we'd come to California was so they could visit a small, home-based fellowship. The informal church had no name, but we referred to it as the "Bay Area home group." Our first week in California found us moving from place to place as different home group members tried accommodating two adults, five children, and a reluctant cat. By the time the Mason family announced we could stay with them, I felt uncomfortable living in the homes of strangers, worried my family and I were becoming an imposition.

"We're not imposing," Mom told me. "If people invite us into their home, it's because they want us to stay with them."

I disagreed. I thought people might invite us to stay with them out of Biblical pressure and guilt. Who would turn away a young family of seven who couldn't afford a hotel, especially if their pastor had notified them of the need? I knew hospitality was an important virtue among members of the Bay Area home group. The apostle Paul repeatedly instructed Christians in the New Testament to open their homes to one another. Romans 12:13 said, "Share with the Lord's people who are in need. Practice hospitality." I guessed my family counted as the Lord's people who were in need. I never got used to the feeling of neediness.

The Mason family hadn't actually invited us to stay in their home. They had invited us to pitch our tent in their front yard. I hated helping Dad hammer the tent stakes into the lawn, where everyone on the Masons' cul-de-sac could see us. The neighbors directly across stared at my family with undisguised confusion. I prayed we wouldn't be there for more than a couple of nights.

One week turned to two and I began missing the stability of my routine in Rockford. I missed my home. I missed my friends. I missed my bed. Even though I shared a room with my sisters, it was better than sharing a tent with my brothers and parents, too. Over a month had passed since I'd slept on a mattress between sheets. Mom and I were kneeling on our sleeping pads one afternoon, folding laundry in our tent, when I asked her if we might be going home soon.

"No," Mom said. She scoffed as though she'd told me this before. "We're not going home for a long while."

I felt blindsided. "What do you mean?"

Mom ignored me.

"When are we going home?" I asked. Her silence gripped me with dread. "Mom, how long are we staying in California?"

"Until God tells us to leave," she snapped. "Now put away your clothes."

I kept my back to Mom so she wouldn't see I was crying. The dots connected in my mind. Mom and Dad had never intended for our trip to be the vacation they'd made it out to be. All along they must have known we might stay in California for an extended period, otherwise they wouldn't have rented out our house to my friend Danika's family. Maybe it was even why Dad had quit his job. I felt tricked.

4

Until God Tells Us to Leave

I f God's not answering your prayers the way you want Him to, it means you're praying for the wrong things."

I couldn't remember which pastor I heard say that. Tidbits of Christian wisdom seemed to pop into my head at the least comforting of times. Like right then, when I stared at the green logo of a seventeen-foot-long Terry trailer as Dad backed it into the Masons' driveway. I hadn't prayed for this trailer. I'd been praying to go home to Rockford. God must be reminding me that going home was the wrong thing to pray for.

It was early November. My family had been in Concord, California, for four months and counting. Our tent was still pitched in the Mason family's front yard. The Masons, who also had five homeschooled children, seemed happy to have us around, though I couldn't understand why. My family brought seven additional people plus a cat to their seven-member household, and with ten kids under the age of sixteen running around, we made a rowdy bunch. The Masons' sprawling one-story house sat on a large, muddy lot. They invited us inside to use the bathroom and shower whenever we needed, and sometimes our families shared meals together. Their easygoing generosity must have come from God.

A woman named Connie Walsh also lived on the Masons' property, in a guest house at the end of their driveway. Connie was in her mid-thirties with a playful personality that matched her springy orange curls. She was Mrs. Mason's younger sister, and she also belonged to the Bay Area home group my parents had plugged into. Connie sidled up to me and plunked her arm around my shoulders as we watched Dad lay down blocks of wood on either side of the trailer tires for added stabilization.

"You like it?" Connie asked.

I nodded. I did not like my family's new home, but since Connie was the one who had given it to us, I figured the moment required politeness more than honesty. I thought honesty was the highest form of politeness one could give. Adults tended to disagree.

I couldn't remember exactly when or how Connie announced she was buying my family the trailer, but I did know why. "God put it on my heart to buy for you guys," she'd said. That was how God usually provided for us, by putting a donation on someone's heart. Sometimes the donation was a grocery bag of food, or a shopping spree at a thrift store. Other times it was an envelope of cash. Dad was still unemployed, but he did occasional handyman jobs for people we knew, particularly those who were elderly or disabled. He did those jobs free of charge because that's what God put on his heart to do, and sometimes the people Dad helped gave him money in return, because that's what God put on their hearts to do. It seemed to me that whatever God put on someone's heart went unquestioned and was nonnegotiable.

The trailer Connie gave us was used, but in good condition. Everything inside and out was the color of soot-blown cream, accented by rust. My family moved out of our tent just in time for the Bay Area's rainy season to start, and while I felt grateful that our new roof kept us dry, we were squished. I slept in the top bunk with Teddy and Madeleine, where we barely had room to turn over in our sleeping bags. Mom and Dad shared the mattress below, where Kate usually wound up at their feet instead of her designated spot with Bryant. Bryant slept in the dining booth-turned-bed opposite the kitchen area. I would have wanted to trade places with him so I wouldn't have to sleep against anyone, but his bed was above Mila's litter box and next to a small closet where Dad installed a portable toilet. The whiff of chemical fluid and poop escaped from the door whenever anyone opened it, so I opted to stay wedged into the top bunk with Teddy and Madeleine.

The best part of living at the Masons' was making friends with Jennie and Jocelyn. They were ten and thirteen, respectively, and since I was almost twelve, I fell right in between them. The sisters and I hung out all day, every day. I thought they were the ultimate girly-girls. Jennie's style was trendy while Jocelyn's took a more bohemian flair, but both girls painted their nails and wore makeup. Being around them brought out a side of me that was impatient to grow up.

Mom didn't allow me to paint my nails or wear makeup, not even lipgloss. She never told me why. She also didn't allow me to wear clothes I thought were cute, like stretchy tops and baby doll dresses, calling them "suggestive." Mom had two sets of clothing for my siblings and me: camp clothes and social clothes. Since I thought we would be in California for a few weeks at most, I'd only brought two social outfits with me. I'd nearly outgrown both of them, and they were now as ripped and stained as my camp clothes. I was tired of feeling like a raggedy tomboy all the time, especially next to Jennie and Jocelyn. I wanted spaghetti strap tanks with shoulder bows. I wanted tube tops and daisy-print skirts. More than anything, I wanted bell-bottoms. Mom forbade me from wearing them and wouldn't tell me why.

In December, my family towed our trailer down the California coast to Torrance, a beach town south of Los Angeles. The Fleming family, relatives of the Masons and Connie, had invited us to visit them for a month. I didn't know why. I figured it was one of those God-put-it-on-our-hearts things. The Flemings were out of town when we arrived at their house, but they'd left us a key and a note to please make ourselves at home. I felt like tiptoeing when I walked through their front door. Their house was spotless. The living room was bright and airy, dappled with afternoon sunlight. The floor had no crumbs. The bathroom sinks were free of trimmed hair, and the toilets looked so brand new that I didn't even want to use them. Three bedrooms boasted the comfiest-looking beds I'd ever seen, all soft and pillowy. I couldn't wait for bedtime when I'd get to sleep in one of them.

Best of all was the Flemings' kitchen. Their cabinets were full of shiny, uncrinkled packages. Froot Loops, Pringles chips, and Capri Suns jumped out at me from the shelves, their colorful labels as organized as a fancy grocery store's. I couldn't remember the last time I'd eaten a brand-name food, like the authentic Kraft macaroni and cheese whose noodles smiled at me, begging to be eaten. The refrigerator practically burst with fresh fruit, Yoplait yogurt, and string cheese. There was real milk, not the cheap, powdered stuff my siblings and I gagged down with our cereal every morning. The freezer was stocked with pizzas and ice cream. I wanted to eat it all.

Mom was hesitant to let us touch the tantalizing foods.

"But here, Mom, see?" I told her, shoving Mrs. Fleming's note into her hand. "It says, 'Help yourselves to anything.' Anything!"

I raced back to the refrigerator. "There's even bubble water here!"

Bubble water was Mom's favorite beverage. She finally cracked a smile and joined our celebration, opting to nurse a cold Corona with Dad while my siblings and I sipped on Capri Suns and greedily nibbled Doritos that didn't even expire until March.

The Flemings came home after my family and I enjoyed three days in their house all to ourselves. Mr. Fleming was good-humored and patient, and Mrs. Fleming was as warm and generous as her sisters, Connie and Mrs. Mason. The Fleming girls, eight-year-old Natalie and four-year-old Tania, were shy at first, not sure what to make of the strange family who had set up a trailer in their driveway. All it took was a four-square ball game for us kids to become fast friends.

The Flemings were Roman Catholics. If that was ever a point of contention between our families, I never knew about it. Natalie begged me to go to mass with her family one Sunday.

"Isn't it really boring?" I asked, a movie scene depicting a Catholic mass flashing into mind.

"Yeah, it's kind of boring," Natalie said. She grinned impishly at me. "But there's doughnuts at the end."

My parents gave me permission to go to mass, and on the drive there, I was startled to learn that some Catholics didn't consider themselves Christians.

"But you believe Jesus died on the cross for your sins, right?" I asked Natalie.

"Yeah," she said. "But we pray to the Virgin Mary and you guys think she's an idol."

I didn't deny it. I vaguely recalled Dad saying something about how praying to Mary and the saints violated the First Commandment. But we all believed in the Father, Son, and the Holy Ghost, and I couldn't understand how that didn't unite us as Christians.

Mass was different from any other church service my family had been to. No one danced or waved banners. No one shook or fell to the floor, or laughed and cried. The greatest difference I noticed was the way the congregation took Communion. They called it Eucharist. The ritual commemorated Jesus' Last Supper before He was crucified, with a cracker representing His body and grape juice symbolizing His blood. I was horrified to discover that, at the Flemings' church, everyone drank the juice from the same goblet. I was used to the juice being divided into thimble-sized plastic cups. I watched in shock as the Flemings took turns sipping from the chalice, not even hesitating at the idea that someone in the congregation might be sick. I was especially surprised because Mrs. Fleming was fearful of germs, habitually sanitizing everything and everyone with antibacterial squirts. I noticed the priest using a cloth to wipe the cup's rim before the next person took a sip. What would that do besides smear everyone's saliva around? I allowed the priest to place a wafer on my tongue, but I shook my head at drinking from the metal goblet.

On the drive back to the Flemings' house, I asked Mr. and Mrs. Fleming why they weren't worried about drinking other people's germs.

"When we drink Christ's blood," Mr. Fleming said, "it's been consecrated to God, so you don't need to worry about germs."

That sounded questionable to me, and I felt the need to clarify something else. "But it's not really Christ's blood," I said.

"Yeah it is," Natalie said. "God turns the cracker into Jesus' body, and He turns the grape juice into Jesus' blood."

I waited for her parents to correct her. They started talking about what to make for dinner that night. I sat back in my seat and wondered who was right, the Flemings or my dad. Dad told me the crackers and juice of Communion only symbolized Jesus' body and blood, which undoubtedly made more sense than the idea that they magically turned into literal interpretations. That would be cannibalism.

~

The next two weeks felt like a vacation from my family's vacation. The Flemings took my family and me whale watching, ice skating, and Costco-raiding. They treated us to meals at diners, pizza parlors, and fast food restaurants. Mrs. Fleming's parents took my family to Disneyland, a place I never thought I'd be able to visit because it was so expensive. Every night, I thanked God for all the fun I was having. Maybe life really could be better when one trusted in Him to provide.

Then one night, Mom and Dad put my siblings and me to bed in the trailer. Hours later, they still hadn't returned. Unable to sleep, I walked up the driveway to peer through the Flemings' windows to see if my parents were inside. Connie had driven down from the Bay Area to visit. Maybe the adults were socializing for longer than they'd intended. There were no lights on when I peered into the living room, and the front door was locked. Then I noticed my family's Suburban wasn't in its usual parking spot.

Panic surged through me. I rang the doorbell several times, but no one came. I kicked the door as hard as I could, yelling for Mom and Dad. The noise made my siblings come out of the trailer, and soon all of us were crying for our parents on the Flemings' front stoop. Or anyone. Though I pounded on the door with all my might, not a sound came from within the house.

"What's wrong, guys?"

I whirled around to find the Flemings' next-door neighbors walking up the driveway, a young couple named Brad and Nancy. Nancy wore a bathrobe.

"We can't find Mom and Dad," I sobbed.

Brad picked up a distraught Bryant and pounded the front door himself. Nancy comforted Kate while Teddy, Madeleine, and I stood in our pajamas waiting for someone to open the door. The house remained dark and still. I had no idea what time it was.

My siblings and I sat on the Flemings' front steps while Brad and Nancy exchanged hushed tones in the driveway. Their voices were low, but I picked up the words "unemployed" and "irresponsible." Then I heard Brad say something about social services. All I knew about social services was that it was for orphans. My heart began to race as terrible scenarios ran through my head. What if Mom and Dad had died in a car accident? What if my siblings and I had to be split up into different homes? I doubted anyone would take all five of us.

A car pulling into the driveway interrupted my thoughts. The squareness of its headlights told me it was the Suburban. Mom jumped out of the passenger's side immediately, her face stricken with alarm.

"What's going on?" she asked. "Is everyone okay?"

The mixture of anger and relief I felt immobilized me. Brad and Nancy explained they'd heard my siblings and me yelling, so they'd come over to check on us. Mr. and Mrs. Fleming stepped out of the Suburban, too, followed by Dad once he turned off the engine. I marched up to Mom.

"Where were you?" I demanded.

"Honey, we went to a church meeting with the Flemings. You guys were supposed to be in bed."

"You didn't even tell us you guys were leaving?"

"No, sweetie, we didn't think you'd be awake." Mom tried to touch me, but I moved out of her reach. She continued trying to explain herself. "Connie was supposed to be watching you guys in case something happened. Where is she?"

"I don't know!"

Mrs. Fleming moved quietly past us and unlocked the front door. Moments later, Connie appeared in the doorway, her curls a mess and her eyes drowsy with sleep. "What happened?" she asked. "Did something happen?"

I listened as the adults explained to Brad and Nancy what had gone wrong. My parents and Mr. and Mrs. Fleming had attended an evening mass, leaving Connie to babysit should there be an emergency. Connie, drugged up on pain medication for a back injury, had fallen into a deep slumber that left her unable to hear us pounding at the door. The Fleming girls somehow hadn't heard us, either. Brad and Nancy seemed to accept the story. They said goodnight to us kids and went back to their home, and Connie apologized profusely to Mom and Dad for falling asleep.

I warned my parents never to leave again without telling us, whether they thought we'd be asleep or not. They apologized, but I knew it would take me a couple of days to forgive them. I had one more question before we went into the trailer.

"What's social services?" I asked.

Dad huffed. "It's the government's way of telling you how to parent your children."

"Shh, not now, Ted," Mom said.

The events of that night left deep scars on my sense of security. A fear of abandonment took root, one that would quake beneath an independent façade well into adulthood. I couldn't be left if I was already detached.

~

Christmas Eve found me homesick for the first time since my family came to Torrance. My stuffed bear, Cinnamon, was a poor substitute for a pillow, but Teddy hogged my real one. Madeleine slept between us in an awkward S-shape with her head at our feet. Her knees kept bumping my butt. We each had our own sleeping bag, but the down feathers did little to cushion our limbs from bruising each other when we tossed and turned.

I wondered how my friend Danika was spending her Christmas Eve back in Rockford. She and her parents were still living in our house. No doubt she was cozy in my bed just then. Maybe she had even switched the summertime sheets for my winter flannels. Where would her family have put their Christmas tree? We always put ours in the upstairs turret, so we could see it twinkling from outside whenever we pulled into the driveway. I missed our ornaments and Advent wreath, and my bejeweled stocking. The only familiarity that comforted me were the mournful strings of Mom's *Winter on the Moors* CD, which played quietly from the boom box on the trailer's kitchen counter. We listened to that album every Christmas, along with Dad's collection of carols performed by The Cambridge Singers and Orchestra. I rolled onto my side and faced the interior of the trailer, where the smell of Mom's Moroccan stew still lingered in the air. I stared down at Bryant and Kate, the reflection of a single strand of multicolored Christmas lights blinking on their peaceful faces from where it hung across the kitchen cabinets. Mila sat nestled between them. She blinked at me slowly, as though sharing my nostalgia. I didn't remember falling asleep.

All of my sadness was forgotten the next morning at the sight of the Flemings' living room. Heaps of presents lie stacked on every surface, extending from beneath the Christmas tree all the way to the front door. Everyone created a nest for themselves out of the wrapping paper that flew about the room in the following hours. It was one of the best Christmases I ever had. I got a camera with a telephoto lens, as well as a brand-new watercolor kit to replace my old one, whose tubes were running dry. Mom and Dad even gave me bell-bottoms. I was so happy to own a pair that I didn't dare question Mom about what had changed her mind.

When everyone finished organizing their pile of presents, I realized that I had received everything I asked for and then some. My siblings did, too. I didn't know how this could be, since Mom and Dad had warned us they didn't have a lot of money that year. The abundance of granted wishes wasn't exclusively from the Flemings, either, or from relatives who mailed us packages. Many of my family's gifts were mysteriously tagged, "From God." That frustrated me, because the tags might as well have read, "From Santa," like some of the Flemings' presents were labeled. I wore Mom down all Christmas day, insistent upon knowing who had really given us the presents. Her argument that God gave us everything held no sway with me.

"Why do you need to know?" Mom asked.

"So I can write them a thank you card," I said. It was partially true. I always hand-wrote thank you cards after receiving presents, per Mom's lessons in courtesy.

Mom finally told me that she and Dad had registered our family with a charity organization that provided Christmas presents for low-income households. A benevolent stranger had taken the time to read the Christmas lists my siblings and I wrote, and they'd given us everything we asked for. I felt deeply moved. I was also confused as to why Mom and Dad would have wanted to keep that information from my siblings and me. Then, in an overdue moment of clarity, I realized that what Mom and Dad called God's provision was really just other people's kindness.

5

Kissing Dating Goodbye

I turned twelve on February 6, 1998. Without warning, boys suddenly became fascinating to me. I went from being mildly curious to viscerally engulfed by desires I never knew imaginable. I wasn't ready to go all the way, as I heard the saying went, but I was eager to know what it felt like to hold hands with a boy, to snuggle him, kiss him, and maybe even let him touch my boobs. Not that I had any yet. I was still as flat as a six-year-old, but I was confident that someday soon I'd awaken with C-cups, and when I did, I planned on going straight to Victoria's Secret for a matching bra and panty set made of black lace. I hoped to have a boyfriend in the near future to show off my lingerie to, even if the near future was still a few years away. My daydreams were taking me to places I knew were premature, but unstoppable nonetheless.

It was my friend Danika who had told me what sex was. When I was ten and still living in Rockford, Danika's mom had been driving me home from a sleepover as my best friend and I whispered in the backseat.

"What do you think sex is?" she'd asked me.

"It's, uh, it's when a guy and a girl make out and stuff."

Danika smirked, then leaned closer to my ear. "Sex," she said, "is when a man puts his penis inside a woman's vagina."

My mouth fell open in horror. Danika tried not to laugh out loud at my face.

"The man rubs his penis inside her until he squirts his stuff out," Danika continued. "That's what fertilizes her egg so she gets pregnant."

I was appalled. I hadn't even known women had eggs, or that sex had anything to do with making babies. Danika laughed at my expression, barely able to contain herself. I could tell she was pleased that she got to tell me something I didn't know, and that she was getting exactly the reaction out of me she hoped for. It made me feel dumb, but my wounded pride was outweighed by the shock I felt. Back at home, I sat on my bed and debated whether or not I should ask Mom if what Danika said was true. I knew I was going to be unsettled until Mom denied everything. That night, I found her alone in my parents' bedroom reading a book.

"Mom?" I asked.

She smiled at me. "Hey, girlbug," she said, folding back three layers of quilts. "Wanna come sit with me?"

I crawled into bed with her.

"Did you have a fun time with Danika?" Mom asked.

"Yeah."

I fiddled with the crochet trim of a pillowcase, nervous. It was then or never.

"Mom, Danika told me something that isn't true."

"What's that?"

"She said . . ." I struggled to get the words out. "She said that you and Dad put your private parts together to have sex."

Mom's face blanked.

"To make babies," I added, as though that made it sound better. Mom silently turned away from me. She wasn't denying it. "Is it true?"

Mom looked embarrassed. "Danika shouldn't have told you that," she said. "But yes, it's true."

Once more that day, shock left me speechless. I wanted to ask Mom more questions, like how she and Dad could do something so inappropriate to one another, but I was thrown off by Mom's awkwardness. Mom rarely got embarrassed about anything. I felt so uncomfortable, I could barely breathe.

"You keep this to yourself," Mom said as I slipped out of the covers.

"Okay."

"It's not your place to tell other kids, okay?"

"Okay," I repeated.

I'd just wanted the conversation to end.

The idea of sex had repulsed me. Now sex seemed to be all I could think about. Barely days into twelve years old, my mind felt seized by a perverted demon who made me notice cute boys everywhere. Whenever I went to a shopping mall or grocery store, I felt mesmerized by the broadening shoulders and cocksure gait of adolescent males. Did they wake up one day swaggering like that, or did they consciously alter the way they walked? It didn't matter to me. I thought the prowling shuffle of skaters was as seductive as a Viennese waltz, which I was sure would be the undoing of my innocence if ever a guy trained in cotillion asked me to dance. I fantasized about meeting a teenage Adonis with shaggy blond hair who raced dirt bikes, wrote poetry, and tangoed in black-tie suits. He'd have an eyebrow piercing, a sleeve of tattoos, and he could crack eggs with a single hand. The type of masculinity I craved was both rugged and elegant, rebellious and gentlemanly. I wanted what nineteenth-century novels called a "rogue." A handsome daredevil with a Robin Hood heart.

As though God whispered to my dad what I'd been thinking about, the topic of dating came up as Valentine's Day approached. My family had returned to the Masons' after our Christmas with the Flemings, and I was reading on the couch of Connie's guest house when Dad's hand extended a paperback to me. Its cover depicted a black-and-white photo of a man holding a fedora over his face. Its title worried me: *I Kissed Dating Goodbye*, by Joshua Harris.

"I'd like you to read this, moppet," Dad said. "I wish I'd read a book like that in my youth. It would've saved me and the young women I dated a lot of heartache."

I didn't know how to respond, so I took the book and said nothing.

"Let's talk about it when you've finished," Dad said.

The nonfiction book opened with the telling of a dream. In the dream, Anna walked down the aisle to David on their wedding day, her heart bursting with love, when suddenly six other women came to the altar as well. She asked her fiancé if he was pulling some kind of joke. He told her that he'd already given pieces of his heart to the six other girls, but she could have what was left.

I Kissed Dating Goodbye's message was clear from its first page: Our hearts, minds, and bodies were to be given to no one until we married. Astonishment and terror glued me to Connie's couch all day as I turned through page after soul-crushing page. By the time I finished the book, I had never feared God more in my life.

Joshua Harris, a 21-year-old Christian, challenged those who were unmarried to commit to a romance based on Biblical scripture. He observed friends struggling like himself to maintain spiritual integrity in the unsupervised, fast-paced dating game of modern day, and so he advocated a different approach: Instead of one-on-one dating, which he felt led to premature intimacy both physical and emotional, he challenged Christian singles to pursue what he called courtship. The word sounded romantic to me at first. I learned it was anything but.

Harris suggested that potential future spouses get to know each other as friends in group settings, or with a chaperone-figure present. That way they could observe each other's character in environments that wouldn't allow Satan to tempt them into sexual immorality. Any sexual activity before marriage, I learned, was a sin. Harris wasn't even going to kiss his future wife until their wedding day. Unless a couple married and could celebrate the physical expression of love with God's approval, men and women were to respect one another as brothers-and-sisters-in-Christ, guarding each other's sexual purity.

God directed the guidelines Joshua Harris wrote of. There were Bible verses throughout the book to prove it. I dug up my own Bible and verified them, discovering passages I'd never read or heard of before. God had a lot to say about fornication, lust, and immorality.

Paul told Christians in First Corinthians, "I say to those who aren't married and to widows—it's better to stay unmarried, just as I am. But if they can't control themselves, they should go ahead and marry. It's better to marry than to burn with lust."

If one didn't marry and gave in to the burnings of lust anyway, they were considered a fornicator and would go to hell, for First Corinthians also said, "Neither fornicators, nor idolators, nor adulterers, nor homosexuals will inherit the kingdom of God."

If one didn't enter the kingdom of God, there was only one other place for the soul to go.

Jesus said in the book of Matthew that merely thinking sexual thoughts was a sin. "I tell you that anyone who looks at a woman lustfully has already committed adultery with her in his heart. If your right eye causes you to stumble, gouge it out and throw it away. It is better for you to lose one part of your body than for your whole body to be thrown into hell."

The extremity of Jesus' command startled me. It seemed so contrary to the love, compassion, and forgiveness He talked about elsewhere. Was that one of the passages pastors said we didn't need to take literally, even though we were to take literally many others? How did one determine which of God's instructions were metaphorical and which were word for word?

Jesus' quote explained why Joshua Harris implored young women to dress modestly in *I Kissed Dating Goodbye*. Harris wrote, "Please be aware of how easily your actions and glances can stir up lust in a guy's mind. You may not realize this, but we guys most commonly struggle with our eyes. I think many girls are innocently unaware of the difficulty a guy has in remaining pure when looking at a girl who is dressed immodestly."

Harris went on to share the stories of two women who purged their wardrobes of anything skin-revealing or body-hugging that might cause a brother-in-Christ to stumble. "Are you willing to be that radical?" Harris asked the female reader.

Harris acknowledged that men needed to take responsibility for their thoughts, but it was my job as a young Christian woman to help them. Otherwise, Harris said, I would be like the wayward woman in the Book of Proverbs who tempted men by provoking lust.

"Then out came a woman to meet him, dressed like a prostitute and with crafty intent," the Proverbs story reads. "She threw her arms around him and kissed him, and with a brazen look she said, 'Come, let's drink our fill of love until morning . . .' He followed her at once, like an ox going to the slaughter."

Women who embraced their sensuality were like murderers. I didn't want to be a murderer, tempting men astray with impure thoughts by what I wore. "For you may be sure of this," read Ephesians 5:5, "that everyone who is sexually immoral or impure . . . has no inheritance in the kingdom of Christ and God."

Terrified of an eternity in flames, I flipped to my Bible's index to look up other verses pertaining to how women should dress. In First Timothy, the apostle Paul said to Christians, "I also want the women to dress modestly, with decency and propriety, adorning themselves, not with elaborate hair-styles or gold or pearls or expensive clothes, but with good deeds, appropriate for women who profess to worship God. A woman should learn in quietness and full submission. I do not permit a woman to teach or to assume author-ity over a man; she must be quiet. For Adam was formed first, then Eve. And Adam was not the one deceived; it was the woman who was deceived and became a sinner. But women will be saved through childbearing—if they continue in faith, love and holiness with propriety."

I was aghast. Women were not only to downplay their appearance. They were to be quiet and submissive, because Eve took the first bite of forbidden fruit in the Garden of Eden. That Adam took the second bite right after her didn't seem to matter. I never knew God was so sexist. I tried to reassure myself that perhaps Paul's mandates on women's behavior were another part of the Bible not to take literally. How could I be certain?

What if it was true that the only way women could be saved was through childbearing and dressing with propriety?

All day, I read and cross-referenced *I Kissed Dating Goodbye*'s message with the Bible verses it sourced. Darkness had fallen by the time I finished. I found Mila curled up in the trailer and laid my head against her purrs as I reflected on everything I'd taken in. Three things stood out to me most: what I was not to wear, what I was not to physically do, and what my future courtship was to look like. Victoria's Secret was off-limits—talk about being a wayward woman. Kissing was out of the question, since it fueled sexual impurity. Dating was no longer a fun milestone to look forward to, but a stifling arrangement to be supervised by God and the spiritual mentors He put in my life. Joshua Harris wrote that a man and woman shouldn't pursue courtship until they were fully ready to commit themselves to marriage, and when they did feel ready, they were to get the blessing of their parents and other godly elders before commencing anything beyond a brother-and-sister friendship. External accountability would help affirm whether they were on course with God's will or with their own fleshly desires.

I wished I could have a conversation with God to discuss what I'd learned. I wanted to know which parts of the Bible were true and which were symbolic, which of Harris's courtship boundaries were strict rules God wanted me to follow and which were only suggestions to consider. For the time being, to err on the side of not going to hell, I had to assume everything I learned was strict and true. God still didn't speak to me directly. I figured He was speaking to me indirectly through Joshua Harris, for why else would his book have come into my life right as I was beginning to think about dating?

I grieved the sexy bra I'd been looking forward to along with the imaginary boyfriend I wished to seduce with it. Seduction was sinful. Beauty was sinful. Just being female now seemed sinful, and sin was what separated us from God.

Dad called me over to where he was painting Connie's guest house the next day. "So, what'd you think of the book?" he asked me.

"I don't know," I said. "I think it sounds really strict."

He considered my opinion. "I'll tell you this, Alice," he said, dipping the paint roller into a tray of ivory-colored slop. "I wished I'd saved myself for your mother, because I left a piece of me with every girl I slept with before her."

My breath froze. I could hardly believe Dad had just told me about his sex life, and the one he had before Mom no less. I couldn't think of what to say, so I turned to leave.

When Dad gave me *I Kissed Dating Goodbye*, which became an international best-seller in the evangelical Christian world, I don't think either of us knew how its message would scar my very sense of womanhood. Neither did we know how harmful its seeds of patriarchal authority would be to our relationship in years to come. I believe my father's intentions at the time were to spare me the hurtful dating experiences he'd had, and to inspire me toward a more fulfilling relationship with God. Dad wasn't aware of how deeply fear and shame took root in my heart, roots I struggled to breathe through in years to come as I wrestled to find the balance between being true to myself and being a woman of God. I couldn't be both.

~

That spring, my family abruptly stopped going to Bay Area home group meetings and began attending a church called Vallejo Vineyard Fellowship. It was at Vallejo Vineyard that Dad met Bob Burke, a middle-aged man who lived alone. I didn't know how it was decided, but one May afternoon, we said goodbye to the Masons and moved into Mr. Burke's two-bedroom apartment. I didn't have time to be shocked. Connie sold the trailer she'd bought for us and I was forced to adjust to new living quarters once more.

My family met another single man through Vallejo Vineyard. His name was Jim Knight and he had kind eyes, a bald head, and a beard rivaling Dad's. Mr. Knight was quite taken with my family and our unconventional life, and, one evening, he invited us to his house for a dinner party. I sat on his deck watching the evening fog roll in from San Francisco Bay as my siblings cartwheeled in the grass. The bench shook as someone sat beside me. I looked up, surprised to see Mr. Knight. None of the other adults came out with him. He smiled and leaned back as though he were relaxing for the first time all day. Then he turned to face me. The respect emanating from his eyes made me feel like I was being seen for the first time in months.

"How do you feel about all this?" he asked.

I didn't need him to explain what "this" meant. I glanced at my parents, who I could see through sliding glass doors chatting at the table.

"I wish I had a say," I said quietly. "Sometimes it feels like God doesn't care about what I think. I want to go home."

My voice caught in my throat. If Mr. Knight noticed, he didn't let on. He just nodded thoughtfully. I blinked back tears that threatened to reveal how much his question meant to me. He might say something to my parents, and they might say something to me that would turn into another argument I knew I'd lose. So instead of telling Mr. Knight how much I appreciated his question, I dedicated a whole page of my diary to him later that evening. He was the only person in California who ever asked me how I felt about my parents' chosen lifestyle.

On June first, my family and I were eating dinner with Mr. Burke when Mom made an announcement.

"Guess what, you guys?" she said. Her tone had that familiar I'm-about-to-upheave-you quality to it. I braced myself. "We're heading back to Rockford in a week."

I hardly dared to believe my ears. Joyous shouts from my brothers and sisters rang around the table. Mr. Burke smiled as my parents explained how God had provided a way for us to go home.

"Mr. Burke got Vallejo Vineyard to put on a garage sale for us," Dad said. "To raise money for the drive back."

I threw a grateful look to Mr. Burke, who dipped his head to me.

"When's the garage sale?" I asked.

"In a few days," Mom said. "We'll need you guys to help out."

I'd do anything to get home.

God provided my family with over eight hundred dollars through the garage sale. It was more than we'd hoped for. He also provided us with yet another trailer, a Palomino pop-up the color of moths that was ours to keep. I hoped to never sleep in it again after we were settled back in Rockford.

6

Setbacks

We ran out of money and gas three weeks later, only 300 miles from home.

The Minnesota plains on either side of Interstate 90 were empty of civilization when Dad dragged out the last few drops of fuel the Suburban had in her. Even if we managed to reach the next town, I didn't know what we'd do. The eight hundred dollars we made from Mr. Burke's garage sale had been eaten up by gas, camping fees, and unexpected repairs to the pop-up trailer.

"There's a Phillips 66 off the next exit," Mom said to Dad.

She had to shout above the wind coming through the open windows. The cool air of the Rocky Mountains had long disappeared, and it was midday and hot as a broiler outside. Mom refused us air conditioning. Her dad had never let her roll down the windows, so rolled-down windows were all she wanted as an adult. I wondered if I would always want the A/C on with my windows up, and if my future kids would beg me to roll them down. Even if Mom did permit us to turn on the air conditioning for once, the extra energy it would take needed to be reserved for our struggling car. The Suburban wasn't old—she was almost five, the same age as my youngest sibling, Kate—but she heaved and sputtered as if she were dying.

"Let's hope we make it," Dad said.

He hunched over the steering wheel as though it might help our car go faster. The wind whipped his dark curls in front of his eyes, trapping them behind his sunglasses. Dad kept trying to shove them back, but they stuck to his sweat, creating a pattern around his hairline that reminded me of paisley.

A green road sign announced we were entering the city of Austin, Minnesota. The car ached with tension. Our entire road trip through the Pacific Northwest and into the Great Plains felt to me like one anxious setback after another, from popped tires to burst freeze plugs. The setbacks were broken up by occasional fun sights, like when we spotted a bear in Yellowstone National Park, but tension remained a steady companion that sat in the middle seat of the front bench row, right between Mom and Dad.

"That's it," Mom said, pointing to a red Phillips 66 sign.

"I can see it," said Dad. His tone was sing-songy. If Mom continued pointing out the obvious, I knew he might shut down, which would cause Mom to amp up. Another fight between them was the last thing we all needed. Lately the smallest things seemed to provoke an argument between my parents, like which way the trailer faced when we erected it for the night.

Dad pulled into the gravel driveway of what appeared to be a modest truck stop. Rust-colored clouds of dust plumed through the windows as he turned off the car, which he'd parked to the side of the pumps even though we wouldn't be gassing up.

"We made it," Dad announced to no one in particular.

Mom left the car first, slamming the door as she marched inside the gas station to use the restroom. Teddy and I waited impatiently for Madeleine, Bryant, and Kate to file out of the middle bench row. Before Kate's sandal even left the running board, I jammed my foot on the pedal making the seat in front of me lurch forward. My shorts stuck to my thighs as I crawled out, along with crumbs from three weeks' worth of peanut butter and jelly sandwiches. I tried to brush them off my sweaty backside. The crumbs only smeared. I looked through Mom's window to check on Mila. She straddled the top of the front bench seat, tethered to Mom's headrest and panting. I took a water bottle and poured some of its contents into Mila's cup. She squinted her yellow eyes at me in gratitude. My siblings tried to balance on concrete parking bumpers, and since I didn't know what else to do, I joined them. I could see Dad inside the gas station through the double entrance doors. He was talking to the attendant behind the cash register. The man's ruddy face looked confounded, then I saw him shrug his shoulders and give Dad a nod. One of the entrance doors opened with Mom's hip, and she slid her way back into the sunshine with a scrunchie in her mouth as she wound her hair into a bun. I could hear the last bit of Dad's exchange with the attendant.

"Thank you very much, sir, I appreciate it," Dad said to him, following Mom out the door. He fell into step with her, but she wouldn't look at him. "He says we can park behind the building and stay as many nights as we need to."

"Great," Mom said. "Let's move."

The Suburban chugged back to life after a few ear-grating seconds. Dad parked it where the attendant told him to, and in silence, he and Mom cranked open the pop-up. We'd only had the trailer for a month, but already Mom and Dad could transform it from a flattened box to a tent on wheels in two minutes flat. Once erected, two sheltered mattresses extended from its sides and in the center was a kitchen and dining area. The pop-up was smaller than the Terry trailer Connie had given us, but somehow, we all fit, plus Mila and her litter box. The plan was to sit and wait for God to provide us with some money. Or gasoline, whichever came first.

I wandered around the truck stop with my diary in hand, looking for a place where I might find some shade and solitude. I'd started journaling more regularly in California, almost every day. Writing gave me a way to speak without being silenced. A semi-truck parked in a corner of the parking lot beckoned me. No one was in it. The space between its trailer and main cabin was the perfect nook to tuck myself into, and I spent the next couple of hours journaling and praying that God would provide money for us to get home.

"Alice!"

I looked up from my diary. It sounded like one of the kids had called for me, but I wasn't in the mood to talk to anyone. I decided to ignore whoever had shouted my name.

"Alice!"

I sighed. That had been the unmistakable voice of Dad.

"Coming!" I shouted.

Irritated, I closed my diary and stood up, using one of the truck's over-sized tires as a step to help me get back to the gravel. I saw Mom and all of the kids gathered around Dad outside of the pop-up. I thought I heard him say the word "cigarette." Had one of the kids been caught smoking? Neither of my parents smoked. I'd never known my siblings to want to try it.

"What's going on?" I asked.

"We're going to look for money," Mom said.

I stopped in my tracks. "Where?"

"On the side of the road," Dad said. "I was just telling everyone to make sure to look in cigarette boxes. I once found a twenty-dollar bill in a cigarette box."

Dad led us all on foot back to Interstate 90 to scavenge for any coins or bills that might have fallen out of someone's car window, or perhaps from the backpack of a hitchhiker. Gas was $1.09 a gallon at the Phillips 66, and every penny was needed to get us closer to Rockford. Cars sped past us. I wondered what their passengers thought as they saw two adults and five children bent over picking through trash on the side of the freeway. I hoped they assumed we were volunteers clearing litter. My pride resisted the truth that my family's poverty had come to this.

We found plastic Coke bottles, wind-shredded magazines, and occasional fast food wrappers, but no money. After a sweaty hour, Dad called it quits on the interstate, suggesting we continue our search someplace more populated. We walked back to the truck stop where Dad asked his attendant buddy to point us in the direction of the nearest shopping area. He directed us to a mall a quarter mile away.

Austin, Minnesota, was a sleepy little town, seemingly unchanged since the 1950s. We moseyed through a quaint middle-class neighborhood, our footsteps heavy with heat-induced fatigue. Splintered tree trunks and strewn branches told us a tornado had recently blown through, and the destruction looked out of place in the brightness of day. My siblings and I raced ahead of Mom and Dad when we reached Oak Park Mall, heaving open its foyer doors and reveling in the icy burst of air conditioning that kissed our sweaty skin.

"Whew! That A/C sure is nice," Dad said, fluffing out his damp maroon t-shirt.

The eyes of women dressed in black stared at my family from behind glass counters. I realized what a sight we must have made, bursting into their shiny cosmetics department all covered in sweat, grime, and dust. No one else in my family seemed to care, but my ears smarted as the ladies' eyes followed us to the mall's main corridor. Eye shadows tantalized me as I walked past, shimmering like sinful potions promising a beauty that would never be mine. The models of Estée Lauder and Lancôme looked gorgeous with their unfreckled skin, their eyes lined to perfection, and their silky-looking hair falling straight and smooth. They were the opposites of me, a buck-toothed, melanin-speckled, frizzy-haired bum.

Teddy discovered a small jackpot in the mall's arcade. "You guys, come here!" he called out.

We scrambled in the direction of Teddy's voice and discovered him lying face down on the star-patterned carpet, his left arm completely buried beneath a *Star Wars Trilogy* game.

"What are you doing?" I asked him.

"Look," he said. Three quarters flung out from under the machine, followed by his hand holding a stick he picked up from the tornado debris.

"Would you look at that," Dad said.

My siblings and I eagerly dashed from game to game in the arcade to see who could collect the most quarters, reaching as far as our scrawny arms could fit. We discovered vending machines were also good spots to look under, and by the end of the day, we had collected close to ten dollars in coins. The amount wasn't enough to get us back to Rockford, but it was ten dollars more than nothing.

The next day passed with sweltering monotony. We walked to the SPAM Museum, Austin, Minnesota's only claim to fame, then headed back to our makeshift campsite at the Phillips 66 and did our best to ignore the heat. I sat in an open door of the Suburban with Mila, hoping God would hurry up with the gas money, until my stomach broke my thoughts with a growl. Stuffed crust pizza. That was what I wanted. I imagined taking a bite of salty mozzarella oozing from a doughy hand-held tunnel. The image of cheese-smothered fries from Beef-A-Roo followed soon after, and I could almost feel the mush of crisp potato on my tongue. I wondered what we had left in our food box. The cooler was almost empty, except for some wilted lettuce bathing in melted ice water. Maybe there was an apple left in one of the pop-up's kitchen cabinets.

I found Teddy sitting at the dining table when I stepped in, drawing on his watercolor pad with an assortment of charcoal pencils laid out in front of him. The art supplies had been a gift from Mr. Burke. I grabbed a half-eaten box of Triscuits from the counter and sat opposite Teddy on the clay-colored dining booth to share the snack with him. Madeleine, Bryant, and Kate played with their Playmobil sets in the dirt outside. Every now and then, their shouts made clear an airborne war was taking place in their imaginations. Just as I wondered where Mom and Dad were, I heard them shouting. I couldn't make out what they said, but the increasing volume of their voices told me they were walking in the direction of the pop-up. I peered out the screened windows. Mom made slicing gestures with her arms to emphasize her words while Dad chased after her. They both looked angry. Concerned, Teddy and I stepped outside just as Mom reached where the other kids were playing. Tears streamed down her face.

"Don't ask any questions and don't argue," Mom told us. "Just get in the car."

I wanted to ask questions, like what was going on and why, but Mom was already pulling Kate by her arm and leading her to the Suburban. Dad stood by the pop-up with his arms crossed and a pained expression on his face. It was clear he wasn't going wherever Mom was.

"Come on," Mom said to the rest of us as she buckled Kate's seat belt. "Get in the car."

Teddy, Madeleine, and Bryant flinched into action. I looked at Dad. He stared at Mom with a mix of fear and challenge in his eyes. I didn't know what to do. I thought I'd be abandoning Dad if I were to get in the car, but I was afraid Mom would abandon me if I didn't. My brain went into snap-decision-making mode. I felt like Dad would understand if I obeyed Mom, but I did not feel like Mom would understand if I stayed with Dad. I couldn't name why. In shock, I climbed into the car with my siblings. All of them looked as bewildered as I felt. Mom got behind the wheel and tried to start the engine. Dad stood in front of the hood.

"How far you think you're gonna go, Jane?" he asked.

"As far as I can!" Mom shouted.

We couldn't even leave the driveway.

I never found out what Mom and Dad were arguing over. I guessed their tension had to do with the stress of our circumstances, but regardless of why they fought, that day was the first time I realized my parents' marriage was not as secure as I'd believed. If Mom was willing to abandon Dad at a truck stop, penniless and miles away from family or friends, their relationship must have been more precarious than I ever considered. From that day on, I knew we were as fragile as any other family my parents called "broken."

~

By the start of our third day at the Phillips 66, almost all of our food supplies had run out. I don't know what we would have eaten if it hadn't been for the waitress in the diner adjacent to the truck stop. She was quite taken with Bryant. My littlest brother looked younger than his seven years, with curly brown hair, black almond-shaped eyes, and a contagious laugh. I never found out what prompted the waitress to give him a free breakfast that morning, but she had, a feast of pancakes, eggs, bacon, and sausage. Breakfasts for Teddy, Madeleine, and Kate soon followed, and I heard all about them when I woke up. My siblings gave me some bacon they'd thoughtfully saved.

Later that morning, a truck stop attendant approached our trailer. "Ted?" he called out.

"That's me," Dad answered.

"There's a phone call for you inside."

I couldn't think of anyone who would know to call Dad at the Phillips 66.

Dad came back from the phone call with a pep in his gait. "That was Glenn," he said to Mom. We kids knew Glenn as Mr. Andersen. "He sent us a FedEx package with enough money for gas to get home. Enough for lunch, too. It'll get here before noon."

Dad must have told Mr. Andersen at some point that we were stranded in Minnesota. I did whatever I could to hasten our packing so we could leave as soon as the FedEx package came.

The six-hour drive flew by. We stopped for lunch at McDonald's, devouring Quarter Pounders and Chicken McNuggets with fries, and when we passed the green sign that read, "Rockford, Population 139,426," we all cheered. I could hardly believe I would get to sleep in my own bed that night.

The familiar crunch of tires on gravel welcomed us into our driveway. Once Dad found the house key he hadn't used in a year, my siblings and

I scrambled to be the first one inside. Lights turned on and everyone scattered. I lingered in the mudroom, where the smell of our home struck me as both familiar and strange, a musty blend of old books and tea leaves. Had it always smelled like this? Mom's Tide laundry detergent sat above the washer and dryer as usual. Dad's deer antler coat rack still hung on the wall to the right. I climbed the mudroom staircase and felt the hardwood planks creak beneath me as I walked to my room. The light bulbs didn't turn on when I flipped the switch, but the ceiling fan whirred to life. I fell face-first onto my quilt, rubbing my cheek into the worn peach fabric. I rolled over and stared at the whirling blades above me whose two pull chains clinked together in rhythm with the fan's rotations. Danika had left the windows open. My room smelled like freshly cut grass and grilled burgers from across the street. I sat up and looked out at the neighboring projects. Girls played double-Dutch in the parking lot as though they'd never stopped. Beats from Cypress Hill vibrated from speakers of a Cadillac. My thin muslin curtains billowed as they always had, and in the buzzing streetlight, I could see the apple trees below me bore green rounds of unripe fruit. This was my view. This was my solace. This was my home.

PART II

Go, sell your possessions and give to
the poor, and you will have treasure
in heaven. Then come, follow me.
Matthew 19:21

Look at the birds of the air; they do not
sow or reap or store away in barns,
and yet your Heavenly Father feeds them.
Are you not much more valuable than they?
Matthew 6:26

7

An Education

My family settled back into home life over the next several months. Mom and Dad said we wouldn't be attending Vine City Fellowship anymore now that we were back in Rockford, and they didn't tell me why. I didn't care to ask. Mom resumed homeschooling my siblings and me, and because she trusted me never to cheat, Mom let me teach myself from seventh grade on. Learning at my own pace and scheduling my own time became my favorite part of being homeschooled, instilling me with a self-discipline I would deeply appreciate in years to come. I found the assignments easy enough, and my hunger to learn never tempted me to look at the teacher's key until it was time to grade myself. I gave Mom a weekly report of my progress every Friday, but academic subjects like pre-algebra and world history wouldn't be all I learned that school year.

A painful twisting in my lower back woke me up one September morning. The sun hadn't yet risen, and I tried to ignore the pain and go back to sleep. The spasms worsened. Did I need to throw up? I couldn't tell if I was nauseous or if I had slept in a disagreeable position. Either way, I had to pee.

I stumbled through the chilly hallway and into the bathroom, moaning as I pulled down my Abercrombie & Fitch boxers and my panties. The flannel shorts were the only item I owned from the brazen retail chain, a hand-me-down from an older cousin. The cold toilet seat made me gasp, then my breath froze at the sight of my underwear. Purple blood saturated the ivory-colored cotton. My knees began to shake. I felt dizzy. All I could do for a full minute was stare back and forth between my ruined undies and the thick droplets of blood falling into the porcelain bowl of the toilet, clumping together at the bottom like dead tadpoles.

I tried to steady my trembling legs as I reached into the cabinet under the sink. Mom kept pads there, Lightdays by Kotex. I pulled out one of the white strips and stuffed a wad of toilet paper into my crotch. Fresh underwear was only several feet away in my bedroom dresser. I wrapped my bloody panties carefully in toilet paper and left the bundle in the trash can, then pulled up my boxers and waddled to my bedroom, the Lightdays pad tucked up the sleeve of my sweatshirt. Madeleine and Kate were still sleeping. I stuck the pad on a clean pair of underwear in the privacy of my closet while my back continued to spasm as though God Himself were wringing my womb. Perhaps He was, in His predetermined way. I wanted to ask Mom if the pain was normal, but my fear of her knowing I started my period made me suffer my first two days in silence. I assumed my irrational fear was some form of embarrassment.

On the third day of my period, I was at the library with Dad and Bryant when the cramps became too intense to ignore. I squirmed at the table as we read our books, unable to find a position that offered relief. Dad couldn't help noticing.

"What's wrong, moppet?" he asked.

I couldn't bring myself to tell him. "I don't know," I lied. "My back just hurts."

My voice cracked and my eyes filled with tears. Dad stood at once, telling Bryant to put his *Calvin and Hobbes* comics back in the section they came from. I let Dad guide me to the elevator and cried the whole way home, no longer trying to hide my agony. Mom was folding laundry in the mudroom when we walked through the back door.

"What's wrong?" she asked as soon as she saw me.

"I don't know," Dad said to her. "All of the sudden she said her back hurt."

Still crying, I walked past them and up the stairs to my room. Mom followed, spooning herself around me on my bed while Dad stood in the doorway.

"What's wrong, chickie?" Mom asked, smoothing my hair.

"I don't know. My back hurts."

"Why is it hurting?"

"I don't know."

She motioned to Dad. "Ted, why don't you get her a Kleenex."

Dad left the room, eager to be useful.

"Can you tell me what's wrong now that Dad's gone?"

Somehow Mom intuited that my father was the last person I wanted to know the real reason of my pain. I didn't want to tell her, either, but the hope of some Advil, which my parents kept hidden from us kids, lured me into confession.

"I got my period," I said into my pillow.

"What?"

I repeated myself more clearly keeping my voice at a whisper.

"Oh. Oh, sweetie, you must have cramps. I've never had cramps, but I hear they can be a major pain in the butt."

I nodded. What an understatement.

"What are you using to control the blood?"

"Pads, but they hardly do anything. I have to change them every two hours."

It was true. Every couple of hours, day and night, I had to go to the bathroom and swap out a soaked and leaking pad for a new one, and not before all the blood ruined my clothes. I was beginning to fear that I was bleeding too much. The box of Kotex said each pad should last me a whole day, yet my flow demanded more absorption.

"What kind of pads are you using?" Mom asked.

"The kind you have in the cabinet, the Lightdays."

"Aw, chickie, no wonder they're hardly doing anything. Those are for something else, not your period. You need thicker pads for your period."

"Then what are the Lightdays for? The white stuff?"

Mom didn't explain cervical mucus or female lubrication to me. I assumed the clearish-white stuff that had been secreting from my body for the past several months was like a pre-period of sorts. My friend Danika said she got it, too, so I thought whatever it was must be normal. Instead of answering my question, Mom redirected our conversation.

"I'm going to have Dad get you some ibuprofen," she said, "and then I'm gonna show you where I keep the pads you should be using from now on."

Later that day as I read on my bed, a much thicker pad adhered to my underwear, Mom came in my room extending a small paperback. Its title read *Preparing for Adolescence* by Dr. James Dobson. Dr. Dobson was the founder of Focus on the Family, a prominent Christian organization promoting conservative values through its publications and films.

"I figured you should read this now," Mom said. She set the book on my bed avoiding my eyes. "Let me know if you have any questions."

The book was sex-ed for Christians. Its pages informed preteens of all the physical and psychological changes they could expect in coming years as their bodies prepared for adulthood, filling out the gaps of my limited knowledge. *Preparing for Adolescence* had illustrations of the male and female reproductive systems, including a sketch of a couple engaged in the missionary position. I found the image inexplicably arousing. Then I learned what I could do with that arousal: masturbate. I had never heard of masturbation before. As I read Dr. Dobson's description of self-stimulation, I realized it was what I'd been doing ever since I was little, when I sat cross-legged rocking on my heels while making my Barbie dolls kiss. Other things that made my private parts throb were bike riding, straddling pillows, and seeing images of men and women lying on top of each other. I didn't know my excitement was normal. I certainly hadn't known there was a way to release it, either, otherwise I would have been having climaxes since age five.

At first, I was relieved to see Dr. Dobson approved of masturbating. "It is my opinion that masturbation is not much of an issue with God," he wrote. "It is a normal part of adolescence which involves no one else. It does not cause disease. It does not produce babies, and Jesus did not mention it in the Bible."

Then Dr. Dobson seemed to contradict himself.

"I'm not telling you to masturbate," he continued, "and I hope you don't feel the need for it. But if you do, it is my opinion that you should not struggle with guilt over it. . . . The best I can do is suggest that you talk with God personally about this matter and decide what He wants you to do."

As soon as I read that I shouldn't feel guilt, I felt guilty. For someone to say that I shouldn't feel something implied that I ought to, otherwise the reassurance wouldn't be there. Dr. Dobson had also said that he hoped I wouldn't feel the need to masturbate, further implying that, despite his other words, the esteemed Christian psychologist thought the act less than ideal. The moral ambiguity vexed me. Was masturbation sinful or not? Did the guilt I carried with me over touching myself, even before I knew what I was doing, signify that it was wrong? If God approved, wouldn't He give me peace about it?

I had my first orgasm later that day. I could hardly believe such a pleasurable experience had been available to me my whole life.

Once the ecstasy wore off, I evaluated my emotions to discern whether I felt peaceful or guilty. Definitely guilty. Any peaceful feelings I had were probably from the sensation of release, and what was left in their wake could be described as nothing less than shame. I masturbated again and again over the following days. My shame deepened, for my orgasms were accompanied by lustful thoughts. As the book *I Kissed Dating Goodbye* had informed me, lustful thoughts were Biblical taboo. I felt like I was personally nailing Jesus to the cross every time I climaxed. He'd died for all the sins He knew I'd commit, including that one. Tears sprang to my eyes when I imagined how grieved He must be over my lust, after all He'd

done for me. I justified my self-pleasure by telling myself that masturbation would be the thorn in my side, the act of deliberate transgression
that would keep me humble before God. My prayers of repentance were
enriched by the acknowledgment that I had become a conscious sinner in
daily need of God's forgiveness.

Perhaps it was my guilt over masturbating that prompted me to read
the entire Bible. I had never read it cover to cover, and I felt I ought to
since I was becoming an adult who professed to be a Christian. I decided
to read at least five chapters of the Bible every day after I finished my
schoolwork. Most of the stories in Genesis and Exodus were familiar to
me, interrupted by long lists of who fathered whom as mankind spread
across the Middle East, but I found things I had never heard of as I went
through Leviticus, Numbers, and Deuteronomy. Disturbing things. God
was supposed to be just, yet He punished children for the sins of their
parents to the third and fourth generations. He was jealous of other gods
and also proclaimed to be the only one. He was a consuming God, but
He was also merciful. He said He wouldn't destroy His people, then sent
venomous snakes to do just that because they were complaining of hunger
and thirst. He claimed to show no partiality among nations, yet repeatedly
expressed that the Israelites were His favorite race.

The injustice that stood out to me most as I read the Bible was God's
misogyny. Sexism screamed at me from the pages of the Old Testament.
God said giving birth to a daughter made a woman more unclean than
having a son. The value of a man was worth fifty shekels of silver while the
value of a woman was only thirty. If a man had sex with one of his female
slaves, she was to be whipped afterward for no named reason, and if she
was a captive from a conquered nation, the man could let her go if he
wasn't satisfied with her. Then there were the poor virgins. If a betrothed
virgin was raped in a town, she was to be stoned for not screaming loudly
enough for help; if she was raped in the countryside where no one could
hear her, then she was allowed to live. If a raped virgin was not betrothed,
God said she had to marry her rapist as long as he paid her father a fine.

If a virgin didn't bleed on her wedding night, all of the men in her village were to drag her to her parents' house and stone her to death. I read of no punishment for men who weren't virgins when they married. Neither did men suffer consequences for being raped or unfaithful to their wives. Only women were punished for having sex outside of marriage, whether they did so voluntarily or by force. The sole exception seemed to be only if a man raped a virgin who was pledged to another—then he was to be stoned, not for raping the woman, but for violating another man's property.

There were two stories I read that troubled me more than others. Both involved fathers offering their virgin daughters for gang rape in order to protect a man from being sodomized. First was the tale of Lot in the book of Genesis. Two angels disguised as men spent the night in Lot's house, and for some reason, a crowd of men wanted to have sex with the male visitors. Lot refused to hand over the disguised angels, saying homosexuality was wicked. "Look," he said, "I have two daughters who have never slept with a man. Let me bring them out to you, and you can do what you like with them." The girls were spared gang rape only because the two angels struck the crowd with blindness.

The second tale about father-offered gang rape didn't have as happy an ending, the story about a Levite man and his concubine. Concubines seemed to me like second-class wives, falling somewhere between spouse and sex slave. In the book of Judges, the nameless concubine of a Levite man decided to leave him. He went to fetch her at her parents' house, and on their long journey home, an old man invited them to take shelter with him. That night, a group of men surrounded the house and pounded on the door, demanding the old man release his male guest so they could have sex with him. The old man said, "No, my friends, don't be so vile. Since this man is my guest, don't do this outrageous thing. Look, here is my virgin daughter, and his concubine. I will bring them out to you now, and you can use them and do to them whatever you wish."

It was unclear what happened to the virgin daughter, but the Levite's concubine was sent outside. The crowd of men raped and abused her all night. She managed to crawl back to the house, and when the Levite man opened the door at daybreak, he found her unconscious with her hands on the threshold. She didn't respond to his command that she get up. The Levite threw her over his donkey and left, and when he arrived home, he took a knife and cut her up, limb by limb, into twelve pieces. The Bible didn't say if the woman was dead or alive when he did this. The Levite then sent her body parts to leaders in various places of Israel as a summoning to war.

I didn't understand the moral of these Bible stories. All I knew was that I felt distressed by every detail of them. I couldn't imagine what God wanted readers to learn from the disturbing tales, and seeing how little God valued girls, I began to worry that He might ask my parents to do something atrocious to me. I needed their reassurance they wouldn't let anything bad happen just because God's Word might allow it, or even command it.

"Did you guys know how much sex and violence are in the Bible?" I asked them at breakfast one morning.

"What?" Mom asked.

I nodded. "If it were a movie, it would be rated R—or X."

"When did you start reading the Bible?"

"A couple weeks ago." I took a breath. "Dad, would you hand me over to a bunch of men to get raped if God told you to?"

Dad looked angry I'd even ask him such a thing. "No!" he sputtered. "What would give you that idea?"

"It's in the Bible," I said.

Dad had studied the Bible extensively at seminary school. He remembered the stories I shared with him.

"You need to keep in mind that the Old Testament is pre-Christianity," Dad said. "Everything changed once Jesus came, so a lot of the laws God talks about in the Old Testament aren't necessarily relevant today."

"There's rape in the Bible?" Mom asked.

"Yeah," I said, surprised she didn't already know. "A lot of it. God even says to stone a girl if she's raped."

"See," Dad said, "that's the kind of thing we don't do anymore. Jesus came to break the old laws."

That confused me, because I thought God didn't change. Numbers 23:10 said, "God is not human, that He should lie, not a human being, that He should change his mind."

"But God doesn't change," I said to Dad.

Dad wiped his mouth with his napkin. "No, God doesn't change," he said. "But sometimes he reveals different parts of Himself to different people, at different times."

I assumed that disclosure was yet to come.

I continued through the Old Testament, which seemed mostly full of bloodshed, poetry, and prophecies. All throughout, God's changelessness was reinforced. The more I learned about His nature, the more I feared Him. God wanted us to fear Him. He minced no words declaring what He would do to people who didn't, including sending wasting diseases and sudden terrors.

"You will eat the flesh of your sons and the flesh of your daughters," God said in Leviticus.

In Isaiah, God said, "I will punish the world for its evil, the wicked for their sins. Their infants will be dashed into pieces before their eyes."

"It will burn like a furnace," God said of Judgment Day in the book of Malachi. "All the arrogant and every evildoer will be stubble, and the day that is coming will set them on fire."

It was a frigid day in January when I completed the Old Testament. I closed my Bible and sat on my bed for several minutes, watching the snow whip past my window. It was hard for me to imagine a day of wrath that would burn like a furnace when I couldn't even see the other side of the street through the blizzard. I tightened my quilt around me, deep in thought.

What I took away from the Old Testament was that God was to be feared above all else. The resounding message seemed to contradict what my parents had taught me: that God was unconditional love. I had now seen for myself that wasn't the case. God had explicit conditions in exchange for His love, which made me question what love was. I thought love meant protection and nurture, caresses when sick, and the removal of suffering when possible. The Bible made love seem inextricable from suffering. To love was to inflict pain. Proverbs 3:11–12 said, "My son, do not despise the Lord's discipline, and do not resent His rebuke, because the Lord disciplines those He loves, as a father the son he delights in."

I realized Dad reinforced that whenever he disciplined my siblings and me. After telling us to get his leather belt from his closet, Dad always crouched to our eye level and held our hands. "I'm doing this because I love you," he'd say, right before he pulled down our pants and lashed our bare bottoms. Once I asked him through my tears why he hurt me if he loved me.

"Because you need to learn to listen to me," he said. "The pain will help you remember."

Sometimes Mom disciplined us. She commanded us to make a fist if she used a wooden spoon on our knuckles, and she used her palm if she smacked our mouths. She always took aim right before she struck, her brow furrowed in concentration as her hand seemed to count to three in pulses that nearly reached our skin. On three, the smack landed. Mom took us into her arms afterward, saying we were only smacked because she loved us and wanted us to obey her for our own safety. If we didn't obey her without question, she explained, one day our lives might be in danger. A car might speed toward us that we couldn't see, and Mom would try to save us by commanding that we move to the sidewalk. If blind obedience wasn't ingrained in us when a moment like that came, we could be dead because she didn't love us enough to discipline us.

I supposed love as inflicted pain made sense. God wanted us to obey His commandments because He wanted to save us from going to hell. In order to train us to obey Him, God needed to make sure we suffered consequences we'd remember, consequences that would set an example to others watching. But I wondered why God had created a hell to save us from to begin with.

I finished the New Testament shortly after I turned thirteen. All the way through the book of Revelation, the Bible never explained why God had made the hell we needed saving from. Two weeks after my birthday, on a cold February afternoon, I was sitting on my bed finger-knitting a scarf when I looked up and saw Mom in the doorway.

"Alice," Mom said. "Come to the sitting room. Dad and I have something to tell you kids."

My belly clenched. Were she and Dad getting divorced? Did a grandparent die? Had Mila been hit by a car?

"What's it about?" I asked.

"We're moving."

8

Homeless

Mom's words cut into me. We'd only been home for seven months since our return from California. In one moment, the stability I'd worked so hard to trust again was shattered.

I sat numbly on the sitting room couch as Mom and Dad explained to my siblings and me that God wanted us to give Him our things.

"He only let us borrow this house," Dad said. "And now He wants us to give it back to Him and trust that He has something better for us."

"Where are we going?" Teddy asked.

"We don't know yet," Mom said.

"Are we leaving Rockford?"

"Most likely."

"When?" asked Madeleine.

"In about two months," Dad said. "As soon as we can sell the house."

"And you don't even know where God's taking us?" I asked.

"No," Mom said. "That's part of the adventure."

I hated adventure. The word once promised summer days with handmade rafts and capture-the-flag. All it promised me now was misery. God-led misery.

"But what about our stuff?" Madeleine asked.

"We're probably going to put some of it in storage," Mom said.

Laughter threatened to spill out of me, which I knew only stifled the raging tears that wished they could come out instead.

"There's a story I'd like to share with you guys," Dad said. The tone of his voice told me he was going into pastor mode. "There was a little girl whose father gave her a necklace of plastic beads. She loved the beads very much, and she slept with them under her pillow every night. One day, years later when the daughter was a teenager, the father asked her to give the beads back. She was confused. It broke her heart to hand over the beads she loved so much. But her father said to trust him, so she did. When she woke up the next day, under her pillow lay not a necklace of plastic beads, but a beautiful necklace of real pearls. Just 'cause she trusted her father."

Dad looked at each of us, letting the moral of the story sink in. Clearly he was making the analogy that we were like the little girl and God was the father who wanted to give us something better. I couldn't let the condescension slide.

"Why didn't the father just tell his daughter he'd give her real pearls if she handed over her fake ones?"

"Because he wanted her to trust him," Dad said.

"Why?" I asked. "Why would he play games with her like that?"

"He wasn't playing games," Mom said. "He wanted to reward the daughter for her faith."

I was disgusted by the story and the implications it left my parents with. The hope it dangled was all I had to cling to in the coming months and years: that God would give me something better than everything He asked me to leave behind.

Less than a week after the moving announcement, Mom, Dad, Teddy, and I were in the dining room wrapping my parents' crystal wine glasses with butcher paper. The glasses had been a wedding gift, and Dad wanted to save them in the storage unit we had yet to rent.

"You really have no idea where God will take us?" I asked Mom.

"All we know is we're leaving Rockford," Mom said. "We'll probably camp our way east."

There it was. We weren't even moving into another house right away.

"We're camping?" I asked.

"Yep."

"For how long?"

"We don't know."

I allowed myself to become more careless about wrapping the crystal, hoping I would accidentally break a glass. I knew it wouldn't change anything, but I wanted to smash every single goblet and listen to their pieces shatter on the table while my parents' mouths hung open in shock.

"Can we go to Florida?" Teddy asked.

"I think we can do that."

"Can we stay in Florida if we go there?"

"We're going wherever God leads us," Dad said. "And we'll stay for as long as He wants us to."

In my prayers, I specified to God that if I was going to hand over my plastic beads in the form of the Victorian house I loved so much, and the friends I'd miss so dearly, He'd better follow through with those pearls. I told Him I wanted my own bedroom wherever we ended up, and I asked that He please change my parents' hearts about letting me go to school so I could make new friends. I knew God wasn't one to negotiate but stating my desires couldn't hurt.

~

By the end of March, my family's house was for sale. The few belongings we wanted to keep were packed into boxes that we moved into the attic. Most of what we saved was irreplaceable, like photo albums and family heirlooms, and Dad said they would go into a storage unit soon. My parents hired a woman named Joanne to appraise what was left of our belongings for an estate sale. Mom told my siblings and me to stay in the sitting room while she and Dad gave Joanne the grand tour, and hearing Joanne's bossy voice place a value on the furniture and decorations I'd grown up with offended me in ways I hadn't anticipated. How dare a stranger decide the worth of the couch we'd snuggled in, or the rugs we'd learned to crawl on, or the copper molds that watched over every kitchen meal from where they hung on the wall?

The night before the estate sale, Mom told my siblings and me that we were going to spend the weekend at the Andersens' home, so we wouldn't be in the way when people came to shop. "Say goodbye to everything," she told us before we left. "We don't know what'll be here when we come back."

I walked through each room of my house and caressed every item one last time. My antique dresser never felt so smooth, and the floral pattern of the sitting room couch never looked so beautiful. I felt as if I were saying goodbye to family members I would never see again. I cried uncontrollably the whole way to the Andersens'. Nothing could comfort me, not even the chocolate chip cookies Mrs. Andersen had waiting for us. As soon as I walked through their front door, I tucked myself into a seldom-used corner of the living room hoping my friend Bethany wasn't watching me cry. I didn't want to embarrass myself in front of her.

"Calm down, Alice," Mom said. She rubbed my back, but I felt her impatience.

"It's happening too fast," I said.

"What is?"

"Everything."

"You just need to change your attitude."

I could tell Mom was bewildered by the depth of my distress. The other kids seemed fine.

The weekend we stayed with the Andersens left me feeling hollow. Bethany seemed heartbroken I was leaving, and there was nothing I could do or say to comfort her when I could barely comfort myself. I couldn't stop thinking about all the people who were picking through my family's things, taking them away never to be seen again. Mom and Dad were happy about it. I overheard them talking to Mr. and Mrs. Andersen in the kitchen one afternoon.

"I used to think I owned my things," Dad said. "Then I realized that my things owned me."

Mr. Andersen quoted a verse from the Bible. "It's easier for a camel to fit through the eye of a needle than it is for a rich man to enter the kingdom of God."

"Exactly," Dad said. "We feel like God's asking us to surrender our worldly things, to follow Him and trust Him to provide."

"So you don't think you guys will be settling down again soon?" Mrs. Andersen asked.

"Probably not, no," Mom said.

"Just whenever it feels right," Dad said. "Whenever we feel in our hearts that God tells us to."

It was as though my parents thought of themselves as modern-day disciples. They felt called to lives of renunciation, lives unencumbered by the material constraints of the world in exchange for the freedom to follow God wherever He led. The first three books of the New Testament were still fresh in my mind, and I figured where Mom and Dad had found their inspiration to sell everything.

"Go," Jesus said in the book of Matthew. "Sell your possessions and give to the poor, and you will have treasure in heaven. Then come, follow me."

In the book of Luke, Jesus said, "Those of you who do not give up everything you have cannot be my disciples."

God must have wanted me to be a disciple, too. Otherwise He would have given me to different parents.

When my family returned home on Sunday evening, I felt as though I were walking through a stranger's house. Joanne had rearranged our furniture into an organized mess and the sight of price tags on our belongings was more than I could bear. Rose and Violet, my two china dolls standing on the hutch of the dining room, had white tags dangling from their velvet dresses. Each read "$85." I ripped the tags off and carried Rose and Violet with me to the kitchen. I didn't expect to yell at Mom.

"You didn't tell me Joanne would be selling my dolls!"

"Well, when you didn't put them in your keepsake pile, I thought that meant you didn't want them anymore."

Mom had a point. I'd overlooked the dolls because they were kept in the dining room, where their deep peach and lilac gowns complemented the "Dusty Rose" paint color of the walls.

"But they're my dolls," I said to Mom. I felt their value was as obvious as if they were my children.

Mom glared at my outrage. "Keep working on that attitude," she said.

I swallowed my protests and nodded. I only yelled when I was trying not to cry. Didn't Mom know that?

My bed was gone. Mom said I could sleep on the sitting room couch until we moved, since our family sofa hadn't sold. Never again would I take its soft beauty for granted. I begged God to change my heart about moving as I lay in my sleeping bag that night. I felt exhausted from crying and trying to control my anger. *Please help me be more cheerful,* I prayed.

I hoped to wake up feeling better. I felt as sad as I'd been the day before.

Mom and Dad sold or donated what remained after the estate sale. We got rid of things so quickly that every time I walked into a different room, it was barer than before. Boxes of clothes were hauled to the Salvation Army, as well as toys, bicycles, and other things we'd accumulated over the years. One day, I heard an unfamiliar female voice talking with Mom in the kitchen. I went downstairs to see who it was and froze at the sight of a young girl trying on a pair of my old figure skates. Her mom laughed with mine over the ridiculous prices of new boots and blades.

"When I saw your ad in the paper," the woman said, "I called right away because Shelly has a competition coming up and she's almost outgrown her last pair. Things are just so expensive nowadays."

"Tell me about it," Mom said. She was smiling in the fake way she did with strangers.

"Those aren't for sale," I said.

Everyone turned to look at me. Their faces were blurry.

"They're not for sale," I repeated.

"Alice," Mom said, walking toward me. "You're never going to use them again—"

"I don't care. You don't have permission to sell *my* things without asking me."

My arms were stiff, yet shaking.

"Excuse us a sec," Mom said to the woman. "Sweetie, how about we talk about this in the other—"

"No, she can't have my skates!"

Despite my best effort to maintain my composure, I crumpled into tears. I heard the woman mumble something about coming back another time, but Mom motioned for her to wait a minute. She gently led me to the mudroom and sat me down on the steps.

"Shh, shh," Mom said. "I'm sorry. I should've asked you first. But chickie, you've outgrown your skates. Why would you want to keep them?"

I didn't know myself. All I could do was cry.

"How about you keep one pair, and we sell the rest?"

I nodded.

"Which pair do you want to keep?"

My words were interrupted by hiccups. "My first pair."

"Okay, I'll have Daddy set those ones aside. Is it okay if I go back to selling the others? Another girl could really use them."

I nodded. My distress wasn't only about the ice skates. It was about my increasing loss of control. Every sale, every donation, every piece of my life that went to someone else made me feel as though I were dying in some way. I knew intellectually that I was more than my things, but my things symbolized my safety. I didn't know how to explain it to Mom. Even if I did, it wouldn't have mattered. My belongings weren't really mine because my parents had paid for them, and their things weren't really theirs because everything belonged to God. God could give and take away what He wanted, when He wanted, and my parents were all too eager to cooperate. What would be the point of telling Mom how important material symbols were to me? We still had to move.

From then on, I worked hard to suppress my emotions. It was the only way I felt I could force the better attitude Mom said would help ease my distress. Tears solved nothing. Voicing my feelings made me feel worse. My parents only told me to "talk to God" if I was unhappy about what He'd called our family to do, for they were only following Him. I learned to replace hope with resignation and fear with numbness. Even so, my repressed feelings attacked me in ways I didn't recognize at the time. Nightmares woke me every night. My jaw ached from grinding my teeth. Without knowing why, I began calling the weather hotline obsessively.

"The temperature is fifty-two degrees," the automated voice would say, "with eighty percent humidity."

I dialed the hotline as soon as I woke up and numerous times throughout the day. It was the first thing I did whenever my family came home from an errand and the last thing I did before I went to bed. Maybe I was comforted to know that no matter what upheavals were going on in my life, the weather robot could be counted on. Its voice was neutral and steady, and it predicted the rest of the week's forecast with unruffled, scientific certainty.

My parents accepted an offer on our house in mid-May, and on June 7, 1999, I said goodbye to my beloved Victorian for the last time. I stroked its crystal doorknobs like they were vanishing diamonds. I memorized the gingerbread molding as though it were a secret code. I ran and slid over the creaky part of the second-floor hallway, where exposed nail heads had snagged many a sock. As a final token to take with me, I crept into the basement and pocketed one of the sparkly white rocks that were mysteriously piled into corners and crevices. Dad said the stones had no value, but to me, they were more special than the rarest of gems.

I stood in the driveway staring at our house until Mom gave me her second command to get in the car. The other kids piled in and I faintly heard the engine start. I wanted to scream as Dad backed out of the driveway. My eyes followed the top of the fourth-story tower until Dad made a turn that blocked it from my sight. With that, we were homeless.

9

The South

The Suburban was packed to its limits. Our green cargo bag bulged against the straps tying it to the roof rack, and the pop-up trailer dragged behind us latched by the tow hitch. Inside the car, my family's seating arrangement was as it had always been: Teddy and I shared the right two spots of the third bench seat, with duffle bags of clothing taking up the left side; Madeleine, Bryant, and Kate shared the middle bench, with Mila's litter box at the foot of whoever sat in the center; and Mom and Dad sat up front.

Giving away Mila was our first stop. Pets weren't allowed in most of the campgrounds Mom said we'd be staying in, so we drove south to Dallas, Texas, when we left Rockford to leave Mila with our Auntie Sandra, who would then pass her on to Mom's brother, our Uncle Frank. His family said they'd take in our beloved cat. When the day came to say goodbye, my siblings and I elbowed each other for one last kiss between Mila's ears, one last scratch beneath her chin. All of us sobbed. Even Dad was misty-eyed. Mila's black and orange fur was wet from all the tears we shed, and she purred as though we were coming back an hour later.

"I'll never forget you, Mila," I whispered. "You're the best cat anyone could've dreamed."

The last time I saw Mila, she was in Auntie Sandra's arms. Her yellow eyes alerted with confusion as she watched the Suburban pull away without her. I burned the image to memory, forcing myself to look back at Mila until she became a speck, disappearing behind a building with Dad's turn of the steering wheel.

We arrived in New Orleans two days later. "The House of the Rising Sun" played in my head as Dad pulled into a campground outside the city. My siblings and I, still grieving the loss of our cat, slumped out of the car and immediately turned damp with sweat.

"See how hot it is, guys?" Mom said. "Mila might've died in this heat."

We glared at her. Nothing would alleviate our anger at the forced surrender of our pet.

The smells of swampland were unlike any I'd breathed before. My family had never visited the South. Live oak trees heavily garlanded with Spanish moss emitted a musty fragrance. Sweet streaks of gardenia interrupted the stench wafting from nearby dumpsters, where a group of kids played hopscotch in the twilight. Woodsmoke rivered through the air in plumes, and I could tell someone in the campground was grilling fish.

Dad sprayed us all with OFF! repellent when the tent was set up. By then, it was too late. We were covered in welts from mosquito bites. Their high-pitched whines were drowned out only by the throbbing buzz of cicadas coming from the woods bordering the campground, which were thick with mystery.

"Teddy, build a fire, please," Mom said. "We're having hot dogs for dinner. Alice, come help me set the table."

"Mom, I have to go potty," said Kate.

"Madeleine, you take Kate to the bathroom."

Madeleine rolled her eyes. "Where is it?"

"I don't know, walk around and figure it out. Take the water jug with you and fill it up on your way back."

Madeleine grabbed the collapsible water container from the back of the Suburban and sulked off with Kate struggling to match her long-legged strides. Bryant helped Dad attach the rain fly to our tent. Trailers weren't allowed in that campground, so our pop-up remained collapsed next to our car.

I helped Mom unfold our plastic tablecloth over the brown diamond grate of the picnic table. The tablecloth was aqua green with colorful fish swimming through coral. We'd had the covering for as long as I could remember. It had become permanently sticky from maple syrup mornings and barbecue sauce evenings. Mom handed me a Ziploc baggie of silver clamps, which helped anchor the cloth to the table so it wouldn't blow away, not that there was even the slightest breeze to break up the humid air. That aqua green tablecloth was now all we had for a dining room.

My family explored New Orleans the next day, then we continued east through the bottoms of Mississippi and Alabama. As soon as we crossed into Florida, the scenery changed from lush swamp to tropical beach. I couldn't believe how stunning the shoreline was. It was like God had dumped bags of white sugar next to a blue raspberry ocean. I wished I were sitting in the middle bench of the Suburban so I could stick my head out the window and let the warm breeze whip the frizzy hair off my face, but no one wanted to trade spots with Teddy or me. Not when Dad was following the scenic route of Highway 30-A all the way to Panama City.

It was after six o'clock when Dad pulled into St. Andrews State Park. We set up camp and everyone scurried into their swimsuits, racing to a silky shoreline tinged pink from sunset. Everyone except me. I was on my period that week. Mom refused to let me wear tampons, saying they'd take away what made me a virgin. I thought about using a quarter to buy one of the tampons in the gas station bathroom near the campground, but what if Mom was right? What would happen if I lost my virginity to anything other than my husband's penis? Would God punish me? The Bible certainly made me think so. While my family dove into the warm water of the Gulf of Mexico, I sat on a beach chair simmering with resentment, my pad bulging through my modest-length jean shorts like a diaper.

"You should really go in," Dad said, walking up to me. "The water's great." He toweled off his hair beside the beach chair I sat on. I could almost feel how refreshed he was.

"I can't," I said. "Mom won't let me."

"What do you mean Mom won't let you?"

I stared at him. His confused expression told me he wouldn't figure out my predicament on his own, but I was too embarrassed to spell it out for him. I rolled my eyes as if to tell Dad that Mom was just being ridiculous. I felt she was.

Sweaty weeks passed as my family camped our way through the Florida Keys and up the Atlantic Coast until mid-July found us at yet another beachside campground, this time on the island bluffs of North Carolina. A fever allowed me to stay in the pop-up by myself one afternoon when my family went for a walk. My latest view from the trailer's screened windows was nothing but sand dunes. Sand had worked its way into everything we owned, and I wasn't sure my sleeping bag would ever be rid of it. From the pockets of my shorts to the cup holder by my spot in the Suburban, and even within the boar bristles of the family hairbrush, fine grains of sand clung to me at every turn, painful to brush off. I decided I hated beach camping. A salty breeze blew through the sleeping area I shared with Teddy and Madeleine, and I rolled onto my back, closing my eyes to try and nap. I'd been fighting a rising temperature for days. My head throbbed, my muscles ached, and I couldn't breathe through my stuffed-up nose. Despite my misery, I was almost grateful to be sick. It gave me an excuse to withdraw from my family.

All I wanted to do was sleep. Dreamless, heavy sleep made time go by more quickly, and I wasn't sure how much time needed to pass before I would want to be awake again. If I wasn't sleeping, I was usually listening to music on the portable CD player Dad let me borrow. The Backstreet Boys' *Millennium* album was the only CD I owned. Normally, my parents forbade secular music, but they made an exception when I convinced them the boy band was Christian by pointing out where they thanked God in their CD cover. Besides, the songs were practically no different from the Vineyard worship music I'd grown up with. I could picture Jesus singing "The One" to me, promising to make all my sorrows undone and take me from darkness to light. "I Want It That Way" reminded me that God should be my fire and one desire, and that my way was selfish and sinful. My parents needn't have worried the Christian filter I grew up with would disappear any time soon.

Mom thought I spent too much time with headphones on. I wasn't "being present," as she said. That was exactly the point. I didn't want to be present. Music helped to drown out the loudness of my siblings playing, of my parents' constant bickering over Dad's driving, and the ever-present white noise of wind blowing through the car windows. Another reason I escaped was to try and regain some sense of privacy. The only space I had to call my own was my seat in the Suburban next to Teddy. I was never alone except when I used the toilet or took a shower in a public campground facility, and even then, the noise of other people never allowed me to feel a moment of solitude. Mom rarely allowed me to opt out of family activities. I had a feeling she'd only let me stay in the trailer that afternoon because of my fever—the thermometer proved I wasn't making it up.

I heard the noise of my family's return from the beach all too soon. "Has your attitude gotten any better?" Mom asked me.

The trailer shook as she stepped inside. Too tired to argue with her, I simply nodded. I didn't think I'd had an attitude to begin with.

I rolled over on my side, my nose brushing against the trailer window. Dad had sewn an extra layer of netting over the screens. The sheer windows the pop-up came with kept out mosquitos, but the square holes of the material didn't keep out no-see-ums. No-see-ums were tinier than gnats and left bites itchier than any other insect I'd known. My whole family's ankles, shins, and wrists were covered in red bumps, and I wondered how much worse off we'd be if Dad hadn't purchased the extra no-see-um netting.

"When are we going to Nannie and Pop-pop's?" I heard Bryant ask.

"We might get there tomorrow," Dad said.

Dad's parents had moved from New Jersey to North Carolina the year before, to a small northeastern town called Camden. I prayed God would tell us to stay there for several days at least. I yearned to shower in a real bathroom all to myself, and a sojourn at Nannie and Pop-pop's house would be a welcome break from driving place to place.

My grandfather was gardening outside a picturesque two-story house when we pulled into my grandparents' driveway the next day. Pop-pop looked dapper as ever, with his silver hair neatly combed back and a striped polo shirt tucked into his buckled trousers.

"There they are," he said, peeling off his work gloves as we tumbled out of the Suburban. My grandmother pulled up behind us a few minutes later. Her chin-length hair seemed whiter than I'd last seen it, but her sparkling blue-gray eyes hadn't lost their delight. After proclamations of how tall we'd grown were declared, we went inside the foyer, which smelled comfortingly like their old home in New Jersey.

"I see you brought the mothballs with you," Dad said to Nannie.

"Oh, you stop," she said, playfully whacking Dad's arm. Everyone in the family teased Nannie about her excessive mothball collection. I'd grown to love the smell over the years. It reminded me of happy times.

"Be sure to take off your shoes," Nannie told us. My grandparents ran a tight ship, which was just fine with me. I craved order and cleanliness.

Mom and Dad took the guest room while Nannie led my siblings and me to what she proudly called the FROG. "It means 'finished room over garage,'" she said, leading us up a staircase to a loft. Nannie showed us where we could put our duffels and sleeping bags, then led us downstairs for cold cut sandwiches.

Nannie and Pop-pop were excited to take us with them to church the following Sunday. Sunday school only went up to sixth grade, which meant I had to sit through the service with the adults. My grandparents' church was the kind Dad would say had no life in it. The hymns inspired no one to jump or clap, and no one wore jeans. Only the handshake interlude felt familiar. Every church had one, when the pastor commanded varying versions of introduction among the congregation.

"Greet the people next to you," said Nannie and Pop-pop's pastor. "Tell them God is doing something wonderful in their life."

When I was a kid, I wasn't expected to participate in handshake inter-
ludes. Almost a year had passed since I'd last been to a church service, and
now that I was over five feet tall and beginning to look like a real teenager,
adults turned to me. I felt as if I were being initiated into a Christian rite
of passage.

"I'm Margaret," said a middle-aged woman to my left, who wore a red
dress suit and heavy jewelry. I tried not to let my nerves show as I shook
her hand. The forced pleasantries felt unbearable.

"I'm Alice."

"God is doing something wonderful in your life," Margaret said.

I mirrored her artificial smile. "God is doing something wonderful in
your life, too."

I felt like a liar. What did we know about each other's lives?

A tall man directly in front of me turned around and stuck out his hand.
"God's doing something wonderful in your life," he said. "I'm Craig."

"Alice," I said. I couldn't bring myself to presume the wonderfulness
of his life.

Back at Nannie and Pop-pop's house, I learned that my grandparents
and I believed in a different God. Only Pop-pop, Teddy, and I remained
seated at the kitchen table when everyone else scattered after lunch. Nannie
stood a few feet away wiping crumbs off the counter.

"It was so hard for us to find a church when we moved here," she said.

"It really was," said Pop-pop. "If we walked into a church and there was
a drum set on the stage, I knew we should turn around right then."

"You don't like drums?" I asked.

Pop-pop grimaced and shook his head.

"And neither does the Lord," Nannie added, joining us at the table.

Teddy and I exchanged a look. "Our old church had drums," Teddy said.

"Yeah," I said. "You don't think God liked our worship music?"

Pop-pop's mouth twitched. Nannie hastened to smooth the table
runner.

"And what about people in remote parts of Africa?" I continued.

"What if all they have is drums? You don't think that pleases God, to hear His people worshipping Him, no matter what instruments they use?"

"Well," Nannie said, "I suppose God would hear their hearts. But I don't think He likes the drums, no."

"But didn't He invent them?" Teddy asked. "Or give people the idea to invent them?"

"The Bible says, 'Make a joyful noise unto the Lord,'" I said. "God didn't specify what noises He doesn't like as long as it's joyful."

"The most joyful music to God's ears is from the Presbyterian hymnal," Nannie said, her eyes gleaming with stubbornness.

I couldn't hold back my tone anymore. "You think God only listens to English hymns?"

"Alright now, that's enough," Pop-pop said.

The kitchen went silent.

"Sorry," I muttered, standing up. I gave them a slight nod of self-dismissal.

Teddy followed me outside into the backyard. The day was bright and humid. Cicadas hummed from the nearby woods, likely worshipping God in their own right. I had never heard a more ridiculous notion about God than that He ignored the worship of everyone in the world except for Presbyterians. The heavenly Father I believed in loved music from every culture.

My family's stay at Nannie and Pop-pop's ended a few days later. I couldn't remember another time when our visit felt so awkward, nor did I know what my grandparents really thought about my family's traveling ways. The overall impression I gathered was that they disagreed with my parents' choices, though I knew they loved us. I didn't realize how badly I'd been hoping God would tell my parents to settle in North Carolina until we pulled out of the driveway and Mom gave Dad directions to the Chincoteague National Wildlife Refuge in Virginia. I slept the whole drive there.

10

The Atlantic

My great-aunt Meg lived in New Jersey in an old colonial built in the 1700s. The floorboards creaked as I walked down a hallway decorated with generations of photographs, and the humid, dusty smell reminded me of my beloved Victorian. Recently widowed, Aunt Meg had invited my family to spend the humid weeks of late July and early August with her. I felt grateful to have another break from camping. I enjoyed wandering from room to room of the creaky house, pondering what other shoes used to tread its hardwood slabs, what hoop skirts once pushed through its doorframes, and what kisses were exchanged on the front porch as lovers said goodbye.

"Alice!"

Mom's voice broke through my imaginings. I walked to the top of the staircase and saw her waiting below with her purse slung over her shoulder. "Aunt Meg wants to take us to the mall," she said.

"The mall?" It sounded too good to be true. I hadn't been to a mall in months.

I basked in the luxury of having the backseat of Aunt Meg's sedan all to myself. Dad and the kids stayed at her home while Mom, Aunt Meg, and

I drove to the Quaker Bridge Mall in Lawrence Township. Mom agreed to let me wander by myself when we got there. I wanted to try on clothes I couldn't buy without feeling the impatience of anyone else.

"Just meet back here at five," Mom said, ascending up an escalator.

The first store I went to was American Eagle Outfitters. I pretended I was the daughter of a wealthy banker with her own credit card, perusing back-to-school racks of ribbed striped sweaters and corduroy flares as though I had a junior high school to attend and an unlimited budget to shop with. I gathered a pile of my favorite items and carried them to the fitting room. A girl with blond highlights opened a stall door for me.

"My name's Stephanie," she said. "Let me know if I can get you any different sizes."

She gave me a look of disdain before shutting the door. I wondered if my lack of a purse told her I didn't really have any money to spend. I slid the lock shut, and midway through taking off my stretched-out tank top, I realized why Stephanie had been put off by me. My armpits reeked of body odor. Shame flooded my ears as I counted back the days to my last shower. It had been at Nannie and Pop-pop's house, so maybe four days had gone by? Five? I let my top fall to the floor and stared at myself in the mirror. My face gleamed with oil and acne. My frizzy hair escaped mismatched clips. My cutoff shorts sagged from protruding hip bones—when had they grown to stick out like that?—and my once-white bra straps were stained yellowish-brown from sweat. I slowly lifted my elbow to examine my armpit, as though I would see my own stink. Instead I saw four sprouts of hair. I stared at them in horror.

"How're you doing in there?"

I recoiled from the door as though it had become see-through. "Fine," I said.

I watched as the pedicured feet in sandals walked away. I couldn't try on any clothes now, not when I knew I might ruin them with my smell. I put my tank top back on and lingered in the fitting room as though changing from outfit to outfit. I unzipped a pair of jeans to make them look like I'd tried them on, and I took a few sweaters off their hangers and threw them sloppily on the fitting room bench. Then I waited. When I felt enough time had gone by, I peeked my head outside the stall to see if anyone was there. The area was empty. I dashed out and hugged the far side of the store as I made my way toward the exit. Stephanie greeted people coming in. I tried to stay behind her, but she turned and saw me.

"Nothing work out for you?" she asked.

I shook my head, not bothering to stop.

After dinner that night, I confronted Mom with a list of demands in one of Aunt Meg's guest rooms.

"I have armpit hair," I said. "So I need a razor, and I'll be shaving my legs, too. Also, I need deodorant. I'm old enough now."

Mom blinked at me. "You have armpit hair?"

"Yes. See?"

I held up my arm and showed Mom the hairs that were almost a quarter inch long. She leaned in close to examine them, then pulled away, staring at me in astonishment.

"Do you have hair in your pubi—"

"I don't know, Mom!"

I flushed with embarrassment. I hadn't even checked my pubic area for hair yet, and I didn't think it was any of Mom's business. All I wanted was a damn razor and deodorant, not a my-baby-girl's-growing-up-so-fast moment.

"So, can you get me a razor or not?"

Mom didn't like my attitude. "Yes," she snapped back. "I'll get you one from the toiletry kit tomorrow."

"And deodorant?"

"You can use the same one I use."

"Mom, that's gross."

"That's all we have right now."

I knew that meant we couldn't afford a brand-new deodorant stick. I decided the next time I had some money, I'd buy my own.

Nobody ever told me puberty would be an easy adjustment, but managing my body's changes that summer proved more difficult than I anticipated. My menstrual cycle wasn't regular. My period lasted for up to ten days at a time and arrived anywhere from two weeks to two months apart. Never knowing when it would start compelled me to wear a pad almost constantly, which gave me a teenage version of diaper rash. I spent half of my waking hours sitting in the Suburban, haunted by the dreadful suspense of lifting my butt to check the blue cushion beneath me for stains. The cramps I experienced made me weep as silently as I could. Two pills of Advil were no match for the sensation of knives twisting in my lower back, and I would have given almost anything for an electrical outlet in the Suburban to plug a heating pad into. I envied girls who could transition into womanhood at home instead of on the road. I reminded myself that pioneer women had it far worse when they crossed America, but I'd already been exposed to modern comforts. My period had been much easier to manage when I lived in a house with bathroom cabinets, where I could store things like pads and painkillers. Instead, all I had was a rose-patterned toiletry kit.

My toiletry kit became my bathroom cabinet and trash can all in one. It held mostly new pads, but two of the zippered compartments carried my used pads, too. This was because I constantly worried that someone might find out when I was on my period. Throwing my used pads in a trash can might give me away. I knew my fear was irrational, but for whatever reason, I couldn't bear the idea of anyone knowing when there was blood coming out of me. I only threw my used pads into trash cans at public restrooms, where they could be anybody's. The rest of the time, I rolled them up in toilet paper, like little pad burritos, and stashed them in my toiletry kit. A foul odor permeated the air whenever I unzipped the section to add a new used pad. The stench reminded me of the dried fish bits I used to feed my pet hermit crab. As more and more used pads were added, I knew I'd have to get rid of them sooner or later. I figured when my family was at the right campground, with the right dumpster hidden in the right spot, I would nonchalantly dump out the contents of my toiletry kit while on my way to the shower. My pad burritos would stay in their compartment until then.

I was on my period during my family's first week at Aunt Meg's. One day, while my siblings rode bikes as I read a Christian romance novel by Janette Oke, Mom called me upstairs.

"What?" I hollered.

"Just come here," she said. Her tone made me feel like I was in trouble, but I couldn't think of any disobedience I'd committed. I set down *Love Takes Wing* and trudged up the stairs and into the guest bedroom I shared with my sisters. Dread clawed up my chest when I saw my toiletry kit laid open on the bed.

"What is this?" Mom asked, pointing to it. Her expression was unreadable. My throat tightened and my vision blurred. I had no idea what to say to Mom, so I just stood frozen in the doorway.

"Are these . . . pads?"

Mom lifted one of the rolled-up bundles, which had unwrapped partway. It began unravelling all over the bedspread. I snapped out of my paralysis and rushed to snatch the pad out of Mom's hand before the whole thing splayed open.

"Yes," I said. I stuffed it back in with the others, then protectively held the kit to my chest.

Mom was silent for a beat. "Why are you saving them?" she asked.

I started crying. "Because I didn't want anyone to see them in the trash and know."

"Why do you care if anybody knows?"

"I don't know."

"It's a natural thing."

I could tell Mom was trying her best to be patient with me, but her face looked as though she either wanted to laugh at my ridiculousness or shake me out of my paranoia. I couldn't explain to her why my period was such a deeply private event for me. I didn't know myself. I expected Mom to scold me for being unreasonable, but she didn't seem to know what to do, or say. After a few silent moments, she gently told me it was the smell that had prompted her to reach under the bed and open my toiletry kit.

"It's like death," Mom said. "Like something died. You can't keep storing them in there."

I nodded and flushed even deeper. She sighed and headed for the doorway.

"Don't tell Dad," I said. I couldn't bear the thought of him knowing about my collection. Mom turned to look at me, still with a mystified expression on her face, then she nodded in promise and left me to my embarrassment.

I nursed my shame for several minutes. Knowing I should take advantage of the near-empty house before anyone else came in, I crept downstairs and snatched a trash bag from under the kitchen sink. I dumped the used pads from my toiletry kit into a billow of white plastic and pulled the yellow drawstrings tight. I carried the bag outside to a large plastic bin, where it would be picked up and taken away forever when garbage day came. The humiliation of being found with dozens of used pads, I decided, was worse than the chance of one being discovered in a regular trash can. From then on, I threw my pads away like I imagined normal girls did. I never stopped wrapping them very carefully, though.

～

"So, you're not gonna believe what I got for my birthday," Danika said.

"What?" I asked.

I sat on Mom and Dad's bed in one of Aunt Meg's guest rooms while everyone watched *With Six You Get Eggroll* downstairs. Aunt Meg's collection of family-friendly Doris Day films kept us entertained when the heat became too unbearable to play outside. I cradled the phone against my shoulder and used Mom's calling card to clean out the dirt from under my fingernails.

"Guess," Danika challenged me.

"A trip to see your dad in Florida?"

"No."

"A new piercing?"

"No." Danika paused dramatically. "I got tickets to an *NSYNC concert!"

She squealed so loudly that I had to hold the phone away from my ear. Envy took a sucker punch to my diaphragm.

"That's so cool!" I said.

"And the best part is I get to bring a friend!"

My heart lurched. I knew she was implying that she wanted to bring me. *NSYNC was our band. Danika and I had spent many a sleepover in her room dancing to "Here We Go," or sitting in her mom's gold Saturn so we could groan along to "You Got It" without driving anyone crazy. Danika said the concert was in a couple of weeks.

"Do you think you'll be back in time?" she asked.

My throat tightened. "No," I said. "Mom and Dad aren't sure if we're ever going back to Rockford."

"Ever? I thought you guys were just doing a drawn-out vacation."

"That's what I hoped, but not anymore. They said they're just going wherever God wants them, and I guess God doesn't want us to go home."

Neither of us could argue with that. Danika, like me, was also familiar with the arbitrariness of living under God's direction. We commiserated over our disappointment until the calling card operator warned I had two minutes of time remaining.

Something inside me died as I hung up the phone. I recognized it as hope. Despite knowing my family had no plans to resettle any time soon, I didn't realize how much I'd been hoping we'd return to Rockford eventually. We had before, after our migratory year in California. The ache in my chest told me I'd been keeping secrets from myself, hoping our current trip would end similarly. That Danika still thought I was in her life enough to plan things with her made me finally admit to myself that I wasn't. I might never be again. It was time to let go of my friendships.

The next day, I decided to cut back on the letters and postcards I sent

Danika and Bethany. I didn't want to abandon my two best friends all at once—my physical presence had done that already. I figured weaning them slowly from my correspondence would be better than an abrupt cease-write. Sometimes they'd been able to write back to me. There had been a letter from each of them waiting for me at Nannie and Pop-pop's, and when Mom said we were going to be staying with Aunt Meg, I gave both Danika and Bethany her address in case they wanted to send me a letter. Neither of them had so far. I knew I couldn't expect them to write at the whim of a sudden address, but it still hurt to look through Aunt Meg's mail every day and find nothing from the friends I'd left behind. Perhaps writing to them less would help ease the pain.

I kept more and more to myself over the next couple of weeks. Staying at Aunt Meg's made my disengagement less noticeable than I would have gotten away with in a campground. Dad helped Aunt Meg with odd jobs around her house, like repainting the walls and replacing her old ceiling fans. Mom spent most of her time in the kitchen cooking meals for all of us. My siblings either played outside or watched Aunt Meg's assortment of black-and-white movies in the den. Sometimes I joined them, but most of the time, I read books or wrote in my journal, feeling increasingly withdrawn. Mom accused me of having a sullen attitude. I wasn't sullen. I was depressed. Loneliness and grief made me cry myself to sleep almost every night. Except for my immediate family, I felt as though everyone in my life had died. The future became something I couldn't imagine. Thoughts of permanent escape began flickering through my mind.

∼

One of Dad's cousins, whom my siblings and I called Uncle Harry, invited us to stay on his empty houseboat for a week during our time in New Jersey. It was docked at a marina on Long Beach Island. I was quiet during the hour and a half drive south. Danika would be going to the *NSYNC concert that week, and I couldn't stop wondering who she would take with her in my place. Reigna? Crystal? It didn't matter. It wouldn't be me.

Closing my eyes, I leaned my head against the car window and wondered just how dangerous it was to hitchhike. I would head west, making my way ride by ride through Pennsylvania, Ohio, Indiana, and then Illinois. It would probably take a week. I fantasized about getting dropped off at Danika's house, knocking on her door, and shouting, "Surprise!" when she opened it. Her parents would have no way of reaching mine, so I'd get to live with them until Mom and Dad thought to call their house. The worry would serve my parents right, making them regret they'd never listened to how sad I was before. They'd be relieved, then angry, and then figure they might as well let me stay with Danika until they settled down someplace. Danika and I would go to the *NSYNC concert together and I'd even get to go to school with her in the fall.

The smell of grilled hot dogs interrupted my daydream. My stomach growled and I opened my eyes. Dad's driving had slowed, and when I looked out the open windows, I could tell we were on LBI. Tourists swarmed the streets the closer we got to Fantasy Island Amusement Park. Invisible strands of cotton candy melted on my tongue in the warm breeze, and Sugar Ray's latest hit "Someday" blared from every gift shop we passed. Summer vacation was at its peak. We left the Suburban in the marina parking lot and walked past long rows of docks until Dad spotted Uncle Harry's small Trojan yacht. It wasn't as glamorous as some of the boats surrounding it, but it had a sparkling blue and white exterior and a spacious main cabin. We all claimed spots in the tiny bedrooms. I chose a narrow mattress where I could look out a window from my sleeping bag. Mom was thrilled to find the galley had a working stove and oven. There was no shower in the tiny bathroom, but Dad said we could use the marina lockers. We unpacked our things and left for the beach.

My family always went to the borough of Beach Haven when we visited LBI. It felt strange to return as a teen, observing with new curiosity what had escaped my eyes when I was younger—lovers making out under the piers, teenagers flirting in front of carnival booths, the ripped bodies of surfers catching my gaze as I stood behind them in line for the ice cream man. Mom preferred the beaches on the eastern coast, which faced the rough and open Atlantic. "It's too crowded," she said of the western side facing the calmer shores of Little Egg Harbor. Little Egg Harbor was where all the cool families went. I fought envy every time I watched them pass on the wooden plank boardwalks, skim boards overhead, floating volleyball nets in backpacks, and coolers of store-bought deli sandwiches and cold soda pops in hand. I wished my family could afford such luxuries, and I told myself to be grateful we could vacation on LBI at all.

Rain flooded Beach Haven one morning. I felt antsy from being cooped up on the boat with my squabbling siblings, and in desperate need of time alone. Mom and Dad surprised me by giving me permission to walk around town by myself. The rain had dissipated by early evening, and I was about to cross a street in search of a library when I noticed a group of kids hanging out on a wooden ramp. They looked to be around my age. The girls wore short shorts and tight spaghetti strap tanks, their long sun-bleached hair swaying in the glow of sunset. They looked so cool. So self-assured and sexy as they laughed at the cute boys trying to impress them with skateboard tricks. If one of the guys was trying to impress me, I wouldn't be making fun of him. He would have my rapt attention and unending praise.

I wondered if one of the boys might notice me and invite me to hang out with them. Immediately I flushed, embarrassed by the notion. Why would the kids want to hang out with me? Scolding myself for even conjuring such an idea, and afraid the group of teens would somehow read my mind and deem me pathetic for lingering around with hopeful eyes, I ducked behind a shrub. It felt wrong to keep watching them, voyeuristic in a way that made me feel ashamed, but I couldn't help indulging a fantasy of what I imagined it was like to be normal. I pictured myself on the ramp with them, sitting coyly on the handrails while a cute guy stood between my knees and slid his hands into the back pockets of my shorts. His lips would taste like saltwater taffy and the gelled spikes of his hair would tangle in my curls. I imagined the girl in pale pink was my best friend, and that the arm she threw around the girl beside her was around me. She'd smell of Bath & Body Works. Plumeria, probably. Her mom would have little rosettes of soap in their guest bathroom, and in the girl's white-carpeted bedroom, we would all play flirty games like Twister until her dad ordered us pizza. I would feel happy, included. Like I belonged.

Tears stung my eyes. I looked away from the laughing group of teens, wondering if I would ever have friends again. *Better to just keep to myself from now on*, I thought. *That way I won't feel so lonely.*

The thought came unbidden. It sunk into my soul with self-protective gravity, a heaviness that told me it would be a long time before I opened my heart to anyone again. It didn't matter where my family and I ended up when we stopped traveling. There was no way of knowing how long we'd stay before God decided to uproot us again. I didn't want to bond with friends only to leave them whenever God felt like telling my parents it was time to relocate.

I hurried back to the marina. No one seemed to be on the boat when I stepped into its back deck, and I found a note left on the kitchen table.

Dad took the kids to the beach for sunset. I'm at the showers. Mom

I couldn't control the emotions on my face, and I felt relieved that Mom and Dad weren't there to ask me what was wrong. Everything was wrong. If I gave them an answer, all they would do is shrug and tell me to talk to God about it, because they were just following Him.

I climbed up three flights of stairs and found myself in the crow's nest for the first time. A white chair sat under the awning and I sank into it, my sobs finally releasing. I curled my knees to my chest as every feeling I'd tried to bury came heaving out of me at once. The anger at having to leave my home. The fear of not knowing where we were going. The frustration of having no privacy. The loneliness of being estranged from my friends and the inability to make new ones. The anxiety about being forgotten. The sensation of being constantly lost that intimidated me with each new place we arrived at. The rage I kept from my parents. Every emotion I'd suppressed wrenched my body with voiceless gasps. I wanted to feel better for letting it all out. I only felt worse.

The realization that my family's trip could never end mocked me with slapping indifference. God didn't care how I felt. My parents didn't care how I felt. My family might never settle down, and I might never know security again. I knew one day I'd turn eighteen and legally be able to care for myself, but eighteen was five years away. I didn't think I could handle five more years of endless instability. I knew I couldn't. If that was life, I wanted to die. I didn't want to live if living meant obeying a God who moved me around ceaselessly to destinations only revealed in His due time. Who was the so-called heavenly Father I'd believed in my whole life, and had always tried to obey? Who was the being responsible for turning my parents into crazy, selfish transients?

I didn't try to censor my thoughts. Nor did I make myself repent for them as they came, searing through my mind with rebellious vengeance. For once, I wanted to acknowledge the raw truth of my unfiltered feelings without condemning myself or trying to temper my judgments with compassion. I was angry with God and furious with Mom and Dad for following Him. I felt disgusted with every single person we'd come across for not stepping in to do something. Maybe my parents fed me food— provided in the name of God—and maybe they met my other basic needs like shelter, if our pop-up trailer and tent counted. But we were homeless, plain and simple. How could anyone meet us and turn a blind eye to five children? If my parents didn't have kids, I felt they would have every right to live their nomadic lifestyle, but how could they drag us into their faith-fueled fantasy and be above some sort of reproach?

I knew my parents loved me. Love wasn't enough, and I hated myself for thinking it. I had intellectually accepted that I would always come second to God and what He called my parents to, but I had run out of grace. I couldn't follow God by following my parents anymore. I was done trying to get through their thick wall that was the Holy Spirit, and I was sick of hearing their excuses about faith and adventure. The only way out was death.

The thought startled me. I'd considered suicide before, but never with the serious conviction that stilled my breath. I wiped my nose and looked out at the darkening horizon. Suddenly, I felt very calm. A shift took place, a surrender so profound that I felt a peace I hadn't remembered in months. Maybe years. I gazed into the murky water of the marina. Did sharks ever come into marinas? Maybe if I floated on my back, a great white would kill me with one swift bite through my midsection. Maybe I could tie weights around my ankles and jump overboard to drown myself. The thought of gasping water into my lungs made me nauseous. My death would have to be quick, however I went.

The sound of Madeleine and Bryant's laughter drifted across the harbor. I twisted and saw Dad and the kids on their way back. Dad carried Kate in one arm and the beach blanket in the other, a bulky bag of sand toys completing their silhouette. Teddy lagged behind everyone, dragging a stick through the water and making oil stains shimmer in the ripples left behind. I couldn't see Mom coming from the bathhouse, but she probably wouldn't be long behind.

I crept down the stairs and into the bedroom cabin before they all arrived. I crawled into my sleeping bag and rolled over to face the wall, hoping they'd think I'd gone to bed early. It worked. I heard Madeleine shush Kate when they opened the door and saw my back to them. I felt grateful not to have to talk to them, or anyone. I decided not to worry any more that night about how and when I would commit suicide. It felt comforting just to have an escape to look forward to.

11

The Northwoods

My family didn't return to Aunt Meg's house right away when we left Long Beach Island. Instead, we spent August and September camping our way through the boreal forests of New England and Canada. All throughout, my thoughts of suicide drifted between resolve and cowardice. I didn't truly want to die. What I wanted was for God to tell my parents to buy a new house so we could settle down, but the disappointment of praying for stability only to have a new destination on the horizon every day crushed me. My siblings were too young to burden or understand. The promise of a sympathetic ear revealed itself in one of the last pages of my battered *YM* magazine, which Mom had made an exception for when no Christian teen magazines were found at any of the grocery stores we went to.

"Feeling sad, lonely, and depressed?" the ad asked. "Do you often think about suicide?"

I tore out the corner of the page and stuffed it into the pocket of my jeans.

One cool evening at a campground outside of Bar Harbor, Maine, I excused myself from the fire ring to use the restroom. I walked past the row of outhouses to the ranger's station at the entrance of the loop road, where I'd spotted a pay phone when my parents paid for our site earlier that day. The box-shaped structure offered shelter from the rain with a small roof, but it had no doors for privacy. I hoped no one else would need to make a call soon.

I pulled the torn advertisement from my pocket. A black-and-white photo of a girl staring out a window accompanied the 1-800 number the ad said was a suicide hotline. I lifted the receiver and slowly began dialing. My heart raced.

"Thank you for calling Teen Line," said a gentle female voice. "How can I help you right now?"

I froze. "Hi, um, I'm calling from a campground because . . ."

Because my family and I were homeless? I couldn't bring myself to say the words. It was as though a voice in my head suddenly reminded me about social services. If I said I was a homeless teen, even one who was with her family, would the woman on the line be obligated to trace the call and send a police officer? The realization of what might happen to my siblings flashed through my mind. We would likely be separated if we were taken from our parents, since I doubted a single foster home would be able to keep us all together. I couldn't bear the thought of being responsible for ripping my siblings apart. All I wanted was someone to talk to, someone who would listen to me and say everything would be alright. I couldn't think of a way to divulge my struggles without revealing my family's homelessness.

"Hello?" the woman said. "Are you there? It's okay to talk—"

I hung up the phone with a clang. My hand trembled as I shoved the ad back into my pocket. Maybe the woman wouldn't have called social services, but it wasn't worth the risk. The thought of Teddy, Madeleine, Bryant, and Kate being sent to live with strangers made me shake my head at my own selfishness. I marched back to camp and resolved to keep my suicidal fantasies to myself.

~

The highway signs in Canada depicted the shape of a maple leaf. That was the first thing I noticed after we drove through the border patrol station. Mom wanted to visit Prince Edward Island and Nova Scotia, and there was no reason not to since we were already so far up the East Coast. The only part of Canada I'd seen before was the city of Toronto, when we'd gone for Toronto Blessing conferences. The days of revival seemed long ago.

We spent our first night in New Brunswick at an RV resort. My parents disdainfully referred to those kinds of vacation parks as "backyard camping." No one there was truly roughing it, with their TV satellites and generators blasting warm heat into color-coordinated living rooms. What was the point of camping, my parents grumbled, if one could have the same comforts as home? They might as well be parked in their backyards. I envied RV campers. I couldn't help gazing longingly at the water hook-ups providing them with hot, private showers. My family showered in public coin-operated facilities where water came out in two-minute drizzles, alternating between icy cold bursts and scalding hot surges. I also coveted the screened awnings attached to RVs, where campers sat on their folding chairs enjoying the evening twilight without the sting of bug bites. Mom and Dad could rough it all they wanted, but if I ever camped when I grew up, I would have no shame in being a backyard camper.

Mom made chicken with cilantro for dinner. The kids were sent to bed when they finished brushing their teeth, but Mom let me stay up later than usual. I didn't know why she decided to give me the privilege that night, and I didn't ask. I plunked myself into a Crazy Creek camp chair and scooted it over the hard-packed dirt until I sat directly in the line of smoke from the campfire. It stung my eyes, but at least the mosquitos wouldn't bother me there. They didn't like smoke. Dad dragged his chair beside me, and when Mom finished tucking the kids into their bags, she sat in her chair to my right. The three of us kept our mouths and noses covered by our jacket collars as we stared into the fire, smoke billowing around us. Being around the modern conveniences of the RV park must have made Dad nostalgic for our old comforts. He bumped my knee with his.

"If you could have any material thing right now," Dad said, "what would it be?"

I smiled as images ran through my head like old film. A down-filled pillow? New boots to replace my outgrown Timberlands? A new backpack? But it was the vision of a soft, clean bed in a warmly glowing room that stood out brighter than the others. I described it to Dad.

"It would be a bed," I said. "A big, cushy bed with fluffy pillows and flannel sheets. Either that or a hot, relaxing Jacuzzi."

Dad's laughter was muffled beneath his fleece neck gaiter. "Yeah, a hot tub sure sounds good right now."

Then it occurred to me that perhaps Dad was fishing for gift ideas. Sometimes he and Mom surprised us kids with little presents, like a new book or Playmobil set.

"If the material thing had to be something practical," I said. "It would be a Conair Steam Straightening Iron."

"A what?"

I pulled down my collar. "A straightening iron for my hair."

I'd seen a commercial for the life-changing invention in a laundromat. I wanted one immediately, fantasizing about having my own bathroom one day where I'd be able to have all my hair tools and products organized in scented paper drawers.

"What would you pick?" I asked Dad.

"I'd pick those pants I saw at that store in New Hampshire," he said. I remembered the olive-green pants. Dad hadn't bought them because they were almost a hundred dollars. He turned to Mom. "What about you, Janey?"

Mom smiled into the flames. "I'd like a large, tall glass of Diet Coke," she said. "With ice in it, and water sweating down the sides." Her fingers made trickling motions as though caressing the imaginary glass. My parents and I sat in the smoke until stars came out, and the lingering embers of the fire pit gave way to black.

~

I sank deeper into depression as my family explored southeastern Canada. From the red clay bluffs of Prince Edward Island to the grassy highlands of Cape Breton, my diary entries grew more and more desperate, begging God for the relief of stability.

Dear God, I wrote. *I'm feeling so alone and helpless. I'm crying inside for help. Could You make me feel more willing to cope with this trip? And make me feel loved and not so alone? Help me to be patient. Love, Your Daughter, Alice*

To my amazement, God seemed to write back. My family returned to Aunt Meg's house in mid-September, and as soon as I finished helping my family unload the Suburban, I raced upstairs to devour the six letters waiting for me. The first I opened was from Connie Walsh, the woman who had given my family a trailer when we lived at the Masons' house in California. Her letter told me that she'd been praying and she wrote down what God said for her to tell me.

Alice, my faithful one, take courage, do not let your faith die. I will fulfill the dreams you have, remember my timing is perfect. Trust me, little one, for I desire to give you good things.

Connie also included a vision God had given her about me.

I see a Queen Bee pollenating and feeding many. Sweet Honey, there is a land of milk and honey set before you. Have faith! Amen.

Connie's words filled me with hope. Was God truly speaking to me through her? I desperately wanted to believe so. I read her letter over and over, repeating, "I will fulfill the dreams you have," like a mantra that would save my life.

Those words became especially important as I read the other five letters. They were all from Bethany. It seemed like she had the life I dreamed of. Bethany was no longer homeschooled like me, since she began junior high at the same Christian school her older siblings had attended. She loved school and had also become heavily involved with a Christian youth group. One of Bethany's cards had a message on the front. "You know how sometimes we get together and talk and eat and talk and laugh and cry and eat and talk?" I flipped the card open. "Can we do that again soon?"

I burst into tears. I missed Bethany so much. Mom allowed me to call her with a prepaid calling card that night, but Mrs. Andersen told me she was out with friends. My heart ached with disappointment. It ached with jealousy, too. Bethany's life sounded so much more stable and happier than mine.

There had been no letters waiting for me from Danika.

~

My family left Aunt Meg's near the end of September and headed west to Michigan. The hand-painted signs advertising homemade pasties told me when we had entered the state's Upper Peninsula. Mom and Dad wanted to continue our tradition of spending the first week of October camping in Pictured Rocks National Lakeshore, a remote twelve-mile stretch of beach that ran along the southern coast of Lake Superior. I knew we were getting close to the campground when the paved road abruptly gave way to dirt. Potholes jostled me against Teddy, and we spread out our limbs to anchor the duffel bags and boxes threatening to fall on us with every bump. A tunnel of maple trees glowed overhead, making flashes of crimson, pumpkin, saffron, and gold paint the forest floor like reflections of stained glass. The brisk air coming through Mom's rolled-down window smelled of birch bark and pine needles. The day couldn't have been more beautiful.

Campsite number nine was the site my family always took if it was available. As soon as Dad pulled into its parking spot, my siblings bolted from the Suburban, heading straight for the end of the bluff. Mom yelled at them to stop before they leapt off the edge and into the sand dunes below.

"You guys need to help set up camp first," Mom said. "Then you can play in the dunes."

"Aw, Mom," Madeleine complained. "We've been sitting in the car all day."

"I know, but you guys at least need to help Dad set up the tarp. Then you can go down to the beach."

Twelvemile Beach Campground had no limit to how long visitors could stay, and I could tell by the way my parents set up camp that they intended for us to be there for a week at minimum. By the time we finished helping Dad set up the tarp, Mom had established clearly designated living spaces throughout our campsite. A kitchen and dining area were at the center of the tarp's shelter, with the propane camp stove and cooking supplies on one end of the picnic table. A living area composed of folding chairs with a stump for a coffee table sat in front of the fire ring, and it relieved me to see Mom and Dad cranking open the pop-up instead of pitching the tent. The pop-up mattresses were more comfortable than sleeping pads. When storms came, as they always did in Michigan's Upper Peninsula, the trailer's canvas-covered frame would offer more security than tent poles.

"Now can we go play?" Madeleine asked Mom.

"Yes," Mom said.

My siblings ran toward the edge of the sandy plateau our campsite sat on. One by one, they leapt into the air and dropped out of sight, their gleeful cries smothered by the wind. I waited until I was sure they'd reached the bottom of the dunes, then I sprinted toward the bluff and kept my eyes on the dazzling whitecaps of Lake Superior, taking a mighty leap off the roots of a tree. Sunlight hit my face mid-air, away from the canopy of pines. The cawing of ring-billed gulls rushed into my ears with the chilliness of the breeze. I landed with a cushioned thud, creating a small avalanche of sand that shimmered with black streaks of magnetite. The sand was soft and heavy, still damp with the previous night's rainfall. I watched as mounds grew around my ankles, knowing my socks were now permanently embedded with granules.

"Come on, Alice!" Kate called from below.

I galloped down the sixty-foot bank to the beach below. Hundreds of small colorful rocks danced in the waves, making the rushing sound of marbles when the ebb and flow of water pulled them in. For a brief moment, I remembered what it was like to feel happy, but Michigan's beauty wasn't enough to keep my thoughts from drifting to suicide.

I didn't want to keep thinking of killing myself. It seemed like the only way I could calm down when anger threatened to lash out of me, and when tears soaked my camping pillow at night. The promising peace of death lingered in my mind like a nagging thought that only grew stronger the more I tried to ignore it. I didn't know how I'd kill myself. Dad hadn't brought any of his guns on our trip, and my parents didn't have any painkillers I could overdose on. Suffocation by carbon monoxide in a closed garage would have been my ideal way to go, because I read somewhere that one didn't feel pain that way. A person simply passed out in the comfort of their car before death took their soul wherever it was doomed to go. My family didn't have a garage. Slitting my wrists seemed to be the next best option. Dad kept carefully sharpened knives in the kitchen utensil box on the picnic table, and there was one in particular I noted, a Wusthof several inches long that I imagined would carve through my wrists like butter. I feared pain and the horror of regretting my actions too late. However I died needed to be quick, as painless as possible, and not endangering to anyone but myself. That ruled out running into traffic or leaping from an overpass.

My breaking point came on our third morning in Pictured Rocks. I awoke to the sounds of rain and Dad and Teddy arguing. I lifted my head from the static warmth of my sleeping bag and peered out the screened window of the pop-up. Everyone but Kate and me sat gathered around the picnic table with steaming bowls of oatmeal in front of them.

"It is not thick and slimy," Dad said.

"But Dad," Teddy said, "I don't like it like this. It's really thick."

"Eat it."

"Can I at least add more water?"

"No."

"Then I'm not gonna eat it."

"You are so ungrateful!"

Then, faster than my eyes could track, Dad somehow lifted Teddy from the picnic bench and wrestled him to the mud, pinning my eleven-year-old brother's arms behind his back. I wanted to scream at them to stop. Instead, I felt frozen.

Teddy eventually stopped struggling. Dad let him go. No one said a word.

Mom, Madeleine, and Bryant resumed eating their oatmeal. Teddy stood and wiped the mud off his face. I saw his hands trembled. He strode to the Suburban and slammed the door behind him as Dad resumed eating his breakfast. I noticed Kate watching through the trailer screen on the other side of the pop-up. I quietly helped her dress, then went to the Suburban, hoping to find Teddy in private so we could talk about what happened if he felt like it. Mom was already there.

"Did you know you scratched Daddy?" she asked him. He didn't respond. "Your anger was demonic. You need to ask God to help you with your self-control."

Mom turned and left. I didn't know the difference between normal anger and demonic anger, but I thought Teddy's anger was justified. If he was supposed to just lie there meekly while Dad held him to the ground, I disagreed. If Teddy had managed to scratch Dad, perhaps it was his budding strength that allowed him to leave a mark, not the assistance of a demon. Their fight that morning would be an isolated incident, and my father would never snap in that way again, but I sat beside my brother in silence wondering why Dad's anger wasn't demonic yet my brother's was.

I barely finished my breakfast. An anxious clench gnawed in place of my appetite, and besides, Teddy was right: The oatmeal did have a slimy texture that morning. Bryant and I lugged plastic containers to the iron pump down the road after breakfast. We were on dish duty that day, and we siphoned icy water from Lake Superior into our tubs and lugged the heavy containers as carefully as we could. If we spilled on our clothes, they would take hours to dry. A light drizzle continued as Bryant and I picked a dishwashing site about a hundred feet from camp, so that if black bears were attracted to the soapy remains, they wouldn't wander directly into our site. Bears were also the reason we didn't just wash dishes at the pump itself. My youngest brother and I squatted above the ground with our makeshift sinks in front of us. Dad poured a kettle of boiling water into Bryant's washing tub, but I didn't look up at him. The image of him pinning Teddy to the ground was too fresh in my mind to forgive. He left without a word. Bryant, his hands still clumsy at eight years old, shot a green squirt of knockoff Palmolive into his newly hot water. My tub of water would remain cold and soap-free for rinsing.

Bryant held out his arms to me. I could see dirt in the creases of his palms as he silently asked me to roll up his sleeves. I tucked my gloves into the waistband of my thermals so they'd be warm for my fingers later, then I rolled up the cuffs of Bryant's coat, his sweatshirt, his fleece shirt, and lastly, his thermal. I readied the dish rack beside me as Bryant plunged dish after dish into the soapy water. His hands turned red from the scalding temperature and the frigid windchill, but he kept soaking bowl after bowl, pot after pot, utensil after utensil. After he soaked and scrubbed the dishes, Bryant handed them to me to swish through the frigid water of my tub, which quickly turned brownish gray. My fingers were so cold, I could hardly bend them. I felt myself fighting tears. A few ran down my cheeks anyway, helped along by the wind that nipped mercilessly at my exposed skin.

"Are you okay?" Bryant asked.

I shook my head and took the plastic plate he held. The slight furrow of his brow told me he felt sympathetic, but he sensed I didn't want to talk. I considered it one of Bryant's strengths to not clutter the air with attempts at comfort or understanding. His silence felt like respect, and I wouldn't have known how to describe my feelings anyway. Maybe my tears were simply another waterfall of depression. Maybe I cried because seeing Dad and Teddy fight had shaken me, or maybe because I longed to wash dishes in a real sink, in a real kitchen, where there were no drizzly gusts or bears to worry about. Something inside me was breaking.

I wiped my nose with my coat sleeve as Bryant dumped the wash water down a small hill. Pine needles lifted off the dirt floor, floating in geometric patterns that bobbed until the water sank into the earth, leaving the needles in a soggy clump. Bryant and I trudged back to camp with our tubs and dishes. I plunked the dish rack on the picnic table and walked straight to the fire to warm up my hands. The tarp occasionally whooshed upward with gusts of wind carrying ashes and smoke deeper into my clothing. I sat in my camp chair and closed my eyes, tucking my nose beneath the collar of my wool coat and pulling my beanie tighter to my scalp.

The scathing in Mom's voice was unmistakable. "Alice!" she hissed. "How many times have I told you to hang up the dish towel when you're done?"

Fear shot through me. I sprang up. Once more, I'd forgotten the simplest of tasks. Mom had warned me repeatedly not to forget to hang up the dish towel, and yet again, I hadn't remembered to follow through. Mom lifted the towel from where I'd left it on the dish rack.

"Why don't you remember?" Mom yelled at me.

"I don't know."

"Why is it so hard to remember to hang up a dish towel?"

My throat ached with steadiness. "I don't know," I said. "It just is."

"What's the matter now?" Dad asked.

"She forgot to hang up the dish towel, again."

Mom's jaw jutted toward me and her eyes narrowed into slits. Dad turned on me.

"How many times do we have to tell you—"

"I don't know!" I shouted. I snatched the towel from Mom's hands and threw it over the clothesline, pinning it with clothespins as Mom told me I was grounded from reading any books for the rest of the week. I didn't respond. I went straight to the Suburban, ripped a page from my journal, and ran to the lakeside hiking trail that ended somewhere I had never reached. The day had come.

I ran until I couldn't run any further. About forty minutes later, when the sun had abruptly returned and my heartbeat had steadied, I sat on a moss-covered log atop a cliff. Azure waves pummeled the limestone floor a hundred feet below. I couldn't see them, but I heard them, the violent tongues of a freshwater ocean that had swallowed ships whole and spat out their driftwood remains like bones. I would be bones soon. The thought made me feel heavy with peace. The torn page from my journal sat folded in the pocket of my coat explaining the reasons for my suicide and apologizing to whoever would find my broken remains amidst the rocks. "At least you'll have one less mouth to feed," I wrote to my parents. "I'm sorry if my death is messy." I'd written the letter almost a week before. At the time, I wasn't sure what my suicide would look like, but I wrote the note in case a perfect moment presented itself and I didn't have time to say goodbye.

A chipmunk scurried past my feet. The tiny creature paused, looking up at me with a disproportionately large black eye. I realized his would be the last eye to make contact with mine. The thought felt surreal. When the chipmunk darted behind the trunk of a tree, I gazed at the view one last time, engaging all of my senses until they were flooded. The scent of pine needles and mushrooms that smelled like black licorice. The chorus of wind rustling the branches accompanied by the lonesome cry of a hawk. The blaze of fall colors that hovered over the shoreline, iridescent from the blur of my tears. The texture of bark leaving its imprint on the back of my thighs. The spice of oatmeal's cinnamon still lingering in my mouth.

I stood, amazed by the thought that it was the last time I would do so. I stepped, marveling at how my foot followed my mind's command. The calmness of my breath surprised me. Though my heart exploded against my ribcage, my inhales and exhales came and went without sound. Even when vertigo forced my eyes shut, and the coldness of the breeze made my nose run, and the anticipation of relief sent tingles through my entire body, my breath remained soft. I inhaled one last time, wondering if my life would flash before my eyes on the way down.

And then something happened. I observed my brain telling my foot to step off the ledge, but my leg felt weighted by something both nebulous and heavy. I opened my eyes, staring at my feet with growing alarm. They wouldn't lift off the forest floor. It was as though someone had filled my legs with cement. Panic quickened in my chest, and I heard myself breathing raggedly. I tried to bend my knees but could only twist my waist.

"No," I called out. My voice snagged with emotion. Piping hot anger shot from my soles through my skull, a fury so blinding and helpless that I gasped. I imagined there was an angel blocking my jump, a winged servant of the Lord sent to stop me from jumping off the cliff. I couldn't kill myself. God wouldn't even allow me that freedom. His urge to control me must be so great that He sent an invisible bodyguard to hold my feet in place. Then the angel seemed to turn my toes without my permission. My left foot rose and fell so that I faced sideways, then my right foot swung around until my eyes saw the deer trail that had led me to the precipice. As if of their own accord, my legs walked me away from the edge and into the thicket. I collapsed after several yards, shaking and sobbing. The angel seemed to let me go.

Years later, I would come to think of the angel as an excuse my mind made up to avoid taking responsibility for failing to jump. It wasn't an angel who anchored my feet with the weight of a thousand bricks. It wasn't a divine being who had turned my feet around. It was my own will to live, my own change of heart. I couldn't admit that to myself in the moment. It was easier to blame God for one more misery than it was to accept that I didn't have the courage to follow through with my own suicide. So, at the time, I decided an angel was what had stopped me.

I found myself face to face with red berries. Wintergreen. The shadows of tall ferns bowed around me, as though offering their condolences for my life. My body shuddered. An arrow of sadness pierced my soul and sent me rising, running furiously past aspen and squirrels. I didn't know how long I ran. My stinging tears blinded me as I crashed into camp.

"Alice, what's wrong?" I heard Mom say.

I couldn't answer. Mom's arms reached me just in time to prevent me from tripping over a stump.

"Are you okay? Did you get hurt?"

"Is anyone else back there?" Dad asked.

But all I could do was cry. Seeing there was no blood on my clothing, Mom took me gently by the arm and guided me to the Suburban. I was too upset to protest.

"Shhh," Mom cooed, helping me into the backseat of the car. "It's okay."

I was bewildered by Mom's sudden compassion. The tender strokes and soothing whispers were almost too harsh a contrast to the scalding beratement of only an hour earlier.

A lesson branded itself onto my psyche as I curled into a ball and let Mom guide my head into her lap: If I wanted to be taken seriously, I had to shut down. For months, I had tried to get my parents' attention. For months, I had told them how unhappy I was, how lonely, angry, and depressed I felt. But it wasn't until the day I nearly committed suicide, running into the campground crying so hard I couldn't speak, that my parents finally took me seriously. They looked at me with a concern that made me want to scream. Did I have to fall to pieces before they'd ask me what was the matter? Did my face have to be covered with tears and mucus before they understood I was suffering? Did I have to refuse to talk in order for them to care what I had to say?

I wouldn't tell them. As Mom rocked my body in the blue bench seat, the only couch we had, I decided that I wouldn't tell them what the matter was. I wouldn't tell them I cried because I hadn't succeeded in killing myself. I wouldn't tell them how much I hated them in that moment for their sudden kindness, which I needed too badly to push away. I wouldn't tell them how the angel had stopped me from jumping off the cliff, because that would be an admission of God's further sovereignty over my life. Instead, I let myself cry and allowed Mom to think she was helping by smoothing my brow, by handing me tissues, and murmuring how okay everything was.

12

A Baptism

I awoke to the pattering of rain. *I'm still here*, I thought. I didn't want
to be, but something seemed to have shifted during the night. As I lay
in the cocoon of my sleeping bag, my thoughts slowly clarifying from the
haze of slumber, I made a decision. It was useless to keep fighting God, to
continue badgering Him with prayers to settle down. My pleas for stability were selfish of me. God had ignored those prayers because they clearly
weren't His will, and life would probably be a lot easier for me if I prayed
not for my will to be done, but His. To ask for anything else, I realized,
was sinful, for self-centered prayers gratified the flesh and the flesh was
what separated us from God. When we were separated from God, misery
was sure to follow. I needed to align myself with the path God had laid
out for me and stop hoping or praying for anything else. I needed to get
into God's good graces. It was the only chance I had at being happy again.

I rolled onto my back and stared at the canvas ceiling of the pop-up,
resisting the urge to scratch my scalp. Days, perhaps weeks, had passed
since the last time I'd washed my hair. I dressed in three layers of clothing
and stepped out of the pop-up, hurrying through the rain to join my
family beneath the brown tarp shelter. I felt every one of them tense. They

didn't know why I'd stumbled back into camp sobbing the day before. I had no plans ever to tell them. My parents had tried to comfort me, but I'd barely said a word the rest of the day.

"You want a bowl of oatmeal, moppet?" Dad asked, scooting on the picnic bench to make room for me.

"Yes, thanks."

"Did you sleep alright, chickie?" Mom asked.

"Yes, I had a deep sleep."

"I figured."

Teddy ate his oatmeal in silence. I could see the scratch on his temple from where Dad had pressed him into the ground, but I sensed everyone trying to forget about the previous day's troubles.

"Do you guys want to go into town today?" Mom asked. The kids cheered and I forced a smile. Mom said as soon as we finished our chores, we could drive to Marquette.

"I'm gonna wash my hair before we leave, Janey," Dad said to Mom. He stood and went to the Suburban to retrieve his toiletry kit. I couldn't resist the urge to wash my hair, too, even though I knew it meant I'd be cold for the rest of the day as I waited for it to dry.

"Can I?" I asked.

"Sure, hon. I'll wait for you to finish eating."

The rain lightened to a soft drizzle as Dad and I walked down the dirt road to the iron pump. Signs in the campground forbade us from using shampoo or conditioner, because anything scented could attract bears, but rarely did we see any rangers to enforce the rule. There were hardly any other campers, either. I knew Dad would make sure there were no soap bubbles remaining when we left.

"You wanna go first?" Dad asked.

I took my coat off and draped it over a parking post. My other top layers followed until the scoop neck of my thermal left my collarbones exposed to the wind. I rolled up my sleeves and took a breath, bracing myself for the cold water of the lake, then I tipped my head upside down beneath the faucet as Dad squeaked the pump to life. My hair was so matted that it hardly fell forward. The water hit the back of my neck with a wide splash, making me gasp. I hurried to get all of my hair wet before an ice cream headache came on, and just as my temples began to sear with cold, I leaned out of the water and held out my palm so Dad could squirt Dr. Bronner's shampoo into it. The scent of lavender smelled exotic in the forest, like a memory of another world. I held my breath and plunged beneath the icy pump once more. My eyes squinted in agony as I forced myself to rinse my hair until no more lather fell on the pebbles beneath me, then I swung to the side and flipped my head right side up, the rush of blood draining from my face making me feel dizzy. Dad handed me a beach towel. I wrapped it around my head like a turban and put my layers back on as quickly as possible, then I pumped water for Dad. We were the only ones vain enough to brave freezing water for the sake of having clean hair.

I felt baptized as we walked back to camp. Reinvigorated, as if my shampoo beneath the pump had washed away my despair and replaced it with hope. I knew the feeling would be temporary. I cherished it nonetheless. Washing my hair seemed symbolic of rinsing away my former relationship with God, which had been filled with constant resentment, pleading, and anger. Now that I had decided to give my life to Him the same way my parents did, letting Him take control and exert His will without asking for anything my flesh wanted, I felt the peace of surrender.

~

My parents invited the only other people in the campground to breakfast the next day. I busied myself slicing strawberries as four guests meandered into our site. Norman and Betsy, an older couple who slept in a silver Airstream, brought orange juice with them. Two men who introduced themselves as Dave and Brian brought fried bacon wrapped in foil. Soon everyone was squeezed around the picnic table eating Swedish pancakes.

The sun was out that day, and a soft breeze blew in from the lake, making the tarp above us flutter happily.

"What brings you guys here?" asked the curly-haired man named Brian.

"We're actually living here for the moment," Dad said.

Our guests listened intently as Dad described how God had led him to quit his job and sell our house, and it amused me to watch them try to hide their shock. People never seemed to know what to say when my parents so freely told our unusual story of living by faith. It turned out all four adults were Christians, too, so I hoped our lifestyle sounded less weird to them.

"Are you guys affiliated with the Rainbow People, by any chance?" Betsy asked.

"You know, that's the third time someone's asked us that," Mom said. "No, we're not. Who are they?"

"Well," Betsy said, bowing her head as though apologizing for any offense. "The Rainbow People are a group of . . . they're kind of like hippies. They're a spiritual group who live in the woods, promoting peace and love."

"I've heard them called the Rainbow Family," Dave added.

Dad seemed to embrace the comparison with a chuckle. "We're not affiliated with any organized group," he said. "But I guess that wouldn't be too far off from what we're doing. We're just going where our daddy in heaven calls us, helping those He puts across our path as we feel led."

I realized Dad's words made us sound like campground missionaries. It comforted me slightly to feel like I had a label for what my parents were doing. Campground missionaries, traveling campsite to campsite like hippies, promoting peace, love, and group breakfasts.

Norman, Betsy, Dave, and Brian asked my parents the usual questions strangers did upon meeting us: where were we from (Illinois by way of the Bay Area), how long had we been on the road (four months so far), when did we think we would settle down (whenever God told us to), what about the kids' schooling (we homeschooled), and the last question, which was always approached with more than a hint of reserve.

"If you don't mind my asking," Brian said, his mustache twitching, "how do you guys support yourselves?"

"God provides," Dad said. "We have some money left from the sale of our house, but God's been providing for us the whole time. Jane has a book of all the free campgrounds in America, so that helps us save, and every now and then we stay with relatives or friends. He provides our food, our clothes, and we're never out of toilet paper."

"Wow," Brian said.

Dave nodded his head in admiration. "You guys are really inspiring."

Mom and Dad deferred their praise, insisting they were only doing what God put on their hearts to do. My siblings wandered off in boredom as my parents shared how their experiences in the Toronto Blessing had shaped and strengthened their faith. I stayed with the adults, grateful Mom didn't tell me to leave. Usually she didn't want me around for what she called "adult conversation." She must have not minded my presence that morning.

"And how do you feel about this?" Betsy asked me.

I hate living by faith so much that I almost killed myself a couple days ago, I imagined saying. I put on a cheerful face and tried not to lie. "It's difficult at times, but it's been kind of fun," I said, nodding as though my head could make up for my half-hearted words. I hoped God and my parents were noting my good attitude.

By the end of the day, my family had three new places to stay when we left Pictured Rocks. Norman and Betsy Leavett, Dave Sullivan, and Brian Murphy all expressed that God put it on their hearts to invite us to visit them at their homes. I was no longer surprised when strangers did this.

We visited the Leavetts first, arriving at their vacation home near Sleeping Bear Dunes in mid-October. I took a proper shower for the first time in almost two weeks. After a couple of nights, my family headed south to Ann Arbor, where Dave Sullivan and his family lived. I knew Dave and his wife Vicky had three kids. I felt especially nervous about meeting their daughter Samantha, who was my age. I figured we would become friends out of the forced situation, the way my siblings and I became friends with any children who lived in the homes our parents brought us to.

The foyer of the Sullivans' two-story craftsman told me they were comfortably middle-class. Samantha, thirteen, Madison, ten, and Petey, seven, smiled politely at my siblings and me while our parents exchanged hugs. Madison was the first to speak up.

"We're playing in the backyard," she said. "Do you guys wanna come?"

My siblings and I mumbled affirmatives. We all moved to follow Madison down a hallway when Samantha motioned me aside.

"Hi," she said. "I'm Samantha. I wasn't playing outside."

"Hi, I'm Alice."

"I was just hanging out in my room. Do you wanna come up there instead?"

"Sure."

We were painting each other's toenails by the end of the afternoon. Samantha, who went to a private Christian school, asked me if I missed my school. I always felt nervous telling my peers I was homeschooled. Their reactions to what I assumed was my dorkiness were always the same.

"I'm homeschooled," I said.

"You mean you've never been to a school?" Samantha asked, flipping her kinky curls to the side. She seemed curious, but not slighting.

"I mean, I've seen friends get dropped off and picked up," I said, thinking of Danika. "But I've never been inside."

Mom rapped on the open door. "Hey, chickie, here's your sleeping bag."

Samantha told me I could lay it next to her bed. I felt embarrassed by the smell of campfire smoke that filled her room as I fluffed out my bag, but Samantha was kind enough not to say anything.

A couple of days into our stay with the Sullivans, Samantha invited me to hang out with her at her friend Megan's house.

"You'll really like Megan," Samantha said as she rang the doorbell. "She's really cool."

She was indeed. Megan was an eighth-grader who went to public school, a slender blond-haired girl who wore thick eyeliner and pink lip-gloss. I soon found out she was a cheerleader. She embodied the stereotype perfectly with her wide smile, musical laugh, and contagious energy. I thought cheerleaders were the goddesses of teenagedom, the golden beings that attracted the cutest boys, had the most friends, and owned a booming confidence I could only dream of having. I worshipped Megan in a matter of minutes, humbled by her casual use of swear words and her exuberant beauty. We sat on the floor of her bedroom while she stretched in the shortest shorts I'd ever seen. I asked her if she wouldn't mind showing me some of the cheers she knew. She sprang up instantly and began a routine full of hip circles, letter chants, and splits that extended her long legs into midair.

"I'll teach it to you, if you want," she offered. Her smile was so genuine that I surprised myself by saying yes. Samantha remained seated on the carpet, giggling at us while Megan coached me to cheer louder, kick higher, and swivel my hips hypnotically.

"If you went to school," Megan said to me as I caught my breath, "you would definitely be a cheerleader."

Her compliment trumped all other compliments I had ever been paid. Megan, the coolest girl in the world, thought I could be a cheerleader. I knew I'd be glowing for days.

Megan had a boyfriend, a senior no less. His name was Scott and they'd been dating for almost two months. He really wanted to have sex with her.

"I'm just not ready to give him my virginity," Megan said to us. "I know I wanna lose it with him, but I need it to be the right time."

I clammed up, shocked at how freely she spoke about sex. Samantha started saying something about why she should wait, but Megan interrupted her.

"I already let him finger me."

Samantha audibly gasped. My mouth fell open.

"What?" Samantha exclaimed.

"Yeah. We were making out the other day, and he was on top of me, and he was already playing with my boobs." Megan looked half-ashamed and half-thrilled to be shocking us. "Then he took my pants off and I just felt like I couldn't say no."

"You can always say no," Samantha said.

"But I didn't want to! At first, he just had his hand outside my underwear, but then he pulled them down a little ways and asked if he could just look at it. Then he asked if he could finger me, and I said yes."

My eyes felt like they were drying from wideness. I could hardly believe I was privy to a conversation that private, that nonchalant, that secular.

Samantha seemed thoroughly appalled. "And you just let him?"

"Yeah." Megan shrugged.

"What did it feel like?" I asked, hoping I didn't sound as awestruck as I felt.

"It felt like a tampon," she said matter-of-factly. "He only put one finger in. He said I felt so tight, and that I was really ripe."

I didn't tell her I had never used a tampon before, much less ask what her boyfriend meant by ripe. It sounded incredibly erotic, but ripe was a term I'd only heard used for fruit. Not vaginas. I stared at Megan, unable to help imagining her with her panties down while her cute seventeen-year-old boyfriend fingered her. It turned me on.

My mind was swimming by the time Samantha and I were picked up and driven home. There was much to contemplate. Megan hadn't seemed like she was from a Christian family, and I had never met anyone my age who wasn't a Christian. I felt as though I'd been exposed to a world I'd only read about in *Sweet Valley High* books, the naughty ones I wasn't supposed to read. It was a world I felt certain my parents would never want me to be a part of, a world I fantasized about joining when I wrote in my diary about the normal life I wished I had. Megan had shown me that world was real. She took my breath away with her innocent sinfulness.

That night I went with Samantha to her church youth group. The junior high girls there couldn't have been more different from Megan. I was back in the world I came from, the world of worship and obedience I didn't think I'd ever be able to leave. As much as I wanted the kind of life Megan had, I had the burden of knowing better. Megan was a wayward woman. Because I knew what being a wayward woman meant, I believed God would hold me more accountable for my sins than He would a person who didn't know the Christian rules.

I chided myself as worship began for even being tempted by the allure of Megan's life. I repented for feeling aroused when Megan talked about her boyfriend, and for not having the courage to stop the conversation when my guilt told me it was wrong to be having. That guilt had been a cue that Satan was chipping away at my armor. The devil had seduced me as an angel of light just as my children's ministry teacher said he would. I didn't know Satan's light would feel so good. I didn't expect his face to be as beautiful as the Bible warned it would be, or that it would appear in the form of a thirteen-year-old girl. Of course Satan attacked me with temptation the same week I surrendered my will to God. That was how he worked. When he saw a person advancing in God's army, he sent out his demons to derail the faithful in the ways he knew they were most vulnerable. My deepest vulnerability was my wish to be a normal girl. Like Megan.

13

His

Rockford was only a five-hour drive from Ann Arbor. After several fun-filled days with the Sullivans, Mom made it clear to me that we would only be visiting the Andersens in Rockford for a week or so. She and Dad did not feel like God was putting it on their hearts to move back, so I was not to get my hopes up. They went up anyway.

The last letter I received from Bethany had arrived right before my family left Aunt Meg's house in New Jersey. Bethany wrote about all the new friends she was making, the parties she attended, and the retreat she looked forward to going on with her new youth group. I realized she would be returning home from the retreat on the same Sunday we'd be arriving at her house. I couldn't shake off one of the lines in her last letter, which stung in a way I knew she hadn't meant: "This summer has been the best summer of my life," she wrote. All I could think about was how it was the one summer I wasn't there to share with her. Taking Bethany's comment personally, even though I knew better, sent cracks through my fragile resolve not to think of suicide anymore. If Bethany's life had become too full to remain friends with me, I felt like I might end my own. I didn't think I'd be able to survive the loss of Bethany's friendship on top of all the other losses in my life.

The Andersens hugged us joyously when my family entered their home. My eyes scanned the entry hallway for Bethany. Instead, I saw her seventeen-year-old sister, Sarah, approaching me.

"I'm about to pick Bethany up from her retreat," Sarah said, twirling a set of keys. "You wanna come with?"

I hesitated. I wasn't sure I wanted to see all of the kids Bethany had just spent the weekend with, all of the kids I feared were replacing me in her life. I determined to override my cowardice.

Bethany was standing in the church parking lot as Sarah and I pulled in. She looked taller, and her hair swung as she laughed at something another kid said. I tried to catch her attention by waving at her through the window.

"She's not gonna see you," Sarah said. "You wanna go get her?"

I stepped out of the car and walked to the curb. "Bethany!" I shouted.

Her eyes lit up when she saw me, relieving a little bit of the clench in my belly. She bounded over and gave me a quick hug. "Let me just finish saying goodbye to everyone," she said.

Before I could respond, she ran back to her group. I fought envy as I watched her hug girl after girl. They rocked back and forth with their arms wrapped around one another, like they were never going to see each other again. A few guys gave Bethany high fives, and at last, she heaved her duffle bag over her shoulder and walked to the car.

All day at the Andersens' house, I endured listening to Bethany talk about how much fun she had on her retreat. Her fun wasn't the kind I'd been expecting. Bethany had become super Christian while I was away. Her version of a good time had gone from pulling pranks to praying prophesies. She talked about how much God did in their hearts over the weekend, how great worship was, and how rad the pastors' sermons were. "Rad" seemed to be her new favorite word.

"Have you heard of a band called the O.C. Supertones?" she asked me as she unpacked clothes in her bedroom. I shook my head. "They're so rad."

A moment later, Bethany's room was filled with the honking of trumpets and a bouncy loop of boys repeating "un-con-di-tional love" over and over. The lyrics were about how unworthy we were of God's love and how, in His grace, He loved us anyway. I'd never known Bethany listened to Christian music. It was all she listened to now.

"We shouldn't be defiling our souls with secular music," she said.

It felt like hearing my mother's words come out of my best friend's mouth. I nodded my head in stern agreement with her, vowing to say nothing of the Backstreet Boys' *Millennium* album that had gotten me through long, lonesome car rides. When the O.C. Supertones song finished, Bethany asked me if I'd heard of a band called Newsboys. Nope. I watched as she relived worship moments from the retreat, singing along to a song called "Shine" about how we Christians should make non-Christians wonder what we've got.

I knew what Bethany got was the Holy Spirit. She had the same glow about her that my parents had whenever they returned from Toronto Blessing conferences. It would probably fade in about a week.

The blast hit me all at once. As soon as I walked through the doorway and into the auditorium of Bethany's youth group, I felt like I had entered a raging nightclub. Music pounded from the stage like the worship team was headlining a rock tour. Neon laser beams of lime, crimson, and purple pierced through the darkness. The roar of the crowd was so loud that I couldn't even hear myself telling Bethany to wait up. Teenagers jumped up and down everywhere I looked, their eyes closed and their hands uplifted as their voices shouted praise to God. At first I couldn't tell if I felt terrified or thrilled. Then I realized I was smiling.

My eyes strained to find Bethany, who had disappeared up an aisle of stairs to my left. The room resembled an indoor stadium, with rows of chairs ascending in a half-circle facing a stage. I spotted her waving at me from a center section.

"This is so cool!" I shouted above the music when I reached her.

"I know!" she shouted back.

I had never been in a room with so many kids my age, and certainly not a room that resembled a scene I'd only glimpsed in music videos. Bethany's youth group was way bigger than Samantha's. I understood why she'd had been having the summer of her life. If I got to go to a rock concert every week, I'd probably be having the time of my life, too. I spotted a few high schoolers who Bethany told me were junior youth pastors. The senior pastor didn't look that old himself, a young man with gelled hair who took the stage when worship began winding down. A spotlight followed him as he spoke.

"Jesus is in the house!" he shouted into his microphone. Everyone cheered ecstatically. "How many of you went on the retreat last weekend?" he asked. Almost every hand shot into the air. "Praise God!"

As we all took our seats, I noticed two teenage girls standing near the entrance double doors. They seemed to be insisting that another girl, who had just walked in wearing shorts and a halter top, put on one of the t-shirts they were handing out. I watched as the halter top girl shook her head, then listened to something one of the t-shirt girls said. The halter top girl's head dropped, and she accepted the t-shirt with the hunched body posture of shame.

"What's going on over there?" I whispered to Bethany.

"Oh, girls aren't allowed to wear spaghetti straps or halters," she said. "It's immodest. We need to guard our brothers' eyes, so we give t-shirts to girls who come in not knowing any better."

Something about that felt incredibly wrong to me. It felt like witnessing a public humiliation, which seemed like the opposite of something Jesus would do. Would Jesus call out young girls who didn't know any better, right there in front of everybody? The WWJD wristbands surrounding me implied the teens in that room thought so. I remembered *I Kissed Dating Goodbye*, the book Dad gave me when we were in California. By 1999, it had become a best-seller in the Christian world. I knew because every Christian bookstore my family went to had piles of copies stacked on tables, front and center. I'd read in Christian magazines that Joshua Harris's message of courtship and guarding against lust had spread to young adult groups across the globe. I guessed Bethany's youth group was no exception.

The youth pastor invited everyone to testify about what God had done in their hearts on the weekend retreat. One kid who took the microphone was a thirteen-year-old boy named Steven.

"So, uh, while I was on the retreat," he said, "I felt God convict me about watching porno."

I sensed the whole room collectively widen their eyes. I knew Steven's admission was a big deal, but I had no idea what porno was.

"What's porno?" I whispered to Bethany. She gave me a look that said, *Come on.* But my question was sincere. I felt like the world's most sheltered idiot, but I shrugged helplessly to let Bethany know I'd need her to answer if I was to understand the magnitude of Steven's confession.

"You've really never heard of pornography?" she whispered to me.

Oh. Pornography I had heard of. I didn't know it had an abbreviation.

"It's a hard thing for me to admit to you all," Steven was saying, scuffing his sneakers on the black surface of the stage. "But I felt like God was summoning me to come clean. James 5:16 says, 'Confess your sins to each other and pray for one another that you might be healed.' So here I am, doing that. I'm sorry that my sin has weakened our bond, brothers. I ask your forgiveness. And you girls, too. I shouldn't be treating you like trash, and that's what Jesus showed me I was doing when I jacked off. Porno infects you with lust. It gets in your mind, and soon all you can see is lust, everywhere. I need to be looking at you girls like sisters. I can't stand before God or any of you when I know my heart, mind, and body have been sinning. So I ask you all to hold me accountable."

The room was silent for several long seconds. I had the urge to throw a blanket I didn't have over Steven's head, to spare him the shocked expressions and open mouths.

"Wow," the pastor finally said, clapping Steven on the shoulder. He seemed as taken aback by Steven's confession as I was. "Steven, that was so awesome of you. You guys should all be inspired by this guy's honesty right now. Let's lift our hands to him."

Everyone in the room, myself included, closed their eyes and extended their palms toward Steven.

"Lord, thank you for this young man's conviction," the pastor said. "Thank you for using him as an example to all of us. Porno is not something to mess with. It's trash, it's of the devil, and we banish his lure in Jesus' name. Lord, we lift Steven up to you right now. Heavenly Father, we thank you for his courage, for his sincere and pure heart. May it be wiped clean of all Satan's lust, right now, Lord Jesus. Amen."

When I opened my eyes, I saw Steven smearing his tears with the sleeve of his hoodie. The pastor hugged him then sent him to return to his seat.

"Who else wants to come up and share what God did for them on the retreat?"

The pangs of conscience in the room were deafening. After several moments of eyes covertly looking around to see if anyone had the guts to follow up Steven's testimony, a girl with long brown hair stood from a row near the front of the auditorium. The pastor handed her the mic and she turned to face us.

"My name's Jessica, for those of you who don't know me," she said shyly. A few people hollered their encouragement. "Um, so on Saturday night, when we were all praying for each other, I really felt Jesus convict me of self-righteousness."

I gulped. I wasn't exactly sure what self-righteousness was, but it sounded like a sin I could relate to, if only because it wasn't as overt as cheating, stealing, or watching pornography. I berated myself for thinking I was above those. I felt sure I had cheated or stolen at some point in my life, but before I could finish agonizing over which sins I must have committed, Jessica's next words stunned me.

"And by the way," she said, "boys aren't the only ones who struggle with porno. Girls do, too. For me, it's reading books I know I shouldn't. Books can make you lust, too."

My soul felt pierced by the nails of Jesus. I was absolutely guilty of masturbating to romance novels. At every library and Barnes & Noble bookstore my family went to, I memorized paragraphs of literary erotica that would bring me to orgasm later in privacy. Jessica was right. Books that stirred lust were just as sinful as porno. I may not have gone on the retreat, but God convicted my heart right then and there. The waves of shame I felt compelled my conscience into vowing I would never touch myself again. Not there.

"But back to what I was saying about self-righteousness," Jessica said, tucking her hair behind an ear. "I've been called a goody-two-shoes all my life. It made my pride go up, and I thought I was better than everyone else because I wasn't tempted by things like swearing, or smoking pot, or cheating on tests. And I really judged people who did those kinds of things. But while I was on the retreat and Danielle was praying for me, I was so frustrated because I couldn't feel the Holy Spirit. Everyone around me was crying and, like, feeling God, but I didn't feel Him. And then Jesus showed me how my pride was the sin that was keeping me from experiencing Him fully."

I felt humbled by how much I related to Jessica. I'd been called a goody-two-shoes all my life, too. I also felt superior for my ability to resist temptations I knew other kids struggled with, and I also had never felt the Holy Spirit. In the quiet of my remorseful heart, I asked God to forgive me.

When the testimonies were over, the pastor instructed everyone to grab a partner and come to the front to pray for one another. Bethany reached for my hand. She held it as we made our way down the stairs. I didn't think we'd ever held hands before. Not unless we were at a dinner table saying grace. I felt a little uncomfortable, both from the hand-holding and because I hadn't participated in a call-to-prayer since the last time I was at a Toronto Blessing conference. I wasn't sure if the elders at Bethany's youth group expected people to fall over on the floor and get slain by the Spirit, or if their call-to-prayers involved something else, some manifestation I'd never seen and wouldn't know how to imitate. I followed Bethany to an empty spot on the carpet in front of the stage. She plopped down on the floor and tugged me down with her. We sat cross-legged in front of each other, and I followed her lead and held out my hands before closing my eyes. Then Bethany began to pray for me.

"Thank you for Alice, God," she began. "Thank you for bringing our families into each other's lives and for making us best friends."

I burst into tears. Bethany didn't know how much I needed to hear those words. God must have told her. Bethany pressed her forehead to mine as she thanked God for all of the qualities about me that she loved, which she named one by one. Never before had I felt so appreciated by anybody. I wasn't sure I could feel any more humbled, any more grateful, or any more relieved. Bethany still loved me. She still called me her best friend, even though my family had moved away from hers and wasn't coming back.

"Thank you that you have a plan for Alice's life, God," Bethany said, echoing the words Connie wrote me. "Give her hope, God, give her peace. Fill her heart with your love and remind her when she's sad that you will give her the desires of her heart."

When Bethany finished praying, she pulled her head from mine and smiled at me. I smiled back at her through my tears. I felt a little self-conscious, but when I looked around the room, I saw other people were crying, too. Boys, even. Some cried for the hope their parents would be saved. A few sobbed with gratitude for God's forgiveness of their sins. We were a puddle of tears and endorphins. We called it God, the flood of serotonin and dopamine that was released in our brains during worship, confession, and prayer. The Holy Spirit was a Christian term for the burst of neurotransmitters allowing us to feel as though we had transcended our insecurities, been forgiven of our sins, and left intoxicated with love. The findings of neurotheology would teach me this years later. That night, all I knew was that I wasn't going to consider suicide anymore. Bethany loved me. God had a plan for me. Everything else would fall into place in His perfect timing.

I made a silent vow to be the most devout woman of God I could be, to heed the words of Jesus in Matthew 5:48: "Be perfect, therefore, as your heavenly Father is perfect." I knew I would never be perfect, because Ecclesiastes 7:20 said, "Indeed, there is no one on earth who is righteous, no one who does what is right and never sins." But I promised God I would die trying.

My life is yours, God, I prayed. *I will do my best to be a daughter worthy of your love and grace. From this day on, I will worship you in every thought, deed, word, and action. Father, I recommit myself to you.*

With that, I became His.

PART III

In the last days, God says, I will pour out
my Spirit on all people. Your sons and
daughters will prophesy, your young
men will see visions, your old
men will dream dreams.

Acts 2:17

There must not be even a hint
of sexual immorality.

Ephesians 5:3

14

The Call

G od seemed to reward my recommitment to Him. By the end of
1999, He'd led my family to Kansas City, Missouri, where He told
my parents we would stay long enough to merit plugging into a new
church. Metro Christian Fellowship was a hotbed of evangelical activity at
the turn of the millennium. Mike Bickle, the senior pastor of the mega-
church, had recently founded what would become the most prominent
24/7 prayer facility in America, the International House of Prayer. Every
time people called it IHOP, I thought of pancakes.

I felt reluctant to join Metro's youth group at first. I didn't want to
make friends only to leave them if and when God said it was time. During
my first youth group event, a pizza party in the basement of one of IHOP's
administrative buildings, I felt keenly aware of my conflicting emotions.
One moment I wanted to be noticed, the next I hoped to vanish. I yearned
for friendship and belonging yet withheld myself from kids who did reach
out because I was too afraid of losing them. We would only both be hurt
when God decided to move my family along. As weeks passed and it
seemed like my family truly might remain in Kansas City for a while, I
allowed the friendliness of the other teenagers to overcome my hesitance.

The kids in Metro Youth took their walks with God seriously. Maybe even more so than Bethany's youth group. Girls dressed modestly, boys raised their hands in prayer, and youth pastors exhorted us to worship God in every action of every day. Desperate to fit in, I made Metro's youth group my own. By mid-December, I had settled into a routine that left me happier than I'd been all year.

My family was living in the one-room attic of the Lees, churchgoers who felt God put it on their hearts to have us stay with them. Mom homeschooled my siblings and me on weekday mornings, and in the afternoons, Dad dropped me off at Metro to rehearse my backstage assignments for the church Christmas pageant. I had youth group on Tuesday nights, church on Sunday mornings, and most Saturdays were spent doing something with Metro Youth. That my fun was solely planned around church didn't bother me the way it might have before I'd recommitted myself to God. Prior to His saving me from suicide and reminding me of the plan He had for me through Bethany, I would have felt like a loser spending all of my free time at church. My newfound love of Christ, as Metro Youth was wont to say, propelled the walking of my faith through acts of service, community, and worship. Those acts also grounded me with the stabilizing routine I so desperately needed.

There were moments during youth group events when I felt like I was living a double life. Like when we volunteered to wrap Christmas presents for underprivileged families one Saturday, and the night we handed out coffees to the homeless in downtown Kansas City. That my family had been on the receiving end of an underprivileged family Christmas program only two years before, and that I currently qualified as homeless myself, were facts I tried to hide from my peers. It felt surreal pretending to be a middle-class suburban girl volunteering to help the poor. Sometimes I had the urge to blurt out to everyone that it should be me receiving presents and being served coffee. Not because I wanted the charity, but because I felt like a liar.

My family's arrival in Kansas City coincided with significant changes taking place within Metro Christian Fellowship. Mike Bickle stepped down from his post as the church's senior pastor to commit full-time to expanding the International House of Prayer. In his place arrived Floyd McClung, a pastor famous in evangelical circles for his former leadership position at Youth With A Mission (YWAM), one of the largest missionary organizations in the world. The excited buzz at Metro made Pastor Floyd seem like a celebrity to me. It was then that I began to consider joining YWAM myself when I was an adult. What greater way could I serve God than through missionary work?

The new millennium arrived without the dreaded fears of Y2K. Most people at Metro seemed to think Y2K was a secular term for what the book of Revelation called the Great Tribulation. The Great Tribulation, I learned, was a three-and-a-half-year period of suffering, an apocalyptic era of destruction when God would release His judgment on humanity. Christians would be spared if they were faithful to Him. They would be "raptured," whisked away from earth to heaven leaving their clothes and unsaved loved ones behind. Almost every kid in my youth group was reading the *Left Behind* series by Tim LaHaye and Jerry B. Jenkins. There was almost an air of disappointment when it did not coincide with Y2K. Then, shortly after the New Year, my parents said God was closing the door on our stay with the Lee family.

"We're not sure what door He'll open next," Dad said, "but we think it'll still be here in Kansas City."

I breathed a sigh of relief. The icy slush of January made the idea of sleeping in a tent seem dreadful.

The next door God opened was Tristan Stafford's. Tristan was a twenty-four-year-old intercessory prayer student at IHOP who lived in Metro's missionary housing, a two-bedroom craftsman near downtown Kansas City that operated as a crash pad for the church's visiting guests. Tristan acted as resident host.

I was rarely privy to what people truly thought of my family's lifestyle, but I knew not everyone was sold on the idea that God had called us into poverty and nomadism. Conversations between my parents that I wasn't supposed to hear informed me that some people thought we were tax evaders or money launderers, or that we were running from the law for some other reason. The only time one of those suspected reasons was brought to me directly happened one evening at Tristan's house when my parents were at Metro for a conference.

"Alice," Tristan said, walking up to where I sat tucked into a sofa reading my Bible.

"Yeah?" I asked.

"What's this?"

I hadn't even noticed the baggie in his hands. The gallon-sized Ziploc contained shrunken flora that was both dried and green.

"That's dehydrated broccoli," I said.

"Really," said Tristan.

"Yes," I said.

"I saw it sticking out of your mother's backpack. You want to tell me what's going on?"

His sternness made me stammer. "Mom's been in a dehydrating phase ever since she found a dehydrator at the Salvation Army."

Tristan eyed me for several long seconds. He opened the baggie and inhaled. He pulled out one of the florets and examined it up close. Then he laughed. "Wow," he said. "For a second I was like, 'That's what this is all about? They're running weed?'"

I laughed with him as though I'd known all along that dehydrated broccoli looked like marijuana buds. I'd never seen weed in my life, but I didn't want Tristan to think I was stupid.

"Nope, not drug runners," I said.

"Because it would be the perfect cover-up, you know? This family, hiding out in churches."

"Yeah, it would."

A family of drug dealers posing as Jesus freaks. I almost wished that were the case, because at least we'd be rich.

~

In early February, shortly before my fourteenth birthday, God told my parents it was time for them to gain worldly employment again. I didn't know exactly how it happened. I only hoped it meant that being settled into a home of our own was just around the corner.

My parents' new jobs were at a mission center providing low-income families with childcare, adult education, and refugee services among other forms of social aid. Mom and Dad taught English as a Second Language to refugees from Vietnam, Bosnia, and Somalia. Dad worked full-time and Mom worked as a substitute teacher, so she could continue homeschooling my siblings and me. Having somewhere to be every day, where they were appreciated for their commitment to helping others, brought back parts of my parents I felt like I hadn't seen in years. Dad walked with a pep in his gait, his head high and confident. Mom danced when she cooked and hummed Oldies like she used to, bobbing across the linoleum with a wooden spoon in her hand.

The announcement that we were officially settling down in Kansas City came a couple of weeks later. In all of the fantasies I'd had about the moment, I never imagined myself choking back tears. They were not tears of happiness. It wasn't settling down that disappointed me, it was the three-bedroom apartment off Gladstone Boulevard that threw painful wrenches into my budding faith.

"I thought you said God would give us a string of pearls if we trusted Him with our beads," I said to Mom, struggling to keep my voice steady. "We left our beautiful house in Rockford for this?"

I gestured around the empty room I would soon share with my sisters. Paint peeled from the walls. Brown watermarks stained the ceiling. The air smelled of garbage and mildew. Our new apartment was a shattering contrast to the Nantucket-inspired cottage-mansion I'd built in my head, the one that sat prettily on the corner of a lemonade-stand sort of neighborhood where I had my own room overlooking a rose garden. That would have been an exchange of plastic beads for pearls. My actual new view overlooked someone's junk-strewn backyard with the drab skyline of the inner city looming above.

"I know," Mom sighed. "It's not what you expected. But this is what we can afford right now and where we feel God's called us to be."

"Will we at least get to be here for a while?" I asked.

"We've signed a year lease, okay? I know it's not ideal, but it would take a miracle for us to move someplace else."

I tried to be grateful that at least God was allowing us to settle down.

Two weeks later, Dad returned from Rockford with a U-Haul truck of all our worldly belongings. Our dump of an apartment turned into what could almost have been one of the floors of our old Victorian. Dad painted the walls my parents' favorite colors, Dusty Rose and Silvery Sage, and my siblings and I covered the ugly brown carpet with our richly colored Oriental rugs. Out came the candlesticks and up went the chandelier, and soon the air was laced with the old book and tealeaf scent of home. Tears burned my eyes when I sank into the floral-patterned sofa. If I closed my eyes, I was in Rockford again.

Late one spring evening, I stood with about eighty other teenagers on the packed floor of Metro Youth's meeting place. Lou Engle had come to visit. Several other youth groups from across the Midwest had traveled to join us that night to hear the renowned evangelist, who claimed he was called by God to spur revival among America's youth and government. By the end of the decade, Lou Engle would be known as the Republican Party's unofficial prayer leader, speaking at Christian Right conferences where United States politicians such as Michele Bachmann, Randy Forbes, and Rick Perry were present. In 2008, Lou Engle would endorse vice-presidential candidate Sarah Palin, calling her a modern-day Queen Esther. In 2000, Lou Engle was simply another famous pastor to me.

"I had a dream in 1996," the tall man said into the microphone, his voice croaking with intensity. "I was with leaders of a prayer movement, and there was a little boy named Joel. I was supposed to give Joel a letter. And I had lost the letter. I looked everywhere for it, absolutely frantic, and when I woke up from the dream, I heard the Lord speak to me. He said, 'Don't lose Joel's letter.' Then the Lord said to me, 'Call the youth of America into fasting and prayer.'"

His eyes burned the crowd.

"At the beginning of this year, there was a woman who came up to me. She prophesied to me that on Labor Day weekend, in the year 2000, one million youth will gather on the mall of Washington, DC. They will gather to fast and pray and worship. A million youth, marching on our nation's mall, crying out for God to move our government and bring our country back to Him." He paused to let the prophesy sink in. "You are *called*," he said.

A few months later, we helped Lou Engle make his prophecy come true.

On the morning of September 2, 2000, I stood with 400,000 young people on the National Mall. The divined day of Lou Engle's rally had arrived, the first event of a movement that would become known in the evangelical Christian world as TheCall. The crowd was 600,000 people short of the one million prophesied. We didn't let that diminish the momentousness of that day. Neither did we let the late-summer rain deter us from our sacred mission to make history. At no other point, we were told, had that many Christian teenagers gathered in our nation's capital. We felt like we were on the verge of something monumental, something profound that would change the world. We were revolutionaries for Christ.

The events of the day blurred together with seamless shifts from worship to prophesies to testimonies and back to worship. It was part rock concert and part conference, part prayer festival and part political rally. Youth groups from around the world clustered on the soggy grass beneath a charcoal sky, jumping in time with music and weeping openly with hands raised. The murmur of prayer never ceased, nor the thunder of voices coming from the stage. As the day went on, the energy of the

crowd grew fervent with purpose, angry with zeal, and dark with har-
kenings of holy war.

"You are called to be martyrs!" someone shouted. "You are called to die
to your flesh! And sometimes this means literally!"

The cries of worshippers lulled as the photograph of a smiling teenage
girl appeared on the projection screens. "This is Rachel Scott," a speaker
said into the microphone. "She gave her life for Christ on April 20, 1999.
Most of you know that's the day Dylan Klebold and Eric Harris marched
into Columbine High School and massacred thirteen people."

Two more men walked on stage. The older man, whom the speaker
introduced as Rachel's father, took the microphone. His voice didn't waver.
"I believe with all my heart that Columbine was a spiritual event," he said.

Darrell Scott's words manifested how the tragedy of Columbine would
be portrayed in the Christian youth groups of my teen years—not as a
high school shooting committed by two teenage boys, but as evidence of
spiritual warfare. Satan's army was advancing across America in the form
of abortion, gay marriage, and prayer banned in schools. God was trying to bring America back to Him, and He used school shootings like
Columbine to get our attention.

Rachel Scott was the first person to be shot on April 20, 1999. Her
father relayed that after being sprayed by bullets that wounded but did not
kill her, the seventeen-year-old was asked if she believed in God.

"You know I do," she told Eric Harris. The boy put his gun to her head
and fired the shot that sent Rachel to heaven.

Rachel's brother Craig took the microphone after his dad. He shared
the story of his experience in the Columbine High School library, where
two of his best friends died beside him, his shirt soaked by their blood.
Craig said he overheard the shooters ask a girl named Cassie Bernall if she
was a Christian. She said yes, and then she, too, was killed.

Christian singer Michael W. Smith wrote a song about Cassie Bernall's
martyrdom. He took the stage after Darrell and Craig Scott finished their
testimony of how Rachel's death was an inspiration to us all. Voices around
me rose in unison, singing along to the Christian radio hit about hoping

to pass the test of martyrdom by saying "yes" if asked whether we believed in God in the face of certain death. Years later, Cassie Bernall's "yes" would be attributed to another girl named Valeen Schnurr, who survived the Columbine shooting. But in 2000, it was Cassie Bernall and Rachel Scott who were extolled as martyrs who had died for their faith. They did not deny Christ. It had cost them their lives.

I wept as the tremble of a cello rocked my body to images of the martyred teenage girls. I couldn't help wondering if I would say yes, too, if a gun were pointed to my head. Rachel Scott and Cassie Bernall would become the heroines of my teenage years. Like modern-day Joans of Arc, they obeyed God even in the face of certain death, sacrificing their lives because they loved Jesus too much to deny Him. They were examples of true godly young women. They volunteered to help the poor, befriended the outcasts, and refused to give in to peer pressure, leaving them shunned for their beliefs. I begged God for the courage to live a life worthy of imitation, as those two girls had done. I asked God for the strength to be a living witness to Him, for Him to give me opportunities to test my devotion to Him, and for me to have the courage to say yes if I were ever confronted with the choice to die for my faith.

I couldn't even fast for Him. My stomach growled as I struggled to focus on prayer instead of hunger. Lou Engle had beseeched my youth group and the thousands of others around us to heed the Bible's words of Joel the Prophet when the Lord said to return to Him with weeping, fasting, and prayer. It was the only way America could be saved from imminent destruction. The key to America's future was in the hearts of the nation's youth, Lou Engle said, and going the whole day without food would show God how earnest we were for revival among our generation. I had never fasted before. If I couldn't make it even one day without food, it meant that I loved food more than God, and that my prayers would be considered insincere in His eyes. I felt the responsibility for the soul of America in the depths of my belly. To eat that day meant to allow the armies of evil a victory. I couldn't let that happen when so many teenagers from across the globe had gathered in my nation's capital to bring our generation back to holiness.

By mid-afternoon, my stomach was in so much pain from not eating anything that I slumped over on the grass. I looked around, desperate to see even one person nibbling an apple or taking a small bite from a granola bar. No one ate anything. Emma, one of my youth pastors who was also a nurse, knelt beside me. I hoped she mistook the hunger pangs on my face for godly weeping. However, she knew the signs of bodily pain too well.

"Alice, are you okay?" she asked.

I nodded. "I'm just hungry. Satan's really trying to test me."

"You don't have to complete the fast."

I looked up at Emma with surprise. "But that's what we came here to do."

Emma sighed. "I told the leadership not everyone's cut out for fasting," she muttered, digging into her backpack and pulling out a box of Triscuits. The basket weave surface of the crackers tempted me like the devil himself, promising salty, crunchy relief if I only gave in.

"But doesn't God tell us to fast and mourn?" I asked.

Emma didn't answer me. I sensed she was struggling herself, trying to reconcile her Christian beliefs with her professional knowledge and experience.

"Are you hypoglycemic?" Emma asked.

"No. What's that?"

"Do you have low blood sugar?"

I shook my head, but my arms continued clutching my stomach. I could barely see straight.

"Do you usually get dizzy and sick when you miss a meal?"

I nodded. "But doesn't everyone?"

Emma shook her head. "No. Most people get grouchy, but some people can get really sick," she said. "Alice, I think you're hypoglycemic. You shouldn't be rocking like this. Can you stand up?"

I wanted to try. I couldn't even sit up straight.

Emma put her hand on my shoulder. "I'm going to leave these Triscuits right here. You help yourself to as many or little as you want, okay?"

I nodded. I wouldn't give in. If I gave in to my hunger pangs, I gave in to Satan. I needed to prove to God that I loved Him more than I wanted food.

Emma caught me dry heaving into a trash can an hour later. Without saying a word, she guided me back to our spot in the grass and helped me sit down. She opened the box of Triscuits without hesitation and tore open the lining of the inner bag. Defiance blazed in her eyes. She handed me a square cracker. I took it. I lifted it to my mouth and let the salt explode over my taste buds, my teeth clamping down on the shredded wheat as my salivary glands burst with relief. I hung my head in shame.

The gravelly boom of Lou Engle's voice brought my attention back to the stage. He paraphrased verses from the book of Joel, the words slamming like poetry, shimmering with bloody images and promising a victory that would be ours should we seize it.

"The day of the Lord is coming. A day of darkness and gloom. A mighty army comes, such as never seen before. You are this army. The youth of America is this army. At the sight of you, nations are in anguish. Even the stars no longer shine. For the day of the Lord is great, the Bible says it is dreadful. Who can endure it? Even now, declares the Lord, return to me with all your heart! With fasting and weeping and mourning!"

"Yes, God!" someone near me shouted. Others echoed the cry.

"Fasting, weeping, and mourning!" Lou repeated. "Rend your hearts, says the Lord. That means tear. Tear your hearts for God. Be overcome with weeping for this nation, for the babies that are aborted, for the homosexuals who are enslaved in their sin . . . But there is hope for America! You are a consecrated assembly, and God is going to pour out his Spirit among you, right now. Right now, Lord Jesus!"

Just as I'd witnessed at Toronto Blessing conferences, the lawn of the National Mall suddenly seemed swept through by an invisible wind that caused girls to shake and boys to weep. The wailing of tongues rose around me, filling the air with chills and battle cries. I was not immune to the contagion. I lifted my arms in swell with the sudden music, tilting my face upward to let the rain blend with the tears that had formed. I

wept for aborted babies, as Lou Engle guided, imagining a sea of slaugh-
tered infants, their tender skin slashed by knives and bruised by vacuum
suction; their bodies blistered from flames while Satan and his demons
speared them with tridents, for they had not received Jesus into their
hearts. Their mothers never gave them the chance. Then I wept for the
homosexuals as Lou urged us. Those men who sodomized each other,
who selfishly defiled what the Lord made good, would not receive the
kingdom of heaven. I wept for the lesbian women who turned their
backs on God's forgiveness, imagining their luscious bodies intertwined
in sin and headed for hell.

"Bring them back to you, Lord!" I cried. "Bring them back!"

The wailing didn't cease until dark.

The next day, Pastor Jeff announced that TheCallDC had made the
morning paper. We all cheered when he held up a copy of *The Washington
Post*. We'd done it. We had made history. Later that day, I bought my own
copy of the newspaper to glue into my scrapbook.

*Tens of thousands of Christian youths gathered on the Mall yesterday in
a dawn-to-dusk prayer rally that called for reconciliation between children
and parents, an end to abortion and sexual immorality, and the return of
school-sponsored prayer*, wrote Bill Broadway. *Although family reconciliation
was a major part of TheCallDC's agenda, more prevalent were the pleas for
renewal of American society, with a new generation of Christians fighting for
what it perceives as the religious values and intent of the Founding Fathers.*

*"A demonic decree has been released on your generation and mine!" shouted
Lou Engle, an associate pastor at Harvest Rock Church. "You're a hated people
by the power of darkness."*

A disquieting feeling cracked through my excitement. Part of me wondered if the author thought we were crazy. Reading Lou Engle's words
in black and white on a legitimate newspaper, accompanied by a picture
of sobbing teenagers with their arms outstretched, made me feel embarrassed. I decided to take the embarrassment as a good thing. It meant that
I was part of a group being persecuted for God.

~

TheCallDC was the last Metro Youth event I would ever be a part of. When I returned to my family's apartment in Kansas City, my parents told me that God had led them to stop attending Metro Christian Fellowship. Therefore, I was to stop as well. They never said why.

I gulped back tears and turned to God in the pages of my prayer journal. It was loneliness that propelled my relationship with Him. When everyone else was taken away, even though it was God taking them, I tried to take comfort knowing He was always with me. Relying on God's invisible companionship was a one-way street I had faith would pay off.

For my fifteenth birthday, and Teddy's thirteenth, Mom and Dad took us all on a family ski trip to Colorado. The trip was the most extravagant present we'd ever received. When Teddy and I told them that was what we wanted for our birthdays, which were only one day apart, we were half-joking. A family of seven wasn't cheap to buy lift tickets for. To our delighted surprise, we spent nearly a week in Boulder, Colorado, skiing at Arapahoe Basin, shopping on the Pearl Street Mall, and binge-watching cartoons at the Quality Inn.

We'd been back in Kansas City for a month when Mom called my siblings and me into her and Dad's bedroom.

"Why?" Teddy asked.

"I just have something important to tell you."

My heart thudded. I picked at a strip of lace peeling from Mom's quilt as she smiled at us.

"You guys know how Daddy and I told you it would take a miracle for us to move?"

My stomach dropped. "Let me guess," I said, unable to stop myself. "That miracle's happened."

"Well," Mom said, letting my attitude slide. "When we were in Colorado, on one of my walks, I passed by this building that said 'Community Housing' on it."

Colorado.

"The lady said they're a nonprofit that helps low-income families, and she didn't have any homes available just then, but I left my number with her just in case. She called me today and guess what? There's a three-bedroom house available that would be perfect for us."

"So we're moving to Colorado?" Madeleine said.

Mom nodded. "Yep."

The nervous smile on her face told me she knew the news of God's miracle might sound bad to some of us. I was no longer the only teenager in the family whose reaction she had to worry about. I glanced at my siblings. Teddy's shoulders slumped, the patches of his Boy Scout sash making it stand stiff. Madeleine's squint seemed suspicious, as though she couldn't process why we were moving all of a sudden. Only Bryant and Kate blinked with indifference. I figured they didn't have as much to lose.

Mom said the house was in Longmont, a town only fifteen minutes away from downtown Boulder. She passed around a Xeroxed photograph of a mid-century ranch. I thought it looked ugly and small.

"When are we moving?" I asked.

"In a couple weeks," Mom said.

"A couple weeks?" I said.

I couldn't bear hearing anything else she had to say. I ran to my room and collapsed, falling onto my bed with heavy sobs. The upheaval of yet another move, accompanied by the dread of having to be the new girl someplace once again, crushed me. I couldn't be angry with my parents, for they were only following God. I couldn't be angry with God, because I feared He might allow something bad to happen. I didn't know what, but something. Having no place to put my anger, I stuffed it inward. I swallowed the searing lumps in my throat. I pounded my twitching eyebrows with my fists. I gasped for relief from the pain in my chest, and I flinched as I held in tremors that wanted to leave holes in the wall. *Die to your flesh, Alice,* I told myself. *Not my will but Yours.*

15

Giving God the Pen

It was dark out when Dad pulled into my family's new driveway. The headlights of the Suburban crept over a single-story brick house with overgrown weeds lining the path to the front door. Dad said we'd unload the moving truck the next day, tossing us our sleeping bags from the roof rack cargo carrier. I barely noticed the rooms of our new house as my hands fumbled for light switches on the walls. Mom helped my sisters spread out their sleeping bags in what would be our bedroom, and in a moment of sympathy, Mom stroked my back in an effort to soothe my tears. I knew I'd adjust as I always did. I just needed to let out my disappointment before it choked me.

The next morning, my swollen eyes opened to a popcorn ceiling. We'd never lived in a place with a popcorn ceiling before. Mom hated them. I looked around the bare room and saw Madeleine and Kate had already left their sleeping bags. The voices of my family drifted down the hallway from what I assumed was the kitchen, judging by the clatter of spoons on cereal bowls. I didn't want to see them yet. I crawled out of my bag and walked across the rough beige carpet to the single window running along the rear wall. The backyard looked beaten by winter. Dried sunflower stalks bowed stiffly in their beds, looking like they'd snap to dust in a breeze. Scraggly shrubs ran along a cyclone fence, and in the distance, hazy rays of sunlight glowed atop endless fields of dead grass. It was almost pretty in a desolate sort of way.

"Oh good, you're up," Mom said, startling me. She stood in the doorway of the bedroom with a pair of scissors in her hand. "You can help me unpack the moving boxes in the kitchen."

Our new house looked plainer than any home we'd lived in before. Mom said it lacked character. Its best feature was the view of the Rocky Mountains from what Mom dubbed the sunroom, but as plain as the mid-century ranch was, its 1,800 square feet gave us plenty of space. The kitchen was small and fluorescent-lit, but functional. The living room didn't have any windows, but it had a working fireplace. Dad said we could plant a vegetable garden in the backyard.

Everyone but Mom went to LifeWay Community Church on our first Sunday in Colorado, since Mom said she wanted to stay home to continue unpacking. The small fellowship overlooking a postcard view of the snow-capped Rockies was nondenominational, and like every other nondenominational church I'd been to, LifeWay had its roots in the Vineyard branch of Pentecostalism. I hadn't been to a church since God asked my family to stop going to Metro almost seven months prior. LifeWay's fellowship seemed much smaller than Metro's, with about a couple hundred people instead of a few thousand, but the hands raised to the same worship songs felt comfortingly familiar. Where my family called home constantly changed, but the churches we went to stayed the same.

A middle-aged woman approached me after the service. She said her name was Sheila and that I should join their youth group, Youth for Truth Ministries. Their annual spring break retreat left the next day, if I wanted to come. When she told Dad they had a scholarship for low-income teens, my parents surprised me by giving their permission to go.

I almost regretted my decision the next morning when Dad drove me back to LifeWay. My chest felt tight with nerves. I wondered if the teens would like me or not. I knew God's was the only opinion that mattered, but my fleshly ego still worried. Twenty or so guys and girls stood in the lobby when I walked through the glass doors, and I tried to be inconspicuous as I moved to a side table covered with bulletins. I pretended to read them until I noticed two girls smiling at me from a corner. One of them gave me a little wave, then they both walked up to me.

"Hi," the blond-haired girl said. "I'm Hailey."

She stuck out her hand with the confidence of a CEO.

"I'm Lauren," said the other girl, whose black curls framed her rosy cheeks.

I introduced myself and shook their hands.

"Are you new to LifeWay?" Hailey asked.

"Yeah, my family just visited yesterday."

"And you're coming with us on the retreat?"

I nodded. Lauren's mouth dropped open in awe. "You're so brave," she said.

The girls' sweet smiles helped put me at ease. They introduced me to everyone else in the lobby, and although my shyness blurred all of their faces together, their warmth and inclusiveness struck me as genuine.

The three-day retreat at Glacier View Ranch focused on what Pastor Eric called the three foundations of Christianity: faith, hope, and love. Faith was the theme of the first day, and I felt grateful to find myself in a youth group that seemed to take their walk with God as seriously as I did. After worship on the second day, the theme of which was hope, Pastor Eric stood up.

"I was planning on giving a message," he said. "But I feel like God wants us to just have an open prayer time." He closed his eyes and prayed. "Father, do whatever you want," he said.

The words had barely left his mouth when everyone broke into prayer. I felt right in my comfort zone, thinking of all the spontaneous prayer sessions I'd had with Metro Youth. I closed my eyes, marveling at how no matter where I was, the manifestations of the Holy Spirit were always the same. Voices prayed in tongues around me, but I prayed in the quiet of my heart. Then I felt the gentle touch of hands on my sweater.

"Thank you for bringing Alice here, God," I heard a girl's voice say.

"Yes, Lord," said another.

I cracked open my eyes and saw Hailey and Lauren standing on either side of me. Their eyes were closed, their voices tender, and their words a balm to my soul.

"Father," Hailey continued. "I ask that you would make Alice feel completely welcome here."

"Yes, God," murmured Lauren.

"That any rejection she might feel would be cast out in the name of Jesus. That any unwantedness she might be afraid of be banished in His name. Father, we love her already."

I started crying. Hailey and Lauren put their arms around me, rocking me side to side and murmuring prayers of thanks as my shoulders heaved. I'd been starving for belonging, and I never expected God would provide me with such caring friends so soon. All of the teens at Youth for Truth made me feel more welcome than anywhere I'd been my whole life, but Hailey and Lauren especially embodied the compassion Jesus spoke of in the Bible. They were living examples of His love, the kind of girls I needed in my life to inspire me toward godliness. I felt overwhelmed with gratitude for how God had blessed me.

Love was the theme of the last day, and I awoke that morning feeling a renewed sense of faith. I'd been scared and angry to leave Kansas City, and even so, God had rewarded my obedience with gifts I didn't feel I deserved. My new friends were better than any I could have dreamed of. I went home from the retreat feeling like I had brothers and sisters in Christ I'd known my whole life. I didn't know how I could feel so close to people I barely knew, and I was tempted to fear that the feeling would fade. I decided to trust God's faithfulness. The prayers of Hailey and Lauren had told me everything I needed to know: that I was right where God wanted me to be. Joining Youth for Truth would take my faith to the next level.

~

My family had lived in Colorado for nearly two months when I visited another church for a special event. The auditorium of LifeBridge Christian Church was packed with teenagers that warm spring evening, but I didn't spot any of my new friends from Youth for Truth in the crowd. We had all come for a conference the flyer in my hands promised would give us "Four Secrets to a Perfect Love Story." Eric and Leslie Ludy were the guest speakers on the stage. They looked like the perfect married couple: young, attractive, and totally devoted to God.

Leslie, a petite brunette who spoke to us the way I imagined a cool big sister might, opened the evening with a story. "I'll never forget the night Brandon broke up with me," she said. "I was a sophomore in high school, and we'd been going out for eight months. I thought we were deeply in love. But by the end of our phone conversation, Brandon had dumped me, and I was left with a broken heart once again."

I listened to Leslie with rapt attention.

"That night I was utterly devastated," she continued. "And a few days later, I cried out to God in desperation. See, I'd been raised in a Christian home all my life. I'd read all the Christian dating books and attended every purity retreat my youth group offered. I had followed the rules of not having sex before marriage and only dating Christian guys. So why was I so miserable? Why did every one of my relationships end in heartbreak?"

She paused as though letting us wonder why all of our relationships ended in heartbreak, too.

"Then I felt God gently say to me, 'Leslie, you keep getting your heart broken because you are holding the pen to your love story. I am the author of true love. I am the creator of romance. I know your heart's every desire, every wish and secret dream. I want to script a beautiful love story just for you. But you need to give the pen of your love life to me.'"

That was the first secret to a perfect love story, Leslie said. "You need to give God the pen."

Eric and Leslie took turns sharing how God had guided every step of their romance. They met the day before Leslie turned sixteen, and almost three years later, they married after a six-month courtship. They said the love they shared was deeper and more beautiful than anything they could have written themselves.

"Because I had been faithful to Leslie long before I met her," Eric said. "Here's secret number two to a perfect love story . . . get a love life! Betcha guys didn't think I'd say that, huh? Now I'm not suggesting you go out looking for someone to woo or seduce. The fact is, you already have someone you can begin loving right now . . . your future spouse."

Leslie agreed, sharing how God revealed this epiphany to her.

"I was sixteen when I came across Proverbs 31," she said. "It says, 'The wife did her husband good and not evil all the days of her life.' And I thought, how is that possible? I'd never met anyone who'd been married all the days of her life. Did this mean the wife did her husband good even before she met him?"

Leslie felt that God told her yes. Then she wondered what doing her husband good meant. She realized it was more than just keeping herself a virgin until she married. She needed to guard her heart, mind, and actions as well.

"I realized there had to be more to purity than just not having sex," Leslie said. "Otherwise I wouldn't feel so dirty and used every time I gave someone my heart as well as my physical body."

"For some reason," Eric said, "today's Christians seem to think that purity stops at virginity. As long as we're not having sex, we're pure. But true purity is deeper than that. True love doesn't just wait. It proves itself in mind and heart as well as body."

He held up two fingers as though making the sign for air quotations. "These are Leslie's eyes."

Everyone laughed, including Leslie.

"Another way to love your future spouse is to imagine they're always watching you," Eric said. "God gave me the idea of what I call the Two-Eyed Principle. I began to live my life as if my future spouse was always

watching me. Wherever I went, there she was." He bobbed his two fin-
ger-eyes in the air. "And if the eyes of my future spouse felt hurt or jealous
through anything I was doing, whether I was flirting with a girl, or whether
a conversation was going a little beyond a level of intimacy than I think
it should, then I would stop and say, 'You know what? This probably isn't
making my future wife feel very loved right now. I want to honor her. I
want her to feel cherished.'"

Several girls in the audience awww-ed.

"And here's another way you can honor and serve your future spouse
even now," Eric continued. "The third secret to a perfect love story is to
be tender. I know guys, tender isn't much of a manly sounding word. But
girls love it, trust me."

Eric told guys they could practice tenderness by learning how to be
more emotionally sensitive to their moms and sisters, and by always noticing when a woman cut her hair. For girls, being tender meant looking
for ways to stroke the male ego of her father and brothers, and practicing
motherhood by taking care of young children and learning how to cook
dinner for her family. Then Eric and Leslie gave us their last and final
secret to a perfect love story.

"Have a winning team," Eric said. "I can't stress enough how important this part is."

Eric told us how valuable it would be to our love lives if we selected a
team of godly mentors—ideally, our parents—to help guide us. "Having
a team of godly mentors to hold you accountable, whether they're your
parents, pastors, or other spiritually mature people in your life, will help
make sure you're on God's path and not your own."

Leslie said that making her parents a part of her team had been pivotal
in her love story with Eric. When Eric started to worry he was spending too much time with Leslie, he took it upon himself to check in with
Leslie's father as her mentor, inviting him to speak up as an authority in
her life if he sensed there was any impurity. Eric said that Leslie's father
had told him he knew his relationship with Leslie was pure because God
would tell him if it wasn't.

"But what he said next shocked me even more," said Eric. "Her dad said, 'Eric, I want you to know that Leslie's mom and I give you our blessing to pursue a relationship with our daughter in any way God would lead you.'"

Eric prayed about it and met with Leslie's father again a few weeks later. "I was super nervous," Eric said. "After hemming and hawing a bit, I finally came out and said, 'Sir, I feel God has shown me that one day Leslie is going to be my wife.' And you know what he said? He said to me, 'Eric, Janet and I have been praying for fourteen years that we would recognize Leslie's future husband when he came into her life. And Eric, we've known for some time that you are the one.'"

I sat back in my seat utterly amazed. If that wasn't confirmation from God, I didn't know what was.

The promise I took home from the conference that night was that if I stayed pure and faithful to my future husband, giving the pen of my love life to God, He would reward my trust with a romance beyond anything I could imagine. I surrendered to Him fully.

Eric and Leslie Ludy's message of purity and faithfulness was a familiar one. Their book, *When God Writes Your Love Story: The Ultimate Approach to Guy/Girl Relationships*, echoed what I'd read in Joshua Harris's *I Kissed Dating Goodbye*. Impassioned by my commitment to love my future husband before I met him, I reread the book Dad introduced me to when I was twelve. When I scoured LifeWay's bookstore for more Christian dating books, I discovered Joshua Harris had written a sequel to his international best-seller. *Boy Meets Girl: Say Hello to Courtship* told the story of how Harris had met, courted, and married the woman God finally revealed to him. The book was part memoir, since it was a personal love story, but it was also peppered with more elaborate courtship advice than he'd been able to give previously. Now that Harris had wooed the bride

God set apart for him, he offered more specific words of wisdom that came from his own experience.

I didn't find many differences between the Ludys' *When God Writes Your Love Story* and Harris's *Boy Meets Girl*. Like the Ludys, Harris and his wife had their courtship externally confirmed as God's will by Harris's parents and pastors. Harris had kept the promise he'd made to his future wife before he'd met her—that he wouldn't kiss her until their wedding day—and Eric and Leslie Ludy had also saved their first kiss until after they said their vows. I began to see this as deeply romantic. What greater gesture of love could there be, the books proposed, than to deny one's flesh, even when two people were engaged, until they were pronounced husband and wife in the eyes of God? That was true selflessness.

I took away three key principles from both books: that courtship was preferable to dating because it distinguished God-led romance from that of the world's version; that God would confirm who my future husband was through my parents and spiritual mentors in my life; and that I was not to be rule-driven in my approach to courtship, but rather let myself be guided by the Holy Spirit when it came to specific issues, like how far was too far physically. Abstaining from outright sex before marriage was a given, but the Ludys and Harris acknowledged how hard it was for unmarried people to know the grayer boundaries of intimacy. Therefore, all forms of physical contact should be subject to prayerful scrutiny. Hugs, snuggles, and handholding could lead down a slippery slope. Only God could show us what was okay, the authors said. Yet I felt it was fairly clear that true Christians didn't kiss until their wedding day.

Saving my first kiss for the altar did sound romantic, but I confessed in my journal that a part of me felt troubled by the forbiddances of physical intimacy. What if my future husband and I saved our first kiss for our wedding day and it turned out he was a bad kisser? What if I was a bad kisser? What if the sex was awful? According to women's magazine headlines, I gathered sex could either be really good or really bad.

A scarier thought occurred to me. What if I wasn't even attracted to the man God told me was my future husband? I desperately scanned the pages of my Christian dating books. Both the Ludys and Harris assured their readers that God created sexual desires so we could find fulfillment in our spouse. He wouldn't punish our trust by giving us a spouse we weren't sexually attracted to. The worries of my heart eased. I hated to admit it, but sometimes I feared God would have me marry a man I wasn't attracted to just because I wasn't supposed to be shallow.

I found ample Bible verses backing up what the Ludys and Harris wrote of.

Charm is deceptive, and beauty is fleeting; but a woman who fears the Lord is to be praised.

Treat younger women as sisters, with absolute purity.

Above all else, guard your heart.

God's will for my love life was clear. I was not to date or betray my future spouse in any way. Flirting, fantasizing about a crush, or leading someone on with words or actions would be emotionally cheating on my future husband. I would be mentally cheating on him if I read pornography or watched a love scene in a movie, or even if I forgot to look away immediately if I saw someone I felt attraction for. Spiritually cheating would be all of the above, because when I dishonored my future spouse by being unfaithful, I cheated on God and the beautiful plan He had for me. I also risked attracting Satan and his temptations that would lead me further down a path of immorality.

I vowed to stay faithful to my future husband before I even met him. Imagining him watching my every move became a compulsive habit, and whenever I found myself in an interaction with someone of the opposite sex, I pictured watching myself through my future husband's eyes. Would he feel honored? Was I being loyal to him? Was there anything in my speech, dress, or conduct that would make him think I was being anything less than faithful? I didn't realize I was priming my mind to accommodate jealous paranoia. I thought I was only loving my future husband the way God wanted me to. My purity of body, heart, and mind would be my gift to him.

16

Friend-Raising

Mom stared at me with wide eyes. "Where are you going to get two thousand dollars?"

"If God wants me to go, He'll provide it," I said.

I couldn't tell if Mom's expression was one of disbelief or awe. Finally, she said, "Wow. You must have big faith, Alice. Even stronger than mine and Dad's if you believe God's going to provide you with over two thousand dollars."

Dad's eyes twinkled with pride.

"So I can go?" I asked.

My parents glanced at each other, then smiled at me. "If God provides you the money, yes, you can go to India," Mom said.

My parents' awe surprised me. Of course I had big faith. I'd learned it from them.

The following Tuesday, I attended a mandatory fundraiser meeting at LifeWay. The leaders told us we needed to mail out support letters to at least fifty people. They also said we shouldn't think of our efforts as fund-raising, but friend-raising, and their instructions to take a parent's coworker out for coffee under the guise of relationship-building felt deceitful to me. I didn't know who could be gullible enough to fall for the friendship of a random teenager who surreptitiously asked for money under the guise of selling them an opportunity to do God's good work. I prayed about it and decided I would only send fundraising letters to the people God put on my heart.

My parents were the first to give money toward my India mission. Dad's new job as an interior painter for a company called Handyman Connection brought in more money than I ever remembered us having. He and Mom paid the $50 deposit I turned in with my mission application. There were only nineteen other people I felt I could ask for money with a clean conscience. Most of them were relatives or people my family had lived with at some point. The idea of asking anybody for money made my stomach roll, but I clung to a quote I once heard some pastor say: "You give other people an opportunity to bless you when you let them know of your financial needs, and in turn God blesses them." Remembering this allowed me to craft my letters with less agony.

The letters I sent out explained how I was going to New Delhi, India, that summer to help share God's love. The organization my group would go with was called Youth With A Mission, or YWAM, as everyone shortened it. Another youth group from Spokane, Washington, would be joining us, and while we were in India, we would minister God's love in schools by performing skits about salvation through Jesus Christ; traveling to rural villages with goods to donate; and evangelizing to local Hindus and Sikhs we met along the way. Our ultimate goal was to convert people to Christianity so they might know the boundless love of God here on earth and have eternal life in heaven when they died. I promised my supporters to update them on the successes of my mission when I was back, and I added that if they didn't feel God put it on their hearts to support me financially, their prayers were just as needed. I didn't want anyone to feel bad if they couldn't afford to give me money.

Fundraising—or friend-raising, for those who preferred the term— proved a bigger challenge than anyone anticipated. The donation account

LifeWay set up for me plateaued at $1,100. The amount was more money than I'd ever had in my life, but it wasn't the $2,200 needed to go to India. No one else seemed able to reach their goal either. With only three weeks left until our departure date, my team was collectively still $9,000 short. The situation looked grave. Pastor Deborah, who seemed to be the director of LifeWay's missions department, invited us to her office for a special meeting. Everything about Pastor Deborah intimidated me, from her perfectly coiffed blond hair to the smile that never seemed to reach her blue gaze. She always spoke in measured tones.

"It's really unusual for a mission team to be so far behind in their fundraising this late in the game," Pastor Deborah said. She took a moment to look at the eight of us from where we sat on the worn office sofas. "I want each of you to consider whether God might be telling you that this summer is not your summer to go on a mission trip. Maybe He's saying wait until next year. Or, maybe He's saying to go on a different trip. There are local outreaches that always need support, you know."

My heart sank. I couldn't deny the truth in Pastor Deborah's words. What if I'd mistaken my own fleshly desire to go to India for God's will? Everyone in the room remained silent until Julia, the youth pastor co-leading the India trip with her husband Anthony, spoke up.

"What if we wait one more week before making any decisions," Julia said. "That'll give everyone time to see how much more money they can raise."

Pastor Deborah nodded. "Okay then," she said. "We're going to pray now, and I want Zach and Alice to go around and lay hands on everyone. The Bible says the Holy Spirit can show us things more clearly with the laying on of hands."

It wasn't the first time I'd been singled out to lay hands on people in prayer, but I always hated how anxious it made me feel. Zach, a seventeen-year-old going into his senior year, began with the person nearest to my right, so I started with Julia to my left. I knelt to her level and thanked God for making her one of my youth pastors, asking Him to bless her leadership and guidance. I prayed something similar over her husband Anthony then made my way around the circle composed of the teenagers I'd hopefully be going to India with. I thanked God for Landon's quiet leadership, for Chelsea's gentle spirit, for Simone's compassionate heart, and for Luke's kind sincerity. I realized I'd learned more about my team-mates over the past couple of months than I thought.

I circled back to Julia just as Zach finished praying for her. He and I were both half-squatted, half-kneeled on the floor, and he looked at me with a question. I nodded. I closed my eyes and felt him place his palms on my shoulders. His forehead hovered inches from mine as he prayed out loud.

"Thanks for making Alice such a woman of God," Zach said. "Thank you for her selfless spirit. Thank you for bringing her to this youth group and for putting her on this team."

I flushed, then put my palms on Zach's shoulders. I can't remember what I prayed because, all of a sudden, our foreheads accidentally touched. The warmth of Zach's skin startled me. I felt his shoulder flinch beneath my hand as I pulled back, my heart pounding in between the silent pauses of my prayer. I was certain Zach could hear its every thud. The scent of his neck so close to mine made me feel dizzy and I had the sudden urge for him to pull me into his chest.

No, I thought in horror. *Satan, I banish your temptation. God, you know I like Zach only as a friend. Please keep our relationship pure and platonic.*

I did only like Zach as a friend. Yet I pulled away from him feeling as though I'd been ambushed. It didn't make any sense to me how one second we could be praying in earnest and the next I could be wanting to fall into his arms. I had never felt such a pheromonal instinct before. Maybe it was the closeness of our faces, or maybe it was how I'd never noticed his amber brown eyes until they bore right into me, or the way his dimples disap-peared like magic when he wasn't talking. Regardless, somewhere during our prayer, I developed feelings for Zach. Romantic feelings. Lustful feel-ings. Feelings I wasn't supposed to have. I didn't know how or why, and I certainly didn't want the burden of a crush, but I suddenly felt shy around Zach in a way I hadn't before.

I felt even more flustered when Zach offered to give me a ride home that night. He overheard me asking Julia if I could borrow her cell phone to call my dad.

"Wait, you're in Longmont, too, right?" Zach said to me.

"Yeah," I said.

"I've got you."

He gave me his signature wink that I wanted to take personally. We said goodbye to everyone else and Zach held open the door of his sticker-covered truck as I climbed into its passenger seat.

"Sorry it's so messy," he said, shoving a Doritos bag and some papers into the back.

We made small talk as he drove us toward the 119 highway. I wasn't sure I'd ever been alone with Zach before, but aside from the butterflies in my chest, I felt strangely comfortable. I attributed the ease to our prayer session. People always felt cozier after they opened up in prayer. Yes, that was probably what my sudden infatuation was. Just a trick of the mind, or a tempting of the devil trying to take my focus off God.

Zach pulled into a Diamond Shamrock gas station. "I'm gonna get something to drink," he said. "You want anything?"

I shook my head no, but thought it was sweet he'd asked. He turned with a shrug and walked into the fluorescent light. I tried not to peek at him through the glass doors and failed. How had I never noticed how cute he was? His buzzed head and roguish grin gave him an edgier look than the other guys in youth group. Zach wore his pants low and baggy, his baseball cap backward, and he always seemed to be chewing gum with a rebel smirk on his face. Yet when he prayed, he bowed his head with the humility of King David. Zach took communion when no other teens walked up for crackers and grape juice. He sat in worship with his eyes closed when others stood with their hands raised. Zach was different, a nonconformist. He was funny, but knew when to be serious, and I realized it was the many paradoxes of Zach that drew me to him. His damn dimples didn't help, either. I forced myself to stare straight ahead when he came back from the gas station.

"You like P.O.D.?" I asked as Zach restarted his truck. The Christian rock band's initials stood for Payable On Death, a reference to how our sins were only payable by Jesus' death. I had noticed the P.O.D. sticker on Zach's dashboard.

"For sure," he said, cracking that smile at me. "You a P.O.D. fan, too? What's your favorite song?"

"I really like 'Hollywood' and 'Set Your Eyes to Zion.'"

"Ah, yes, good tracks, good tracks."

I couldn't help myself. By the time Zach dropped me off at my house, I realized the unfortunate had happened. I had a full-blown crush. There was no denying it as I watched his taillights fade. If he liked me, I couldn't tell. I picked up no indication that he thought of me as anything more than a sister in Christ. Zach might've been a badass, but he was a godly badass. His parents were leaders at LifeWay and he volunteered as a leader for the junior high youth group. Zach was so godly I figured he probably wouldn't even be attracted to a girl who would have a crush on anybody other than her future husband, which made me feel ashamed of my uncontrollable feelings. I would just have to repent for them constantly.

～

Two Sundays later, my mission teammates and I waited in LifeWay's empty auditorium with hopeful faces and bated breath. More money had come in for each of us, but it still wasn't enough. Pastor Deborah had taken a special collection for us during service that morning. The India team was $4,000 short of their goal, she'd announced. Anything would help.

The churchgoers were long gone. Only my teammates and I lingered in the empty auditorium. I sat on the edge of the stage next to Simone, my legs swinging with restlessness. Pastor Deborah was counting the offering money in a back room. She said she'd divide up the sum equally and whoever had reached at least 80% of their goal was going to India. LifeWay's scholarship fund would cover the rest. In minutes, we would find out who would go and who would stay behind.

I had the peace of knowing I'd already reached 82% of my goal. A couple at LifeWay I didn't even know had given me $350 because God led them to, and someone else had anonymously deposited $300 into my missions account. I never found out who, but I thanked God profusely for their generosity. All I hoped now was for the rest of my teammates to be going to India with me.

"Here she comes," Luke said.

I looked up. Pastor Deborah walked down the aisle toward us with an expression that gave away nothing. We all stood and faced her.

"Let's open with a prayer," she said.

I could almost hear the silent groans of suspense as we bowed our heads.

"Heavenly Father, we thank you for the plan you have for this team," said Pastor Deborah. "It's been a difficult journey, but they have remained full of faith and hope. Let your will be done here now, Lord. Amen."

Our eyes opened to our fate.

"So," said Pastor Deborah, looking at each of us. "What do you guys plan to do with the offering money? Do you want to divide it up evenly among you all, or do you want to give it to those who already have the most money so at least they can go?"

I thought we'd already decided to split the offering evenly. Pastor Deborah's options told me the collection must not have been enough to cover everyone. My smile fell. Luke spoke first.

"How much did we make in the offering?" he asked.

"Well, I don't want to tell you that yet," said Pastor Deborah.

"I just figured if we knew how much we had, maybe we could better decide what to do with it." Luke's manner was nothing if not polite—he was the most courteous teenage guy I'd ever met—but I could tell he was also annoyed by Pastor Deborah's mind games.

Pastor Deborah smiled evenly. "How about you just tell me what you want to do first, then I'll tell you the amount. I want to see where your hearts are at."

I wondered how much pleasure she got from toying with our hopes. No one spoke.

"What do you guys want to do?" she asked again. "Do you want to divide the money evenly, or do you want to give it to those who already have the most?"

I couldn't stand her patient stare any longer.

"I don't think we should do either of those," I said. "I think we should give the money to whoever has the least. Then maybe we can all reach eighty percent. I know I already have enough, so I don't need any more. Splitting the money among those who have the least should be an option to consider."

I hoped I didn't sound belligerent. Or like I was trying to be noble.

Pastor Deborah eyed me thoughtfully. "That's a generous way of looking at it," she said. "What do the rest of you think we should do?"

"Well, I kind of agree with Alice," said Landon. "We should give the money to those who need it."

Everyone else chimed in their agreement.

Pastor Deborah took a breath, then allowed a small smile. "I can see you all have generous hearts," she said. "The offering made thirty-six hundred dollars. With the money some of you turned in today, all you need now is two hundred more."

We gaped at her. The offering was more than we'd dared to hope for.

"And that's not all," Pastor Deborah said. "I have a friend who said he would make up the difference for whatever was left. So when you leave this room today, you can all say that you are fully funded for your trip to India!"

Praise Gods and woohoos echoed through the auditorium. Anthony threw his arms around Julia and Luke and told everyone to circle for a group prayer. I heard him thanking God for His faithfulness, but my attention was on the joyous faces around me. Landon looked stunned.

Luke chuckled with excitement. Zach grinned as though he'd known all along God would pull through. Chelsea's eyes twinkled softly, and even reserved Simone's lips were curved into a shocked smile. My eyes felt misty. We were going to India.

~

Five days later, the eight of us said goodbye to our families and drove to a YWAM base camp in Colorado Springs for three days of missionary training before our flight to New Delhi. Colorado Springs seemed to be the very embodiment of America's glorification of military power and Christian values. Signs for Army and Air Force bases hung from nearly every church-dotted street we passed. The overwhelming military presence was noticed by my teammates, too.

"Isn't the base camp right next to NORAD?" asked Zach.

Anthony answered from the front seat. "I think you're right about that."

"What's NORAD?" I asked.

Anthony, who had served in the military, explained that NORAD stood for North American Aerospace Defense Command.

"What do they do?" I asked.

"Well," Anthony said, "they're who the government calls if crap hits the fan. There's a bunker up the mountain and it's where the president could be flown for hiding if America was ever attacked." Anthony pointed out a tall barbed wire fence partially hidden by trees as the van made a turn up a windy mountain road. "See that?" he said. "That's the border of NORAD. Cross that fence and you'll meet a bunch of guys with machine guns."

We pulled down a dirt driveway where a blue sign hung between two pine trees. It read, "Welcome to Mission Adventures!"

A petite girl with a heart-shaped face led the girls and me to our cabin. She said her name was Lindsay and that she would be our skit instructor.

"We'll rehearse your skits later today," she said. "For now, you guys can set yourselves up in the bunks here and then come to the main lodge."

We met the seven-member Washington team from Spokane during lunch. They seemed friendly and I looked forward to getting to know them better. The first day of our missionary training involved skit rehearsals, a briefing on culture shock, and a sermon based on the importance of teamwork. Sean, the twenty-four-year-old YWAM leader guiding our trip, warned that third-world travel often brought out the worst in people. Jet lag, stress, stomach issues, and the emotional impact of seeing poverty we weren't used to could take a toll on us, resulting in arguments with each other we might not have under normal circumstances. He said that communication and conflict resolution would be the focus of the next day.

"We have an obstacle course set up in the woods," he said. "And you're all gonna have to work as a team to get everyone through each obstacle."

My team handled the obstacle course like pros. The following afternoon, we deftly overcame every challenge set up for us, from tightrope walking between pine trees to climbing over a twelve-foot wall with no ropes. It felt like we were game contestants who had successfully won the day.

"I have to say," said Sean as he walked us back to the lodge, "you guys have the best communication and teamwork of any group I've seen do this."

We all gave each other high fives. I couldn't imagine a scenario where we would have any conflict, but it felt good to know we'd probably handle it with flying colors. I smiled to myself. I still couldn't believe that only months earlier, I'd been so upset to move to Colorado. Here I was having more fun than I'd ever had in my life. I had awesome youth pastors, budding friendships in my teammates, and I was going on a mission trip to India. My life had purpose.

17

Martyrs and Missionaries

I awakened to someone shoving my shoulder.

"Alice, get up!" a female voice hissed. "We have to leave, now!"

I rolled over in my bunk, disoriented. The light was turned on. The girls in the cabin were packing frantically, shoving their things into backpacks and whispering to each other in urgent tones. My youth pastor Julia stood at eye level with me; her face was set with worry.

"Get dressed quickly and take only what you can carry," she said. "We have to evacuate."

My first thought was NORAD, the military base next to the YWAM camp. Had America broken out into war while we slept?

"What happened?" I asked, yanking back my covers.

"We have to leave the country," Julia said. "We've been found out."

I didn't know what she meant, but the terror in her voice compelled me to move without further questions. Fear raced through my veins as I got dressed, yanking on a long blue skirt and a hoodie. I slipped on my sandals, then thought better of it, swapping them out for my tennis shoes in case wherever we were going had rough terrain.

My family. "Is my family okay?" I asked Julia.

"Yes, your family's okay, but we need to leave. Now."

I grabbed my Bible from the bedside shelf and stuffed it into my backpack atop Clif bars, toiletries, and my journal. Someone whispered for me to hurry, and I heaved my backpack over my shoulders. I was the last one to leave the bunkhouse.

The night was lit only by stars. I heard someone say it was two in the morning. I shivered in the mountain air, scrambling to keep up with the rest of the girls, but I could barely see the dirt path we walked on.

"Here's your train ticket," Julia said to the girl ahead of me. Then Julia turned and shoved a slip of paper into my hands. "Here's your train ticket," she repeated urgently. "Keep it with you."

I made out the words "Train Ticket" scrawled on the piece of paper.

"Train for where?" I asked.

Julia ignored my question. Something felt off, even more so than it already did. I was about to ask Julia what was happening when I stumbled over a cluster of tree roots in the darkness.

"You there!" shouted a male voice. "Stop!"

I turned and saw the silhouette of a man with a gun coming toward us. His rifle was aimed at me and he wore a black balaclava over his face. I froze in complete terror. A girl screamed.

"Please, don't hurt us," Julia cried. "We're just on our way to the train."

My heart missed beats. I could barely breathe.

"You're not going to the train," the man said. "You're coming with me."

Suddenly three more people with guns and balaclavas appeared. I could barely process what was happening. They shone bright lights in our faces, blinding us.

"Move!" said one of the gunmen.

They herded us single file in a new direction. My body went through motions as my mind alternately raced with questions and blanked with panic. I heard one of the girls whimper, and I tripped and felt the hard muzzle of a gun jab into the base of my neck. It stayed there, pushing me forward.

"Keep your hands where I can see them," my gunman said.

I put my hands in the air.

"Help!" one of the girls screamed out.

"Shut up! Keep walking!"

"Where are you taking us?" someone asked.

No one answered.

We stumbled through the dark forest until another masked gunman, a woman, told us to stop. She looked right at me. "You," she said. "Inside."

She pointed with her gun to the door of a tiny cabin.

"No," Julia said. "We're not splitting up."

"Shut up," said the third man. "Or I'll shut you up."

I moved toward the cabin door before he could hit Julia. The head gunman kept the cold barrel of his rifle against the top of my spine as he shoved me inside. The door shut behind me. I was in pitch black. Was I alone? I heard someone yell at Julia and the rest of the girls to march, then a bright flashlight pierced my eyes. The head gunman and female gunman had followed me inside the small space, which I saw was no bigger than a closet. I shielded my eyes with my hands and backed into a wall, tripping over something on the floor.

"Clumsy one, ain't you?" the man said.

The light blinded me from seeing his masked face. It was so bright. So dark, and so bright.

"Sit down," he said, shoving a footstool in front of me.

My knees trembled as I sat.

"What's your name?"

I couldn't speak.

"What's your name?!"

"Alice," I whispered.

"Louder, I can't hear you!"

His gun waved inches from my face.

"My name is Alice," I repeated. My voice sounded foreign to my ears. Its calmness belied the fear surging through me.

"Alice, where's your passport?" the woman asked.

"In my backpack," I said.

"Remove the backpack," said the man. "Slowly."

I sat my pack down in front of me. My hands shook. "It's in the front zipper pocket," I said.

"Get it out."

I did as he said and handed him my brand-new passport. I'd only gotten it two weeks ago at the post office with Mom. Mom. Where was she? What was happening?

"You're American?"

"Yes."

"Open the rest of your backpack."

I unzipped the main compartment. His flashlight shone on the first thing on top.

"What's this?" he asked, lifting my Bible. "Is this your business here in China? Are you a missionary?"

My mind felt like it was splitting with confusion. We weren't in China. We were still in Colorado Springs.

"Answer the question," the man barked. "What is your business here in China?"

"I don't know, sir," I said. Then I remembered what a YWAM leader had told me to say when I went through customs in India. "Tourist, I'm a tourist."

"Why do you have a Bible? Are you a Christian? Are you here to poison our people's minds with your false god? You know we kill Christians here in China. Do you want to be a martyr?"

I shook as he berated me with questions. Something in me knew it had to be pretend, but it felt too real.

"Are you a Christian?" the woman yelled at me. Then I recognized her voice. It was Lindsay, my skit instructor. These weren't soldiers from NORAD. They were YWAM staff members.

Lindsay put a gun to my head. Its cold barrel pressed hard into my temple. A black-and-white image popped into my mind of Rachel Scott, the Columbine martyr. This must be how she felt right before she died.

"Are you a Christian?!" Lindsay yelled again.

"Yes!" I said. "Yes, I'm a Christian."

"Then you're gonna die."

I couldn't breathe. I couldn't swallow. My vision tunneled and warped. I waited for Lindsay to pull the trigger, but the gun's muzzle came off my face.

"Stand up," the man said. Somehow, I stood. "Leave your things and put your hands behind your head. I'm taking you to the execution room."

Stunned, I did as he said. They marched me out of the cabin and down a long hill. My mind resumed some of its rational thinking without the brightness of a flashlight blinding me. I felt confusion. I felt betrayal. Mostly, I felt fear. The guns looked and felt real. No orange tips capped their barrels indicating they were toys, and the force with which I'd been shoved hurt. The combination of sleepiness and terror made everything seem hazy, like I was living in a movie scene that was part stupid hoax, part horrific nightmare. I didn't know what to believe.

We arrived at the cafeteria building. "Get inside," the man said.

"We have a Christian," Lindsay called out.

A new soldier appeared. He, too, wore a balaclava, camouflage pants, and carried a handgun. His gaze slid over me. "So," he said, "you want to die for your faith, do you?"

I felt a fresh wave of fear rising. It was silly, I knew. Surely they wouldn't really kill me. But their performances seemed too cruel to be a prank.

"I'll finish her," the new soldier said. My captors vanished into the night.

I stared at the new masked soldier, wondering who he was. He looked too thin to be Sean, and too tall to be Victor, the worship guitarist going with us to India. It had to be one of the other YWAM staff members who lived on site. They must have all lost their minds.

The soldier pointed his gun at my head. "Lie on the floor," he said. "Face down."

I did as he commanded. The cement was cold against my cheek.

"Hands behind your head."

I interlaced my fingers and put them against my neck. I could see the legs of the folding tables I'd eaten at, their chairs stacked upside down on top of them. The fluorescent light emitting from the kitchen cast an eerie glow around the concrete room, and my guard's voice echoed when he spoke.

"You stay here. I'm gonna get you a piece of paper and you're gonna write a letter to your family explaining why you died."

I managed a nod. His footsteps faded behind a wall. I didn't know whether to be angry or afraid. One moment I felt a seething hotness, the next an icy nausea. A minute later, I watched the guard's boots come back. He threw down a pencil in front of me and a white sheet of paper floated after it.

"Write," he said.

I sat up. I took the pencil in my hand and debated whether to object to the twisted exercise or play along.

"Write!" he shouted. "Tell your family why you died! Tell them you're a martyr!"

I flinched into compliance.

Dear Mom and Dad, I wrote. Tears began rolling down my cheeks. *Teddy, Madeleine, Bryant, and Kate. If you're reading this, I've been martyred. Don't worry, it's an honor to die for God. But please know how much I love you guys. Each one of you. I'm sorry for the times I was disobedient and mean. I love you guys more than I could ever express. I*

"Finish up!" my guard yelled.

love you. Love always, Alice

The guard snatched my paper from the floor. "Back face down!" he yelled.

I was still crying as I put my face to the cement again. The man squatted beside me. I felt the cold barrel of his gun press above my ear. He clicked the trigger.

"Boom," he whispered. "You just died."

He stood up slowly and sauntered to a pillar. I lay on the floor, shaking with silent sobs.

I didn't know how much time had passed before someone came and announced I could get up and go to the lodge. I looked to my guard to make sure he wasn't going to stop me. He took off his ski mask and nodded, smiling. It was Kyle, one of the YWAM staffers. He offered me his hand. I stood up without his help.

Everyone else had already gathered in the lodge by the time I got there. I saw the Washington team, then Anthony and Julia. I spotted Landon, Luke, Zach, Chelsea, and Simone. I couldn't read anyone's face. It was as if none us knew how to act. I sat on a couch toward the back of the room, and Simone came and sat beside me.

"That was so messed up," she whispered.

"Yeah, it was," I said.

Sean walked in front of the massive fireplace. He clapped his hands together with a smile. "So," he said. "That was your persecution training."

I wanted to slap him.

"We did that exercise so you guys could have an idea of what it feels like to be a missionary in a country where Christians are persecuted," Sean continued. "Christians around the world go through this all the time. They get interrogated, beaten, and killed, all because they're trying to spread the Gospel and save people's souls. How many of you guys died tonight?"

I looked around the room. The only person with their hand raised was Jed, the eighteen-year-old from the Washington team. I raised my hand, too.

"Only two of you?" Sean said. "Wow. You guys are supposed to die for your faith."

He said it jokingly. I felt appalled. They'd terrified us just to stage a mock persecution. I realized my youth leaders must have known about the prank ahead of time, which was why Julia had handed me a sorry excuse for a train ticket, yet reassured me my family was okay. I was livid.

"Let's give a hand to Jed and Alice for being martyrs tonight," Sean said.

Everyone clapped, then we sat there while Sean preached about persecution conditions around the world. Some Christians in North Korea had been slowly rolled to death by a road paving truck. Other Christians in South America had been shot up with arrows. Still other Christians were stoned to death in the Middle East, and all because they were trying to share Jesus' love.

I didn't know at the time how to process the mock persecution. My spine would bruise from where the gunman had jabbed me as he marched me through the woods. My neck ached for days from lying on the cement floor after I'd been "shot." The physical discomfort was second only to the psychological ramifications. The confusion, chaos, and fear of that night left me feeling like I didn't know who I could trust anymore. I didn't know when another gunpoint interrogation or something worse might happen. Would they stage a kidnapping next? A torture chamber? Part of me understood that my youth pastors and YWAM leaders were only trying to open our eyes to what Christians in other countries went through. It was supposed to inspire us to pray for the missionaries being held in prisons and for the proselytizers being tortured for refusing to deny their faith. It worked. And deep down, I knew what happened was wrong.

~

Our first days in India passed in a blur of jet lag. I nearly fell out of a rickshaw and into traffic on our first outing in New Delhi, where open motorcars, buses, scooters, bicycle taxis, and other vehicles raced each other for a meter of open pavement. Animals stood in the middle of the lanes like barriers in an obstacle course, unbothered by the honks and shouts urging them to move. Humpbacked cows wearing necklaces of orange flowers blinked slowly, and wild dogs trotted in packs through wheels that threatened to run them over. I spotted a few pups who had not been lucky, limping through the traffic with their mangled legs held off the ground. It brought tears to my eyes. I reminded myself that this was what people meant when they spoke of culture shock.

Despite the sights that troubled me, including the jolt of seeing a man masturbate on the sidewalk in broad daylight, I felt energized by the exotic sounds and smells. One moment carried the delicate whiff of incense, the next brought the reek of open sewage. Broken glass jingled beneath tires, and I felt as if I could hear the music of a hundred stereos at once. India was a feast for the senses.

I felt nervous when we pulled up to the school where Sean said we'd do our first program. A program was the heart of our missionary work, starting with worship music followed by the skits we'd rehearsed at the YWAM training camp. The skit I was part of was a mime-like, wordless routine called "King of Hearts." I worried I'd mess up my role, a beauty queen who hated herself beneath a smiling façade. Anthony as Jesus would heal my broken, Velcro heart, replacing it with a whole one. The thought of being onstage made me feel anxious.

Children raced past as we filed down a tiled hallway to meet the school principal. The kids appeared to be between five and sixteen years old, and all of them wore crisp white uniforms and stared at us with uncontained curiosity. A few of them smiled and waved, seeming tickled when I waved back. The principal, a mustached man with glasses, ushered us into a large auditorium where long rows of chairs faced a stage. "This is where you can perform," he said.

No air conditioning pumped through vents to cool us. Muggy air seeped through screened windows as Sean and the other YWAM leaders began setting up their instruments on the stage. Worship ran smoothly, and the performing of our skits elicited enthusiastic applause from the students. I didn't mess up, much to my relief, and the program ended with the principal saying we could stay a bit longer to visit with the kids. I wondered if this was the part where we were supposed to evangelize to them.

My palms felt sweaty when I stood from my chair. I couldn't tell if the dampness was from the heat or nerves as I rehearsed opening lines in my head. *Where do you think you're going when you die?* No, too dark. *Do you believe in Jesus?* Neutral, but kind of pointed. *Did you know God sent His only Son to die for your sins?* That didn't feel right either. I realized there was no nice way to tell someone I thought they were going to hell unless they believed what I did. It seemed rude, even though my motives were good. I had to find a way to get past my reluctance. I looked at the children's shining faces, picturing them contorting with pain over hell's flames. I imagined them crying for mercy as demons gnashed at their innocent flesh, except these children weren't innocent. We were all sinners from the day we were born. If I didn't tell these kids about Jesus' offer of eternal mercy, they might go to hell. I couldn't let them perish just because I was afraid of offending their feelings.

"Miss, may I have your autograph, please?" asked a young boy.

A waist-high crowd had gathered beneath me while I sorted through my inner dilemma. I smiled back at the boy and took the notebook and pen he offered.

"And please, miss, add your email address?"

"You wanna be pen pals?" I asked him.

He smiled shyly and nodded. Everyone else wanted an autograph with my email address, too, and when I managed to look up in between signing notebooks, I saw everyone on my team doing the same thing. It was as if the children thought we were celebrities. I wondered how we could possibly manage to save all of them.

Then I overheard a conversation between Anthony and the school principal.

"Yes, we are a Christian school," the principal said.

Immediately, my heart felt at ease. I checked with the kids in front of me to make sure. "Are you guys Christians?"

They nodded with enthusiasm. I gave them a thumbs-up and felt stupid for it. I was off the hook.

My team and I visited more schools over the next two weeks. Our routine was pretty much the same. We began with worship, performed our skits, and hung out with the kids for about an hour or so afterward. No one ever converted to Christianity. Most of the kids we met already professed to be Christians, and there was never time to find the few that weren't. I felt relieved of my duty to evangelize, but the lack of conversions also made me feel a bewildering sense of letdown. I didn't understand why we were performing salvation dramas to people who were already saved. It felt like both a waste of time and anticlimactic to the anticipation of personally having a role in rescuing souls from hell. Wasn't that the whole point of a mission trip? I told myself I should be happy no one needed converting. It was selfish of me to want to meet someone bound for eternal damnation just so I could be God's tool of deliverance, but I couldn't help wishing I'd gotten to lead at least one person to the Lord. It would have meant God was using me.

YWAM made sure our youth groups got to do non-mission stuff, too, taking us on a field trip to the Taj Mahal. The palace was the most beautiful piece of architecture I'd ever seen. I felt someone grope my butt as we walked through one of the looming gates on the property, but whoever touched me vanished into the crowd before I could even process what had happened. I felt shaken, but okay. I decided not to tell anyone in case the leaders said we had to leave early.

It was during a rainy excursion through the marketplace of Old Delhi that my crush on Zach went from being mildly under control to helplessly overwhelming. We were all shopping for souvenirs in the bustling walkways when Zach pointed out an elderly woman following us. She wore a tattered sari and had no shoes.

"What do you think she wants?" asked one of the girls from the Washington team.

Zach shrugged. The rest of us continued inside a market stall boasting sacks of fragrant cardamom and rows of hand-carved spice grinders. I bought a soapstone incense burner for Mom, and when I went outside to wait for the rest of the group, I was startled by the sight in front of me. There, in the middle of the muddy walkway, Zach knelt on the ground placing brand-new sandals on the old woman's feet. His movements were slow and tender. The woman held the top of his head for balance as she smiled down toothlessly at him. Her feet were filthy with grime and disfigured by callouses, but Zach handled them as though they were the feet of a queen. I had never been more smitten.

"You bought her those sandals?" Julia asked.

"Yeah, I mean, she had no shoes," Zach said, almost stammering. "And there's, like, glass everywhere."

I could tell he felt embarrassed that his secret act of kindness was turning into a spectacle. It only made him more attractive to me.

"Does anyone else wanna pitch in and get her a new sari?" Zach asked us.

We all agreed. We led the woman to the nearest sari stall and watched tears flow from her eyes as the shopkeepers swathed her in fresh pink cotton. It was one of the most meaningful moments of the entire trip for me, for it was the only time I felt like I'd done anything remotely Christlike. Jesus' love had to be shown through practical gestures, I realized. Not through corny skits. Zach's spontaneous generosity proved that to me. I'd already liked him for his contrasting depth and humor, for his rebel attitude and his wry, dimpled smile. That I'd just watched him place brand-new sandals on the feet of a homeless beggar in the pouring rain brought tears to my eyes. I didn't know compassion could be such a turn on. I could hardly look at Zach, I admired him so much.

18

Shame

Zach stood before a narrow crevice in a rock wall hidden by flowering vines, looking at me with an impish gleam in his eyes. "What do you say, Alice?" he asked. "Shall we go in?"

We were in Nek Chand's Rock Garden. Our time in India had almost reached its end, and our team had taken a bus to the northern city of Chandigarh to spend our last few nights. The town's botanic attraction lies beneath the cool foothills of the Himalayas, and from the moment I ducked under its arched wall entrance, I felt like I had entered the mystical India of storybooks. Waterfalls cascaded down ancient stone walls. Stone staircases spiraled upward to pillared structures looking like the remnants of a vanished civilization. Blooming flowers laced the air with fragrance while an emerald river sparkled along a dirt pathway. It was like stepping into a fairytale.

I didn't know Zach had followed me down the small path from the main walkway. He'd moved past when I stopped in front of the mysterious sliver in the rock wall, and the careful way Zach peered through it told me he felt as intrigued by the crevice as I was. His mischievous stare awaited my answer. I grinned and nodded.

Zach motioned me to duck first through the narrow opening. He followed close behind, and we found ourselves on another dirt path lined by moss-covered walls. We followed the path through a maze of winding tunnels and archways leading from one corridor to the next, our footsteps taking us faster with every beautiful turn. It felt like we had discovered an enchanted labyrinth, our very own secret garden. We reached the end of the path and before our eyes opened a dripping cavern, weeping with waterfalls and gushing with greenery. Sunlight filtered through gaps in the trees, making the mist look like gold dust wafting through the humid air. It was the most romantic place I had ever seen. That I got to be there alone with Zach made me feel even more intoxicated by the thrill of our secret adventure. Neither of us could stop smiling at the overwhelming splendor around us.

"It's like that ape palace in *The Jungle Book*," I said.

Zach laughed. "Yeah. Or like Indiana Jones's *Temple of Doom*."

No film I'd seen had been able to capture the lush glory of India's natural beauty. Zach and I lingered in the cavern as long as we dared, maybe for only a few minutes. They felt timeless. When my gnawing sense of responsibility told me we should rejoin the rest of our group, Zach reluctantly agreed. I knew the others would be wondering where we had gone.

We got lost in the maze on the way back. I started feeling anxious thinking of how much time had passed. Had it been fifteen minutes? Thirty? I didn't know. Zach was ducking through yet another stone archway when his head nearly crashed into Luke's.

"There you guys are," Luke said. "Everyone's been looking for you two."

Luke smiled, but he seemed irritated. I figured the stress of searching for us must have worried everybody. I apologized to Sean, Anthony, and Julia for wandering off. They said not to worry, the important thing was that we were all together again. We all exited the Rock Garden and lined up to take bicycle rickshaws back to our hotel.

A bicycle rickshaw consisted of a two-wheeled passenger cart pulled by a one-man bicycle. Each guy on the team was supposed to ride with a girl, and I tried not to smile when Zach climbed up next to me. I told myself it was probably just a coincidence. Maybe everyone else had already partnered up and I was the only girl left.

The ride back to our hotel was almost as exhilarating as our visit to the Rock Garden. Zach kept hopping out of the cart to run alongside the rickshaw while pushing it to go faster. Our rail-thin peddler looked both grateful for the boost and terrified of trying to steer us through the traffic at high speed.

"Gotta live life to the fullest," Zach said as he hopped back in the cart grinning.

"You're one of the few people I know who actually do," I told him.

He gave me an embarrassed shrug. "I try."

He stood in the cart and reached up to snatch a handful of leaves from the trees above us. He picked out a nice one that hadn't been torn and handed it to me.

"You want it?"

"Sure," I said, laughing.

"Have another," he said, reaching up to pluck more.

I giggled and tucked the leaves carefully into my passport holder. "I'll put these samples of Indian agriculture in my scrapbook," I said with exaggerated solemnity.

Zach laughed. He tried to pluck me a bunch of purple flowers, but they were too high. I told him not to worry. The crush of my dreams had followed me on a secret adventure through the Rock Garden and given me a bouquet of leaves. I didn't think I'd had a more exciting day in my whole life.

Our rickshaw ride ended too soon. As Zach and I stepped out of the carriage back at our hotel, I saw Simone making a beeline for me. Her expression was unreadable, but her hurried pace told me something was the matter. I wondered if she felt sick again. She'd thrown up several times at the Taj Mahal from dehydration.

"Alice," Simone whispered, linking her arm in mine. "I desperately need to talk to you."

"Are you okay?" I asked.

"Yes, yes, I'm fine. I'll tell you in our room."

Simone was my assigned roommate at the Hotel G.K. International. She and I were the youngest team members at fifteen, and though I'd gotten to know her a little bit over the past few months, we never hung out one-on-one until we became roommates. I had always thought of Simone as shy, hiding behind her long hair as though it were a protective veil. Spending one-on-one time with her allowed me to realize we were actually a lot alike. Not shy at all, just a little reserved in group settings.

Simone urgently led me up the hotel stairs and into our double queen room. I locked the door behind us and turned to see Simone brushing her hair viciously. After a few silent moments, she set down the hairbrush and whirled to face me.

"Alice, do you like Zach?"

Her question caught me off guard. I had already confided in Simone that I struggled with my feelings for Zach. Seeing him put those sandals on the old lady in Old Delhi had left me too infatuated not to tell someone. I'd also told Simone that I knew my attraction was wrong, because I was supposed to be faithful to my future husband.

"No, I'm trying not to," I said, attempting to be as dishonestly truthful as possible. Acknowledging out loud that I did like Zach made me feel sinful. I could barely acknowledge it in my journal.

"Well, do you like Luke?" Simone asked.

"What?"

"Okay," she said, flustered. "Here's what happened."

Simone relayed the conversation she'd had with Luke in the bicycle rickshaw they'd shared from the Rock Garden. "You and Zach were ahead of us," she said. "And Luke turns to me and goes, 'Does Alice have a thing for Zach?' I was like, 'Um, what would make you think that?' And he said, 'Well does she? Because I really like her, but if she likes Zach, I'll back off.'"

My heart thudded. "What did you say?"

"I didn't know what to say! I was really nervous and I just started giggling. But you told me not to tell anyone. So I told Luke I'd ask you if you liked Zach or not, so he knows to back off."

Simone looked miserable with excitement. I felt miserable with dread. I appreciated she'd kept my confidence, but I felt sick with anxiety about the knowledge that Luke liked me. It explained why he'd seemed bothered when he found Zach and me in the Rock Garden. That Luke also sensed I liked Zach made me feel even worse, and I wondered if my crush was obvious to anyone else. I thought I'd done my best to avoid Zach the whole trip. I couldn't help that he'd followed me through the hidden crevice in the Rock Garden, or that he'd hopped into the rickshaw with me when we left, or that he'd picked me leaves on our ride home. I was sure Luke and Simone had witnessed the exchange. It was innocent, but it might have looked like something more. I felt caught.

"So if Luke doesn't know I like Zach, he's gonna pursue me?" I asked.

Simone bit her lip and nodded.

"And if he does know, then Zach will probably know, and Luke's feelings will be hurt."

Simone shrugged, then nodded again. I collapsed on the bed face down.

"I hate this," I said, my words muffled by the comforter.

Simone sat down beside me. "It's okay. You can't help who you have feelings for."

"But I shouldn't be having them for anybody."

We spent the next half hour with me moaning over how horrible it all was and Simone regretting she'd ever gotten involved in the first place.

"I know," I said, rolling over to face the ceiling. "How about you just tell Luke that I don't like either of them as more than a friend?"

"But, you do," Simone said.

"Not really. Because even if Zach did like me back, I still wouldn't date him."

Simone seemed torn by my wanting her to lie. I didn't blame her. We were both too conscientious for our own good.

"Please?" I begged. She reluctantly agreed.

I was tying the drawstring of my pajama bottoms when someone knocked on our door.

"Who is it?" I asked, dreading the answer.

"Luke."

I looked at Simone. She nodded for me to open the door.

"Hi!" I said, hoping my smile disguised my nervousness.

Luke smiled back at me. The eighteen-year-old was one of the tallest guys in our youth group, with light brown hair and green eyes. "Hey," he said. "I was hoping to talk to you for a second."

"Sure."

I let him into the room. He looked at Simone apologetically and she took her cue to leave, giving me an encouraging smile on the way out. Luke stood in the center of the room staring at the floor. I sat on the foot of the bed opposite him. After what felt like minutes, I couldn't stand the silence any longer.

"Just say it," I blurted out.

He glanced up at me. "Say what?"

"Whatever it is you came here to say."

"Um, okay. Well, uh . . ."

"Simone told me that you wondered if I liked Zach."

He looked at me gratefully. "Yeah," he said.

"Well, I don't like him as anything more than a friend."

My ears smarted from lying. Luke let out a sigh, his demeanor resuming its usual confidence. I was just about to tell him that I didn't like him as anything more than a friend, either, when he spoke again.

"I just want you to know that I think you're a really cool person," he said. "And I'd really like to get to know you better."

Luke's eyes looked straight into mine. He had made a statement, but I knew there was an unasked question in his words. I smiled at him, hoping my voice sounded as kind as I meant for it to.

"Thanks, but I don't really want to be in a relationship right now," I said. "I like you, but as a friend. I don't want to have anything more, with you or anyone else."

"That's fine," Luke said. "I can respect that. Could we still get to know each other better? As friends, I mean?"

"Yes, that'd be fine."

Our formality helped cover our awkwardness. I almost couldn't believe how easy it had been. I worried he would try to ask me more questions about Zach, or that he'd attempt to persuade me to give him a chance. Instead, Luke had behaved like a perfect gentleman. I followed him to the door and stuck out my hand.

"Friends?" I said.

He smiled and shook my hand. "Yeah. Friends."

We opened the door and saw Simone sitting on the floor of the hallway. She looked up at us, her blue eyes wide with curiosity.

"All good," Luke said to her. "Thanks for waiting."

She smiled and stood up. Then Luke stopped her as she walked into our room. "Why were you so nervous and giggly in the rickshaw?" he asked.

"Because I didn't know what to say," Simone said.

"Wait a minute," Luke said. My heart began to panic. "Alice just told me that she didn't like me or Zach as more than friends. So why wouldn't you know what to say?"

Simone looked at me. Luke crossed his arms. "Simone," he said. "Does Alice like Zach?"

Any thoughts I had about Luke's gentlemanliness vanished. I couldn't believe he put Simone on the spot in front of me, and my eyes begged her to say no.

"Yes," Simone said meekly.

I felt stabbed by her betrayal. Yet I also knew I was the one in the wrong for asking her to lie for me. No one said anything. Just then, Chelsea came in from the hallway.

"Hey, guys," Chelsea said, shaking out her ponytail. None of us responded. "Whoa. Everything okay?"

Luke looked at me. "Why didn't you just tell me you like Zach?"

"Because I don't!"

"Chelsea, do you think Alice has been flirty with Zach?" Luke asked.

Chelsea glanced at me. "I mean, kinda."

I winced with humiliation. Had my feelings been so obvious?

"But she's been flirty with, like, every guy on this trip," Chelsea continued.

My head shot up. "What do you mean?" I asked.

"You've been flirting with all the guys," she said. "I mean, maybe you don't realize you're doing it, but you kind of are."

I looked at Simone. "You are a little flirty," she said, emphasizing "little."

At first, I felt angry with them for ganging up on me. Then I realized that for all three of them to say the same thing must mean there was truth in their words. I sat on the bed, struggling to hold back my defensiveness. The Bible instructed Christians to call each other out on their sins. Maybe Luke, Simone, and Chelsea were only looking out for my spiritual health.

"Can you give me an example?" I asked.

"Like, when we were on the bus coming here," said Chelsea.

"Oh yeah, with Jed?" said Luke.

Jed had been sitting next to me on the bus ride from New Delhi to Chandigarh. I couldn't think of a single time I might have flirted with him.

"What do you mean?" I asked.

"Alice, come on," Chelsea said. "You put your bare legs right in front of his face hoping he'd notice you."

I realized what Chelsea was talking about. Just after we'd left New Delhi, the bus's air conditioner broke. The heat during the five-hour drive was almost unbearable, and I'd unzipped the bottom half of my cargo pants to convert them into shorts. Restless, I tried to put my feet up on the headrest in front of me. My toes would have touched Landon's head, so instead I propped my feet on the empty headrest in front of my seatmate, Jed. I supposed my legs had been in front of Jed's face, but I certainly hadn't been trying to get him to notice me. I explained my blunder to Chelsea, Luke, and Simone.

"Okay," Luke said. "Maybe that time wasn't on purpose. But you do flirt a lot, especially with Zach. Like how you guys disappeared at the Rock Garden."

"Or like the time you were hanging on to Landon's arm when we were at that museum?" Chelsea said. "And when you were stretching in front of everyone in the lobby?"

"I noticed you don't really reach out to the girls on the Washington team," Luke said. "But you reach out a lot to the guys."

Their voices felt like judgment disguised as concern. I believed them. In that moment, I believed God was convicting me of being a wayward woman, like the book of Proverbs warned against. It didn't matter that my heart was pure if my actions were being perceived as a harlot's. Hot waves of shame washed over me. I couldn't look anywhere but my hands.

Simone tried to make me feel better. "We know it's not your intention," she said. "You're just really innocent. Like when you didn't get the joke about the Kum Pool."

The sign above the pool at the hostel in New Delhi had made Luke and Simone crack up. I'd had no idea why they were laughing, never having heard the term "cum" used in reference to male ejaculate. It was hard for me not to feel patronized when they explained why it was funny. I blamed my ignorance on my sheltered, homeschooled upbringing.

Luke, Chelsea, and Simone continued pointing out more ways I'd behaved like a tease.

"To be honest," Luke said, "there were a few times I thought you were flirting with me. Like when you held my arm at the Taj Mahal."

"I can see that," I said, stammering. "I get how that looks now. It was because some guy had just grabbed my butt. I was scared and I wanted to stay close to a guy on our team, and you were the closest guy."

"Wait, a guy grabbed your butt?" Simone asked.

I nodded. "Yeah. At least, I assume it was a guy. It was when we were walking through the gate. All of the sudden, I felt a hand grope me, like this."

I cupped my hand to my right butt cheek and squeezed it. Then I froze, jerking my hand off my rear and looking up at the three of them. I realized they were right. I was a flirt. I'd just behaved inappropriately in front of Luke, for how could a guy not be distracted by the sight of a teenage girl gripping her own butt? More hot waves crept over my ears.

"Oh my gosh," I whispered. "Like that?"

They nodded. I looked down at my feet.

"It's okay," Luke said, seeing my distress. "Like Simone said, we know you don't mean to. But you should probably be more aware of the messages you send out."

I felt both grateful for my friends' accountability and mortified for not catching myself flirting sooner. After all of the Christian courtship books I'd read, and all of the long paragraphs I'd taken to heart about helping guys guard their hearts from lust; after all of that reading, it was as if I'd never paid any attention. I blinked back tears of shame.

"I'm so sorry," I said.

Luke smiled at me. "It's okay," he said. "I forgive you."

I looked at Chelsea and Simone. "Would you guys help me?" I asked. "Could you let me know whenever I do something that looks flirty, even if it's small? I don't want to be a flirt. I want to treat our guys like brothers."

"But, maybe that's part of the problem," Simone said. "Maybe you've been treating our guys too much like brothers."

"Yeah," said Luke. "It's like you treat us like we're your real brothers, forgetting we're only your brothers in Christ."

I nodded my head. Simone handed me a Kleenex so I could blow my nose.

"I'm just curious," Luke said. "Why don't you want to date anybody?"

"Because God wants me to wait for my future husband," I said.

"What?" Chelsea asked.

"He wants me to be faithful to my future husband. So I don't give my heart or body away to someone else. I'm saving myself for the man I marry."

Luke, Chelsea, and Simone exchanged looks. I felt embarrassed, like I had revealed further depths of my naiveté.

"Well, that's probably not gonna happen," Chelsea said.

Luke shook his head. "No, probably not."

I was surprised. "You guys don't believe in waiting 'til marriage?"

"To have sex, yeah," Luke said. "God doesn't say anything about dating."

My Christian courtship books had warned me I'd come against back-lash for my beliefs, even from fellow Christians. I knew not every teen in Youth for Truth felt the same way I did about purity. We could all agree it was an indisputable sin to have sex outside of marriage, but aside from that, I observed there were varying levels of commitment to a pure lifestyle.

"I know it might not make sense to you guys," I said, "but I just really feel like God's called me to save myself completely for my future husband."

They gave up trying to convince me how unlikely it was that I'd date only one man throughout my life. I apologized to Luke once more for being flirty and then we all said goodnight.

Simone fell asleep quickly, but I felt too wretched to sleep. I tossed and turned until I finally allowed myself to weep silent tears of shame. Shame that my crush on Zach had been exposed. Shame that I'd lied about it. Shame that I'd been caught, and shame that I'd been flirting with all the guys and everyone had seen it. I felt like a disgusting whore and begged God for forgiveness.

～

I didn't go to breakfast the next day. My shame was still too great. When Simone came up and told me it was time to visit a Mother Teresa home, I made sure to avoid even a glance at the males on our team the whole time we were there, and I went straight back to my room the moment we returned to the hotel. I didn't have an appetite for dinner, but I forced myself to eat a Clif bar. A knock on my door interrupted my lonely meal. It was Simone and my youth pastors, Anthony and Julia. I hoped they couldn't tell I'd been crying.

"Hey, sweetie, what's wrong?" Julia asked. She sat next to me on my bed. "Simone said you weren't feeling well, are you okay?"

I couldn't help it. I cried fresh tears as I told Anthony and Julia about the events of the previous night. I also expressed how regretful I was that I hadn't even noticed I'd been flirting with practically the whole team. They listened patiently as Simone handed me Kleenexes.

I would never be able to remember how the decision came about. I may have suggested it myself. Somehow, it was determined that Julia would escort me to the hotel rooms of each guy on the team so I could apologize to them personally. I had been a distraction, whether I meant to be or not. I needed to ask forgiveness for how I had led my brothers astray.

Room to room, guy to guy, I went, barely able to look any of them in the face. I apologized for bringing them down by taking their attention away from the mission. The boys seemed surprised by my admission, but they forgave me. A couple of them said they hadn't noticed anything, but I thought they were just trying to make me feel better.

Julia and I went to Zach's room last. I felt more nervous knocking on his door than I had the others. I didn't know if he'd heard that I liked him or not, and all I could pray was that he hadn't. Zach's roommate, a YWAM leader, opened the door.

"Hey, is Zach in there?" Julia asked.

We saw Zach poke his head within view of the door. "Hey!"

"Hey, Zach, you got a minute? Alice has something she needs to say to you."

I wished Julia hadn't phrased it like that. Zach had a nervous smile on his face as he followed us to Julia and Anthony's room next door, where we could talk privately. I could only imagine what was in his head. The three of us sat on the bed. I took a deep breath.

"Zach," I said. "This isn't easy for me to say, but I need to say it. It was brought to my attention that I've been really flirty with the guys on this trip. Especially with you. And I'm really sorry."

Zach's face grew serious as I proceeded to tell him what I'd told the other guys about being a spiritual distraction and treating them too much like brothers. He listened patiently and never once laughed or interrupted me. I finished by explaining that I wanted to be held accountable and asked him if he'd noticed any way I'd flirted.

"Kind of," he said.

My heart sank. "In what ways?" I asked.

Zach hesitated.

"Zach, please be completely honest with me," I said. "Everyone else already has, and I'm as raw as I can get."

I let out a small chuckle to help ease my nerves.

"Well," Zach said. "I kinda noticed it, but I knew you weren't doing it on purpose."

At least Zach knew my intentions. It allowed me a smidgen of relief.

"Yeah," Julia said. "You're just being you. You have an innocence about you, and sometimes people might mistake your sweetness for something else. But it's just who you are."

Zach nodded. "I'll let you know if I see anything, but yeah. Like Julia said, I knew you were just being you. And I wanna say, I'm really impressed with the way you've handled this. How you were just honest with me. I really appreciate it."

The three of us said goodnight, and when Julia walked me back to my room, she told me how in awe she was of my commitment to God. "When I was your age, I had way more to repent for than just having a crush!"

She gave my shoulder an extra squeeze and told me not to be too hard on myself.

It was hard for me not to be hard on myself. Being accused of flirting wasn't the only thing making me feel ashamed—I also felt as though I'd been caught cheating. Others might not live in faithfulness to an unknown spouse, but I believed deeply that God had called me to such fidelity. It devastated me to think how hurt my future husband would be if he had witnessed my behavior. I had betrayed him. I had also betrayed my teammates, and most importantly, I had betrayed God. I had been selfishly naive to the effect I had on men. I had caused my brothers in Christ to stumble.

Despite the reassurance of Zach and the other guys I apologized to, it wasn't outweighed by the humiliation of being confronted by Luke, Chelsea, and Simone in the first place. I knew they probably had the best of intentions. After all, there were numerous verses in the Bible instructing Christians to point out each other's sins, so that one bad sheep wouldn't ruin the whole flock.

Galatians 6:1 said, "Brothers and sisters, if someone is caught in a sin, you who live by the Spirit should restore that person gently."

Jesus told His disciples in the book of Matthew, "If your brother or sister sins, go and point out their fault, just between the two of you. If they listen to you, you have won them over. But if they will not listen, take one or two others along, so that every matter may be established by the testimony of two or three witnesses. If they still refuse to listen, tell it to the church; and if they refuse to listen even to the church, treat them as you would a pagan or a tax collector."

It was verses like these that made me feel defenseless. I believed that if I had refused to take responsibility for my actions, no matter how innocent they were, it might have only brought more attention to my sins. I feared I would have been ostracized. As I ruminated over the confrontation in the following days, I became aware of a voice inside arguing that other people were only projecting their own motives onto my actions. I rejected that voice as pride coming from the devil. Who did I think I was to be above the gentle reproach of my fellow Christians? I'd felt praised for owning up to their judgment. It affirmed that I had indeed been in the wrong.

19

Rites of Passage

Without warning, Mom announced she was done homeschooling me that fall. She said she'd taught me everything she could and that it was time for me to graduate high school by getting a General Education Diploma (GED). A career counseling center in Boulder evaluated what school subjects I was weakest in, and I received passing marks for every assessment they gave me but math. To pass the GED test, Mom registered me for private math tutoring. I was in the middle of a tutoring session when I learned two airplanes had crashed into the Twin Towers of New York City.

The terrorist attacks were all anyone could talk about at my next youth group meeting. Pastor Fred, the speaker that night, based his sermon around the tragedy that would be called 9/11. "Guys, this is just spiritual warfare breaking into physical warfare before our eyes," he said. "The symbolism here is crawling with spiritual references. Think about it. September eleventh. Nine-eleven. Nine-one-one, the call for help. And get this—the World Trade Center is located on the corner of Church Street and Liberty Street. Satan attacked what he knows is most important to us: our religious freedom. Amazing, isn't it?"

Pastor Fred pointed out that great spiritual events happened every 2,000 years. "Two thousand years ago, Jesus was born. Two thousand years before that, Moses led the Israelites out of Egypt. Two thousand years before that, the spiritual history of the world began," he said. "Satan thinks he won a victory yesterday. He and his legion of demons are celebrating in hell right now for the lives they took, for the fear they've instilled in the hearts of Americans and the world. He stabbed us where it mattered most: on the building that symbolized the heart of our nation in DC and the buildings in New York that symbolized freedom of trade. There will be war. But I believe this war will be won with prayer. Now, more than ever, we need to be sold-out warriors for Christ."

By that point in my life, I had learned to filter everything through a spiritual lens. The events of September 11th, 2001, were no exception. Pastor Fred's words weren't those of a Christian conspiracy theorist, but the words of a prophet affirming the ultimate battle between good and evil. 9/11 was not only a terrorist attack. It was a sign of the end times. As Christians, Pastor Fred told us, we needed to work harder to beat Satan and his forces. We needed to pray more, to evangelize more, to fast and worship more. We needed to save more souls by being fearless, living examples of Christ's love, with the goal of converting as many people as we could to Christianity so they'd be assured a place in heaven when the prophesies in the book of Revelation came true. That was what it meant to be a spiritual warrior.

It felt like some Christians almost rejoiced over what happened on 9/11. As more details came out and Al-Qaeda eventually took responsibility for the attack, I observed the evangelical Christian world tie the events of that day to the ongoing crisis in the Middle East, where the intensifying wars were a sign of Jesus' Second Coming. Christ's return was a good thing. Therefore, any signs indicating His imminent arrival were met with praise. I felt conflicted. I wanted to grieve in my heart and simply chalk up the terrorist attacks to the senselessness of humanity. Instead, I mitigated my sorrow with the trite reminder that tragedy was all a part of God's perfect plan, and it wasn't for me to understand His ways. I wouldn't know how to cope with the horrors in the world otherwise.

~

I became a college student at fifteen that winter, before I had officially graduated high school. My early enrollment in college wasn't because I was brilliantly smart or academically gifted, though I would have liked to think so, but because the state of Colorado wouldn't let me take the GED test until I turned sixteen in February. Classes started in January.

The realization I had in India, that Jesus' love had to be shown through practical gestures, led me to believe God was calling me to nursing. What could be more practical than ministering God's love to people through health care, I thought. My parents' low income qualified me to receive a Pell Grant and other financial aid through Front Range Community College. I planned on becoming a registered nurse and joining YWAM or Mercy Ships, the Christian version of Doctors Without Borders. I pictured opening my own hospital in India and working alongside a handsome doctor while we evangelized to the needy without uttering a word.

My first day of college went better than I hoped. The teachers and students paid me no mind, and at first, I thought the general education courses were a breeze. As the weeks wore on, I wondered what I'd gotten myself into. School kept me busier than I had ever been before. I wasn't used to working on anyone's schedule but my own. Homeschooling had instilled me with a ruthless sense of self-discipline, but I soon learned it had also crippled me from knowing when to be subservient. I was used to being submissive when it came to spiritual matters. God was in charge, that I had never been allowed to challenge. When it came to my education, I didn't expect to feel like there were too many questions one could ask. School was for learning, I thought. The impatient tone of my teachers and the glares from my peers told me learning in college meant shut up and take notes. When I objected to being graded on a bell-curve, believing each person should be assessed as an individual rather than lumped into a pre-allotted score, my teacher asked me where I'd gone to school.

"I was homeschooled," I said.

"Well, that explains it," she muttered.

I tried to shrug off my humiliation, but there were times when I couldn't. Like when my sociology teacher had everyone in the class proclaim what they wanted to be when they graduated.

"I want to be a missionary nurse," I said.

Snickers filled the room. One guy laughed out loud, saying, "Wow," as though I were a sad joke.

It was then I realized I had entered the real world. I had always been exposed to it, the secular society I'd been told was lost, broken, and dangerous. Yet I had never been a part of it, skirting around its edges like a shy child passing a playground. The playground had thorns. I was no longer surrounded by Christians who spoke the same language I did. In the real world, one had to take responsibility for his or her choices, not hide behind the guise of God's divine calling. No one said God put anything on their heart, or claimed to have prophetic insight, or even tried to hide their judgment of others. I wondered how my Christian friends in secular schools handled mockery from their peers. Maybe they never let on that their beliefs ruled so much of their life. We were all told repeatedly to be unashamed for Christ, to be living examples of His purity and goodness at all times, and now I knew why this was drilled into our heads over and over. The world was a harsh place. It took courage to stand for one's beliefs. It was brave how stupid we had to be to open ourselves up to the cruelty of the unsaved. Not everyone was unkind to my beliefs when they leaked out, but enough were that I began to develop a thick skin indifferent to the opinions of others.

Nowhere was my Christian homeschooled upbringing more evident than in my anatomy and physiology class. Science was the subject my parents knew the least, and as a result, I'd read maybe two or three science-related books from a Christian curriculum. They taught Creationism instead of evolution and proclaimed the first woman, Eve, was created from Adam's rib. I had no idea what else I might have learned that was improbable or untrue. Whenever I sat in my anatomy and physiology class, a crucial prerequisite for nursing, I was lost within minutes. I ended up withdrawing to avoid having an F on my transcript. Frustrated with my parents for not anticipating that one of their kids might go into a scientific field, I resigned myself to taking an introductory biology course the next semester and working my way back up to A&P from there.

My parents had done an excellent job homeschooling me in other areas. When I passed the GED test after I turned sixteen, the above-average scores I got in language arts and social studies attested to Mom's skill as a teacher, and my tutoring sessions at Workforce allowed me to pass the math portion of the GED test in the average range. If science was the one subject where I wasn't up to par, at least it was something I could work toward.

To celebrate my high school graduation, Mom took me to get my driver's license. Dad had been giving me driving lessons all winter, and while I didn't have a car of my own yet, Mom often let me borrow hers. Driving allowed me an independence I'd never known. I drove myself to school, to youth group, and to friends' houses for sleepovers, relishing moments of solitude from place to place.

It was during a sleepover with my friend Lauren that I began exercising even more freedom. Lauren and I had become good friends since I met her on the youth group spring retreat, when my family had first arrived in Colorado. Lauren and I were both in love with the idea of saving ourselves for one man only, and many a sleepover was spent dreamily thumbing through bridal magazines as we planned our future weddings. We were sitting on her bed one winter night flipping through an issue of *Modern Bride* when I felt a familiar ache in my lower back. I went to the bathroom and saw my period had started. Lauren's cabinet only had tampons. I stuffed toilet paper in my underwear and went to check my purse for a pad. Lauren saw me rummaging and I told her what I needed.

"You use pads?" Lauren asked.

"Yeah," I said.

"But they're so uncomfortable."

"I know. My mom won't let me use tampons, though."

I sighed. There were no pads left in the zippered compartment of my purse. I'd have to go out and buy some.

"Why won't she let you use tampons?" Lauren asked.

"She thinks they'll take away my virginity."

Lauren laughed. "That's a little ridiculous," she said, tucking a flyaway curl behind her ear. "God knows you're still a virgin. Virginity's about the purity of your heart, not just the purity of your body."

I felt struck by her words.

"You've really never used a tampon?" Lauren asked.

I shook my head.

"Want me to show you how?"

I nodded.

Lauren got up and retrieved the instruction sheet that came in her box of Tampax. We giggled at the illustration of a woman placing one of her legs on a bathtub for easier insertion. "You don't really need to do that," Lauren said. "You can just reach down while you're still sitting on the toilet."

She handed me the instruction sheet and told me not to come out of her bathroom until I had successfully inserted my first tampon.

It didn't hurt at all. In fact, I barely felt a thing. Only the white string hanging between my legs told me I had anything up there.

I marveled at how no sudden gush of blood seeped out of me when I laughed. I went to sleep unworried about adjusting my pad when I turned in the middle of the night. When I awoke the next morning, I could almost laugh at how life-changing the tampon truly was. There were no leaks on my underwear. No diaper rash in the crevices of thighs. It was as if I wasn't on my period at all, and changing a tampon was easier than swapping out a Band-Aid.

Back at home, I told Mom I wasn't going to be using pads anymore.

"I'll buy my own tampons if I have to," I said.

"You realize that once you use a tampon, your body will never be the same," she said.

"Well, it's too late," I told her. "I already used one at Lauren's and I'm not going back."

Mom was speechless at my defiance. I looked her straight in the eye.

"And besides," I said. "God knows I'm still a virgin. He cares more about the purity of my heart than He does my body."

I marched to my room, triumphant.

It was also because of Lauren that something else happened, something far more life-changing than using tampons. Neither of us would realize its significance at the time.

Lauren and I were waiting for my mom to pick us up from the mall when a woman's voice interrupted our conversation.

"Excuse me," the voice said.

I ignored it.

"Excuse me?" she repeated. Lauren motioned with her eyes that the voice was addressing me. I turned and saw a young woman in a business suit extending a blank form from French-manicured nails.

"Hi, I'm Sofia," she said. "I think you should sign up to win our scholarship. We're at that John Casablancas booth over there."

She pointed to the table in the center of the mall. It was draped with a banner that read, "Do You Want To Be A Model?"

Something like embarrassment shot through me. "Sorry, what is it exactly?" I asked.

"John Casablancas is a talent company. We're scouting today for kids who want to be models and actors. Have you ever thought about modeling?"

Flustered, I shook my head. The very idea seemed offensive for reasons I couldn't name in the moment.

"Well, you should," said Sofia. "I'm a modeling scout, and I see a lot of girls. You have a great look and I think you'd be a perfect fit for our agency."

"Oh, um, thanks," I said. "But I'm not interested."

Sofia persisted. "If you enter our sweepstakes, you could win a chance to go through our program for free. We would train you to do runway, photo shoots, commercials."

I felt acutely aware of Lauren standing beside me. Sofia hadn't acknowledged her at all. I glanced out the glass doors of the mall foyer, hoping to see Mom had arrived, but the Suburban still wasn't outside. I looked at Lauren. Despite the fact that Sofia continued ignoring her, my friend wore an encouraging smile.

"Why not?" Lauren said.

"Okay," I told Sofia, accepting the blank form. "I'll fill it out."

If anything, it would make her go away. I followed Sofia to the John Casablancas booth and wrote down my name, age, height, measurements, and phone number. I slipped the form into the slotted box and tried to push the incident out of my mind.

My family's phone rang that night while we were eating dinner.

"Hello?" Mom answered. "Yes, this is Alice's mom. What?" Mom looked at me. "No, she didn't tell me. What's this?"

I watched as Mom listened to the person on the other end of the line. It had to be Sofia. I felt bad I hadn't given Mom a heads up, but I truly didn't think the John Casablancas people would call.

"So, you're telling me Alice won a scholarship for, what, modeling school?" Mom asked. "Oh. Well, if she didn't win, may I ask why you're calling? Oh, I see. Mm-hmm. Really? Well, let me talk with my husband and Alice about this and I'll let you know. Can I have a number to call you back?"

Mom wrote down the number and hung up the phone with a curious smile. "You entered a modeling contest?" she asked me.

One of my siblings snickered.

"Well, not a contest," I said. "While Lauren and I were waiting for you at the mall, this lady came up to me and said she was a modeling scout. She wanted me to enter this sweepstakes they were having, I guess it's to train you to become a model."

Mom sat at the table. "Well, she says you didn't win the sweepstakes, but she thought you were really pretty and wants you to audition for the program anyway."

"Hey, Janey," Dad said, his eyes twinkling. "She gets it from my side. Those Greczyn genes."

Mom rolled her eyes. Dad liked to tease Mom by taking credit for their kids' good looks only because Mom was clearly so beautiful. Dad was handsome, too. I thought he looked like a cross between Yanni and Burt Reynolds, but there was no celebrity who looked like Mom. With her high cheekbones and almond eyes, I thought she looked like a Polynesian goddess. People always said what an attractive couple my parents made. I supposed my siblings and I were good-looking, but I didn't want to admit it because vanity was a sin.

"So they want me to audition?" I asked.

"That's what it sounds like," Mom said. "She said they're a modeling school with an agency you could join when you graduate. What do you think?"

The conversation felt surreal. I had secretly fantasized about modeling ever since I used to make Bethany and Danika play dress up with me, but I could hardly imagine doing it for real. The profession seemed to embody everything worldly and sinful I was supposed to stay away from. Plus, I wasn't tall. I'd plateaued at around five-foot-seven that winter, and while I was thin, I thought models were supposed to be at least five-foot-nine and super skinny. And gorgeous. I could admit I wasn't homely, but I didn't think I was anywhere near beautiful enough to be a model.

"I don't know," I said.

"Why don't you just go to the audition and try out?" Dad said.

"Yeah," said Mom. "Maybe this is a door God's opening."

I could hardly believe my ears. The last thing I'd expected from my parents was their encouragement. Modeling seemed more like a door Satan would open than God. I was about to say I didn't want to go, then it occurred to me that models made a lot of money. What if—maybe—this was God's way of providing the funds for the missionary work He wanted me to do? The notion seemed ludicrous. How many teenage girls were approached to be models that actually went on to have careers? I wondered. But with God, one ever knew.

"Okay," I said. "I guess we could find out more about it."

∽

Three months later, my modeling school instructor handed me a black portfolio of the pictures I'd taken in class.

"I've selected your best photos," Donovan said, flipping his flowing charcoal hair over a shoulder. "You'll find an editorial look, a sporty look, some beauty shots, and some pics from the avant-garde shoot. It's important to have a portfolio that shows photographers and casting directors a variety of your looks."

I opened the cover. A black-and-white closeup of a girl stared back at me. At first, I thought my portfolio must have been mixed up for someone else's. The girl looked too beautiful, too mature and elegant to be me. Then I noticed her freckles. I gasped. It *was* me. I slammed the portfolio shut, my heart pounding. I didn't know why. All I knew was that I didn't want to look at any more pictures until I was alone.

I drove back to my family's house and went straight to the bedroom I shared with my sisters. I shut the door and sat on my bed. The portfolio lay in front of me, and I lifted its cover with a trepidation I still didn't understand. Slowly, I turned through the pages. I barely recognized the young woman in the nine-by-twelve photos. Her beauty didn't feel like it could be my own. The girl in the photos had smooth dark hair that fell long onto her shoulders. Her brown eyes were wide with eyeliner, accentuated by long, mascaraed lashes. She had full lips. A slender waist. Small boobs. Long legs. Perfect posture. She wasn't me.

I closed the book with a lump in my throat, realizing why I'd been afraid to look at the photos. I felt ashamed. A toxic blend of pride and guilt coursed through me. Bible verse after Bible verse bombarded my mind, warning of the dangers of being a beautiful woman.

Your heart became proud on account of your beauty, said the book of Ezekiel. *You corrupted your wisdom because of your splendor. So I threw you to the earth; I made a spectacle of you before kings.*

The women of Zion are haughty, said the book of Isaiah, *walking along with outstretched necks, flirting with their eyes, strutting along with swaying hips . . . Therefore the Lord will bring sores on the heads of the women of Zion; the Lord will make their scalps bald . . . Instead of fragrance there will be a stench; instead of sash, a rope; instead of well-dressed hair, baldness; instead of fine clothing, sackcloth; instead of beauty, branding.*

One verse in particular gnawed at me most, Proverbs 11:22. *Like a gold ring in a pig's snout is a beautiful woman who shows no discretion.*

I had been that gold ring in India. When I'd thoughtlessly distracted the guys on my mission team by being a flirt, I had shown no discretion. How much less discretion was I showing if I were to become a professional model? The job necessitated the flaunting of one's beauty. The industry thrived on the exploitation of young girls, on seductive poses, sultry gazes, toned flesh, and naughty smiles. To be successful, I would have to become the woman of Zion the Bible warned against. I would have to be a wayward woman.

I reached for my Bible from the nightstand. There had to be positive verses about women's beauty, for God had created us. My index directed me to the story of Jacob, Leah, and Rachel, the love triangle that led to the twelve tribes of Israel. Rachel's lovely figure, as Genesis pointed out, was the reason for it all. Then there was the story of Ruth, who used her beauty to seduce Boaz into marrying her, which led to the birth of Jesus Himself. But it was the story of Queen Esther that finally gave my heart peace about modeling.

Esther was a Jewish girl, one of many virgins summoned to a king as a possible replacement for his former queen, who wouldn't undress for his friends. The king was attracted to Esther more than any other virgin. She kept her Jewish heritage a secret and he married her. She "had a lovely figure and was beautiful," said the story. When Esther's cousin told her the king had authorized the slaughter of all Jews in the kingdom, Esther finally revealed to her husband that he would have to kill her, too, or else spare her and her people. She dolled herself up and seduced him with wine first. It worked.

Esther used the beauty God gave her to save lives. Maybe the notion of God using my beauty to do the same wasn't as vain as I feared. If I were to model professionally, I could save up enough money to join any nursing program or missionary organization I felt called to. By traveling the world as a nurse, I could save lives, like Esther. God had a reason for everything. What if He had Sofia approach me so the looks He'd blessed me with could bring glory to His name?

I was offered the coveted modeling contract when I graduated from the John Casablancas program. After praying about it and discussing it with my parents, I accepted. My first modeling job was for a hair product company called Matrix, followed by a second job for Gillette Venus Women's Razor. The money I made wasn't thousands of dollars yet, but the few hundred bucks here and there would definitely help toward buying nursing school supplies. Whenever I felt myself enjoying compliments about my looks, I repented for it and allowed shame to lower my eyes. It was the only way I thought I could be a model and not become vain or proud.

∽

That summer, for the first time since I was four, my family moved to a new home without relocating to a new city. Our new two-story house sat behind a maple tree in a suburban neighborhood where kids rode their bikes to the community pool. I couldn't remember ever living in such a nice middle-class area. The three-bedroom traditional boasted central heating, a swamp cooler for A/C, vaulted ceilings, and a deck in the fenced backyard. The best part was that I got to have my own room. Mom and Dad let my brothers take over the basement to use as their sleeping lair, where Bryant's LEGO pieces waited to ambush bare heels and Teddy's art supplies were scattered between black lights and incense burners. That left one bedroom for my parents, one for Madeleine and Kate, and Mom said the last one was for me. I couldn't thank God enough. For the first time in years, it felt like I could finally trust the appearance of stability. Dad's work seemed steady. My family seemed settled. My schooling and career seemed set. Then, through a fluke accident, God seemed to be closing the doors on my pursuit of a nursing degree.

I'd been taking a Certified Nurse's Aide course that summer semester. It wasn't required for enrollment in the fall nursing program, but I figured it wouldn't hurt to have the extra experience. I aced every assignment in my class. Then I failed the state certification exam—twice.

"You didn't wash your hands properly," said the judge both times.

I knew I'd washed my hands correctly, soaping above my wrists for the required twenty seconds and turning off the faucet with a paper towel to avoid the spread of germs. That God had allowed me to fail my exam two times in a row shook my confidence. *Is there something else you're calling me to, God?* I prayed.

Just then, I noticed the song playing on my radio. It was "Lucky" by Britney Spears. As Britney sang about a Hollywood girl, an eerie sensation crept over me. What if God was answering me through Britney's song? My spine prickled. Me, a Hollywood girl? Hollywood felt as far away from being a missionary as I could get. The future I saw for myself was one of poverty and servitude, of long, sweaty days giving immunizations to orphans and air condition–less nights spent under mosquito netting. I'd never heard of God calling anyone to a life of luxury, to an industry that was the very embodiment of sin. God called people to give up their comforts. He didn't call them to seek fame or fortune.

The timing of "Lucky" coming on the airwaves was just a coincidence. I brushed it aside and forgot about it.

~

I was holed up in my room with a fever one day when Mom knocked on the door. She said my modeling agent had called to say a talent manager from Los Angeles wanted to meet with me. I told her I didn't want to go—I felt too sick and besides, what was I going to do, fly to L.A. every time I had a casting?

"Are you sure, girlbug?" Mom said. "Dad's going to Denver tomorrow anyway. You could meet with this guy and just see what he's offering. Maybe it's an open door."

The next day, with a 102-degree fever and a pounding headache, I met Lorenzo Moretti. He was a short Italian man with a shaved head, a gold chain necklace, and an accent that sounded more New York than L.A. A cigar would have looked right at home on his lips, along with an order to beat the shit out of someone until he talked.

"I'm Lorenzo Moretti," he said. "I'm from L.A. and I'm very picky about who I meet."

The two boys sitting on either side of me straightened. Even though we were indoors, Lorenzo kept his sunglasses on, and his flashiness made him seem like a quack to me. I regretted coming. I wondered how long I'd have to sit through his spiel before I could go back home to bed.

"Have you guys heard of Kristen Stewart?" Lorenzo asked us.

I shook my head.

"She played Jodie Foster's daughter in *Panic Room*."

I'd never seen *Panic Room*. Apparently the two boys had.

Lorenzo stuck his thumb to his chest. "I discovered her."

Lorenzo explained that his job as a talent manager involved overseeing acting careers. I zoned out of his speech, immediately dismissing the possibility of ever acting. Modeling in front of cameras made me nervous enough without having lines to remember. When Lorenzo's talk finished, I started following the two boys out of the office, but Lorenzo stopped me.

"You're Alice, aren't you?" he said.

"Yeah," I said.

He smiled at me. "How do you pronounce your last name?"

"Gre-chen," I said. "Like the girl's first name."

"Alice Greczyn. Nice to meet you. Where's your parents? I wanna talk with you guys."

"Oh, it's okay," I said. "I don't think I can go to L.A."

"Bring 'em in here," Lorenzo insisted.

I didn't have the energy to protest. I leaned into the lobby and motioned for Dad to follow me back to the office. Lorenzo and Dad made introductions while I sat in a chair wishing for some Tylenol. Eventually, I realized Dad was taking the meeting seriously.

"The best time for her to come out would be January to April," Lorenzo said. "For pilot season."

An image of flight school popped in my head. I didn't know that a pilot was the first episode of a TV show, one of many that were shown to television networks in hopes of being produced to a full series. Lorenzo went on about things like headshots and temporary housing.

Dad looked at me. "Does that sound like something you might like, moppet?"

I didn't want to hurt Lorenzo's feelings by showing him we'd wasted his time, so I nodded. "Sure, it sounds interesting."

"We'd have to talk with my wife about this," Dad said. "But it certainly sounds like a rare opportunity."

"Absolutely," Lorenzo said, thumbing a business card from his wallet. "Call me anytime. I really think she's got a great look. Casting directors will love her."

"But you haven't even seen me act," I said.

Lorenzo looked at me with a confident smile. "Honey, I got good instincts."

On our drive back to Longmont, I told Dad I had no interest in going to L.A. for whatever pilot season was. "I'm just getting comfortable with school," I said.

"You don't have to go to L.A.," Dad said. "But you might wanna pray about it. It could be a door God's opening for you."

Then I remembered the premonitory feeling I had when "Lucky" came on the radio. What if the invitation to L.A. *was* a door God was opening? I indulged a daydream about starring in a period piece where I'd get to wear a hoop skirt and fall in love with a dashing Civil War soldier. I pictured myself walking a red carpet and smiling into all the cameras. I almost laughed. Thousands of teens moved to Hollywood every year hoping to land an acting job, and they had probably worked for it all their lives. Why should I get to move there and potentially take a job away from them when I was perfectly happy heading toward another career?

But it seemed that nursing was not meant to be. A few days after my meeting with Lorenzo Moretti, Mom told me she had some bad news. "Front Range just changed the policy for their nursing school requirements," she said. "You have to be eighteen to enroll now."

All I could do was sigh in response. I'd twice-failed the state board exam for my CNA certificate, and now I had to wait a year and a half to start the program I'd wanted to do all along. Either God was testing my faith, or He was closing the doors to nursing. Mom and I went over different programs I could enroll in instead. The EMT basic certification course was only six months long and allowed seventeen-year-olds. I decided I would become an EMT the following year to make my health care experience more well-rounded. Then, when I was eighteen, I would continue with nursing school and eventually join YWAM or Mercy Ships.

God had other plans for me.

20

L.A.

"Fuck," I said, alone in the hotel shower where Mom and my siblings couldn't hear me. "Fuck fuckin' fuckity fuck."

I'd been in Los Angeles for a month. EMT school didn't start until summer, so my parents had encouraged me to come to L.A. for what my new manager, Lorenzo Moretti, called pilot season. The first acting audition my agent sent me challenged all of my Christian values at once. The supporting role was for a TV movie, a crime drama where my character was to be found dead in her college dorm room. The part required me to say and mimic things I'd never done. Things like using the f-word and smoking a joint.

"Fuck."

I'd never smoked anything. I'd never sworn out loud. My audition scene required me to inhale a blunt, blow it out coolly, and say, "What the fuck did you think was gonna happen?"

The word wouldn't get comfortable in my mouth. "Fuck." I felt like the poser I was. "Fuck." Like a nerdy homeschooled Christian girl who said things like gosh-dang instead of goddamn, and fudge instead of the word my voice kept wavering over. I knew I didn't have to actually smoke a joint in the audition, but I would need to say all of the dialogue. I had to say fuck as naturally as I said God.

Crossed out in the lines of a black Sharpie on my audition pages was another scene, a montage of my character getting wasted and having sex with her boyfriend. *Lost in bliss. Tearing off each other's clothes. Humping.* I hadn't so much as held a boy's hand, except in youth group prayer sessions. How could I play a girl I'd never even met the likes of before?

Everyone in my family but Dad had been living at the Days Inn on Ventura Boulevard for four weeks. Dad had stayed behind in Colorado for work. It was February, but the scent of night-blooming jasmine drifted through the bathroom window like it was July. L.A. was nothing like the concrete city I thought it would be. Vibrant foliage burst in its hills. The freeway medians overflowed with fuchsia bougainvillea. Palm trees lined the way to the Starbucks at Coldwater Canyon where Mom got her latte every morning. L.A. tasted like fresh flour tortillas and hand-squeezed orange juice. It sounded like ocean waves of traffic and leaf blowers, interspersed by sirens, hip-hop, and mariachi. It glistened with sunshine and smiled with optimism. People came to L.A. to make dreams come true.

Acting wasn't my dream. I knew I'd been handed an opportunity that thousands had sacrificed everything for. I had arrived in one of the world's most competitive cities with a manager and agent already signed, and I didn't know it then, but those two things alone took most people months to attain. All I knew was that God had opened doors making it impossible for me to deny He might want me in Hollywood. Maybe it was only for a short time. If in that time I booked a job, it would be a sign that I was supposed to stay, at least until I turned eighteen and could go back to Colorado for nursing school. If I didn't land an acting role by the end of pilot season, I'd return to Longmont with my family and chalk up my time in L.A. as a nice vacation.

I had acting lessons twice a week in Studio City. A jovial man named David Wells taught a class for teens in a small room resembling a theater, and it was there, shortly after my seventeenth birthday, where my Christian upbringing collided with Hollywood for the second time.

"I happened to notice you had this inferiority complex," said Mitch, my scene partner.

He continued reciting his lines from Tennessee Williams's *The Glass Menagerie*. It was the first time we were performing our assigned scene from the play, and already I regretted agreeing to it. My hand trembled on Mitch's shoulder as we swayed to imaginary music. He pulled my waist, bringing me closer to his. I tried to avoid his gaze, focusing on the blond scruff that gave away he was the oldest student in class, a twenty-four-year-old trapped in a sixteen-year-old's body.

"Somebody needs to build your confidence up," Mitch continued. "And make you proud instead of shy and turning away and blushing."

Heat flushed from my heart to my ears. I wondered if our teacher could tell my nerves were mine and not those of my character's.

"Somebody ought to . . ." Mitch paused, moving even closer. Everything in me wanted to yank away from his embrace, to run out the door of the acting studio before it was too late. Mitch's voiced lowered.

"Somebody ought to kiss you, Laura."

I had no more time to think. Mitch's lips met mine, warm and thin. I forced my eyes shut, thankful my character would close hers just as awkwardly. There was no going back now. I had betrayed my future husband and given my body to Mitch. It could never be undone.

Mitch pulled away with a tender expression on his face. A wave of nausea swept over me. I wanted to cry. Our acting teacher, David, led our class into applause.

"And scene!" David said, allowing my eyes to break away from Mitch's. "That was great, you guys. Just wonderful. I knew you two would make a perfect Jim and Laura."

I tried to smile at David's praise, but all I could manage was the stiff widening of my cheeks. Mitch raised a hand to high five me. I avoided his eyes as I smacked his hand as quickly as I could, shifting my weight away from him. Suddenly, everything about my scene partner repulsed me.

Mitch invited me to share a hummus platter with him in the cafe downstairs after class. Mom hadn't arrived to pick me up yet, so I couldn't think of an excuse not to join him. We sat at a table in awkward silence waiting for our order. Mitch sensed my nervousness, but he had no way of knowing my shame.

"Well, that went well," he said, trying to make conversation.

"Yeah, it did," I said.

"Our timing of the waltz was perfect," Mitch said. "I'm glad we decided to get up when we did. Worked out nicely."

We complimented each other's costume choices—his a button-down shirt with pressed khakis, mine a polka-dotted dress. We expressed relief for not having forgotten any of our lines, and we voiced our regret that we'd had to settle for a miniature figurine of a horse instead of the script's written unicorn. We talked about everything but the kiss.

Kiss. I'd kissed him. My mouth had kissed the mouth of the guy sitting across from me. I'd always known actors had to kiss other actors, but I never thought I'd be practicing so soon. I never thought I'd be an actor. I felt robbed.

Later that night, I asked God for the strength to do what the career He called me to required of me. Mitch probably wouldn't be the last guy I had to kiss. My heart was still pure, I told myself, because it still waited for my future husband. God was still holding the pen of my love story. Even so, I wrote a letter to my future husband asking his forgiveness. I explained that it wasn't really me, Alice, kissing Mitch. It was Laura kissing Jim. My first grown-up kiss as myself was still waiting for him. The wild romance of my dreams was still in God's hands. All I had to do was remain faithful.

~

One day in March, Dad called to say that an old friend of mine heard I was in L.A.

"You remember Luke Brenner, don't you?" Dad said.

I doubted I would ever forget the guy who confessed his feelings for me in India and then accused me of being flirtatious. It had been almost a year since I'd last seen Luke. Neither of us had ever brought up the incident, and the times we'd seen each other at youth group had been polite enough. Even so, I felt anxious as Dad explained how Luke had called him asking for my number.

"He's moving to L.A. in a week," Dad said. "I told him I'd have you call him."

My heart pounded. "Luke is moving to L.A.?" I asked, stalling.

"Yep," Dad said. "He's in real estate now and he just sold his first house. I guess his brothers live out there, in Santa Monica."

"Is he wanting to get together?" I asked.

"Why don't you ask him?" Dad said.

I waited a couple of days and dialed Luke's number, feeling more nervous than excited.

"Hello," Luke answered.

"Hey, it's Alice. My Dad said—"

"Oh, hey! How's it going?"

"Good," I said. "How are you?"

"Great, I'm actually living with my brother now in Santa Monica. Just got here yesterday, in fact."

I didn't know what to say, so I let out a half-giggle that sounded breathier than I meant for it to.

"So," Luke said. "I was wondering if maybe you wanted to hang out or something, since we're both out here."

I'd been anticipating his suggestion. While I didn't particularly want to see Luke, it seemed rude not to, at least once.

Two days later, Luke stood outside my acting studio to greet me when class ended. He seemed taller than I remembered, appearing to have plateaued at around six-foot-two. His sage green eyes, close-cropped sandy hair, and gentle smile were the same. He moved to give me a hug.

"Long time no see," he said.

"I know," I said, careful not to let my boobs reach his chest.

Our conversation felt stilted as Luke drove us to a nearby restaurant. By the time dinner ended, his laid-back affability had drawn me out of my shell. What happened in India seemed to be forgotten, and I realized Luke was actually an easy guy to talk to. He asked me how I liked Los Angeles and if I thought I'd stay.

"I don't know," I said. "I felt like God was calling me to be a missionary and minister to people through health care. But sometimes I wonder if Hollywood is my mission field now. Maybe I'll minister to people through my performances as an actress, or just in day-to-day life out here. The people of L.A. are broken, too."

Luke sighed and nodded his agreement. "I know, there's so many homeless people here."

"And not just the homeless people," I said. "It seems like everyone here is consumed by sin. Like, I saw a line for an ATM the other day. All the people standing in it were so representative of what L.A. symbolizes. There was this girl with fake boobs wearing a skimpy outfit, a guy who wore a really nice designer-looking suit, and a skater kid wearing a hoodie with a swear word on it. Even a man who was dressed up like a woman."

Luke knew how each of the people I described represented lust, greed, rebelliousness, and sexual immorality. I was blind to how my faith had reduced human beings to stereotypes of sin, and blind further to my own sin of passing judgment. I thought I was seeing people as Jesus saw them, as lost individuals held in the grips of Satan who prevented them from being who they really were: pure children of God.

It comforted me more than I'd anticipated to talk about L.A. with someone who understood the Christian lens through which I saw it.

"We should do this again," Luke said when he took me home at the end of the night.

"Yeah," I said. "It's nice to talk to somebody from back home. Someone who's not my family, I mean."

We smiled and said goodnight.

Luke and I continued seeing each other. He never minded picking me up and dropping me off. At first, I hung out with him because I didn't want to hurt his feelings by saying no. After a few weeks, I realized I looked forward to spending time with Luke and genuinely enjoyed his company. Every time we ate out, Luke insisted on paying, and because I had grown up receiving the generosity of friends and strangers, I didn't think anything of it.

One night, after a dinner of mozzarella sticks and burgers at a west-side sports bar, Luke drove me back to my family and asked me how I liked acting.

"I love it," I said. "It's fun being someone else, saying things I'd never say, doing things I'd never do."

"Things like what?" Luke asked.

"Like, I had to do this scene in my acting class. It was from *The Glass Menagerie*, a Tennessee Williams play. I had to kiss my scene partner, which, as you know, is something I would never do."

I didn't know why I brought up that scene. Luke pulled up to a stoplight. "Wait," he said. "You had to kiss somebody?"

"Yeah. And it was challenging, because I still don't even date."

Luke stared at me. "You mean that's not what we've been doing this whole time?"

My face froze. I couldn't read his expression.

"Just kidding," he finally said, breaking into a smile.

I breathed a sigh of relief. "Oh good. For a second, I thought you forgot where I stood on all that."

"No," he said, laughing. "How could I forget? After that conversation in India?"

I laughed too. "Yeah, that's what I thought. We're just friends, right?"

"Of course. Just friends. And I'm lucky to be your friend."

In May, just as I was beginning to think my time in L.A. had come to an unfruitful end, I booked my first acting job. It was a commercial for a stuffed animal uncreatively called "The Dog." All I did was dance around in a polka-dotted dress with a toy Dalmatian that looked like a fish-eye lens had blown it to life, but booking "The Dog" was the sign I'd been waiting for. God wanted me to stay in Hollywood, at least for a little bit longer.

My parents decided to let me stay in L.A. by myself. They said they would pay my rent at least through summer, and some leftover money from my college Pell grant also helped to support me. Looking back, I would understand why people thought it was crazy for my parents to leave me alone in L.A. at seventeen. It felt like just another God-led adventure to us at the time. I had already graduated high school a year previously, and my GED meant I could legally work as an adult in the entertainment industry, an advantage for a teenager who wouldn't have to have a tutor on set. Perhaps if I'd grown up in the same town all my life, being suddenly on my own in a new city would have been scary. But I was used to big changes.

I flew to Colorado at the end of May to collect my things. Dad drove back to L.A. with me in my first car, a maroon-brown sedan with an air conditioner that no longer worked. I didn't mind. The car was a gift from my parents, an '87 Chevy Celebrity.

"It's an omen," Dad said, grinning at me. "Maybe you'll be a celebrity one day."

As we drove through the night on our road trip to Los Angeles, I discovered my father's musical taste had changed. Dad played a few secular albums, among them *Busted Stuff* by the Dave Matthews Band and *Weathered* by Creed.

"So you don't think it's wrong to listen to secular music?" I asked Dad.

He cocked his head. "You know, Alice," he said. "I feel like it's about what's in your heart, between you and God. But with your mother gone, I've been expanding my horizons." He gave me a sly glance. "It's been nice to listen to something other than classical."

Classical was the only genre Mom listened to besides Christian music.

Very rarely, she would put on the Oldies station. Hearing Dad's shift in perspective surprised me. It also gave me the courage to confess to him my latest CD purchase. When the last strains of Creed's "Lullaby" faded away, I popped open the disc player and slipped in Daniel Bedingfield's *Gotta Get Thru This*. I glanced at Dad to watch his reaction. When the electronic drumbeat kicked in, his head bobbed along and an impish smile crossed his face.

"I'm guessing this is secular, too?" he asked me.

"Yeah," I said.

I couldn't help smiling. My father the former pastor and I were listening to music that didn't glorify God. And we liked it.

My family left L.A. after helping me move into a one-bedroom bungalow in Santa Monica. My new roommates were two girls a couple of years older than me—Bella, a gorgeous and outspoken Dominican New Yorker who I met in acting class, and Juliett, a native Angeleno who looked and sounded like a cross between Shakira and Beyoncé. Both girls shared the only bedroom in our 600-square-foot space. I slept on their living room futon for $400 a month.

I'd been at the bungalow for no more than a week when the girls introduced me to a lifestyle I'd only read about in books. Nothing could have prepared me for my first house party. I felt overwhelmed from the start. Our tiny bungalow was too small for the thirty or so people the girls had invited. Music by the Black Eyed Peas throbbed from the stereo speakers. I watched from a corner of the living room as a girl carelessly spilled beer on the futon that was my bed. Several guys smoked weed in the kitchen. People in the bedroom danced like they were in a nightclub, and someone said a couple was making out on the hallway washing machine. I wanted to scream at everyone to shut up and get out.

"How you doing?" Luke yelled at me above the loudness.

"Good," I shouted, smiling to cover up my anxiety.

Bella and Juliett had said to invite anyone I wanted. Since Luke was the only friend I had in L.A., I invited him. He laughed easily with a group of guys while I tried to busy myself restacking red cups that had knocked over. I envied Luke's natural extroversion. I remembered he had gone to public school, which helped explain to me why he seemed at ease in such a secular crowd. That and the fact he would be turning twenty in a month.

Just then, someone knocked over a cup of Jack and Coke. I watched as it spilled all over the corner of my white down comforter. Furious, I knelt to try and stuff my blanket further beneath the futon, and then another guy crashed into me, knocking me off balance.

"Sorry," the guy said, obviously drunk. "What are you doing down there? You're really hot."

I had to leave before I snapped at someone.

The June air felt chilly when I stepped outside. I wished I'd worn jeans and a hoodie instead of the mini skirt and slinky black halter I thought I'd feel cool in. *Coolness might be unattainable for me*, I thought. I found cement steps behind the bungalow and sat on them. Bass vibrated through the stucco walls, but at least I could hear myself think again.

"There you are."

I opened my eyes and saw Luke. I smiled at him wearily as he sat next to me.

"You okay?" he asked.

"Yeah, I'm okay."

"You don't seem like you're having a very good time."

My grievances came tumbling out. "Everyone's being so inconsiderate," I said. "They're spilling everywhere, making a mess, and the music's too loud to even hear anyone talk."

Luke smiled at me sympathetically. "Well, it is a party."

"It's my first party," I confessed. "I didn't know they were like this."

"You've never been to a party?"

"No. The only people I know are from youth group."

Luke's eyes widened. "So the only parties you've been to were at youth group?"

I nodded. "If this is a party, I hate it."

Luke laughed. I wondered if he thought I was a total loser. Then he quieted and looked at me, kindness beaming from his eyes. "Parties are lame," he said. "Everyone just gets drunk and tries to hook up."

I glanced at the red plastic cup he held. "Are you drinking?" I asked.

"A little," he said. "Are you?"

"No. I've never had alcohol before and I don't intend to start now. At least not in this environment."

"That's why you're so miserable," Luke said.

I laughed with him, grateful for his company. Luke felt like the bridge between my two worlds: my old world in Colorado, where all I'd known was Christianity and community college; and my new world in L.A., where I was being introduced to secular culture and the hedonism it offered. Luke could navigate both. Suddenly, I felt glad that God had called him to California at the same time as me.

⁓

Luke and I became good friends that summer. Best friends, the kind who saw each other every day. Los Angeles offered a slew of day-trip adventures, and Luke and I eagerly explored them all, from off-road ATV rides in the hills above Santa Clarita to sunset strolls along the Santa Monica pier. We didn't let the city's notorious traffic stop us. Luke never made any romantic advances toward me, and I never harbored any feelings of attraction toward him. His respect, and the fact that we had cleared up any misunderstanding about us dating, left me relaxing into his companionship with a heart full of gratitude. Luke felt like the older brother I never had. We even cuddled sometimes. I missed the closeness of my family, and when Luke let me link my arm through his when we watched movies together on the couch, it felt comfortable, safe. I trusted him and thanked God for giving me a friend in an otherwise lonely city.

By early fall, I did start to make more friends, mostly through Bella and Juliett. Our bungalow felt like a revolving door of musicians, dancers, actors, and students, and with the exception of my roommates, guys tended to like me more than girls. I didn't care if it was because they thought I was pretty. Guys were the only people who made an effort to get to know me, the only ones I felt I could talk to and be myself. I knew where I stood with guys. With girls, I always wondered.

Building a social circle in L.A. helped give me confidence. I still wasn't sure if I'd be back in Colorado by the end of the year, but in the meantime, it felt good to be establishing relationships with people outside of Luke. I didn't want to solely depend on him for companionship. It didn't seem healthy. So, I also began hanging out with Gabe, a talented musician; Travis, a model whose sexiness gave me a crush I repented for; and Miguel, a street racer bound for the Air Force.

One day, I was telling Luke about a recent hike I went on with Miguel. It was just the two of us in the bungalow that afternoon, since Bella and Juliett had gone to their boyfriends' homes. I stood at the stovetop making biscuits and gravy for dinner while Luke sat at the kitchen table. He seemed quieter than usual, like he felt on edge about something.

"You okay?" I asked.

"You've been hanging out with Miguel a lot," Luke said.

"Yeah, I guess I have been."

"What do you guys do?"

"Mostly hike. He drag races, so he's gonna take me racing sometime. Not like in a real race, just a spin at the place where he usually does it."

"You're going street racing with this guy?"

Luke's tone was neutral, but I detected a hint of suspicion that puzzled me. I told myself he was only being overprotective.

"Yeah," I said. "Why?"

"Seems dangerous."

"Well, he's been doing it since he was fifteen. He's twenty-one now, so I think he knows what he's doing."

I didn't like the sarcasm creeping into my voice, but it felt like Luke was patronizing me.

"Do you like him?" Luke asked.

"Yeah, I like him. I wouldn't hang out with him if I didn't like him."

I knew what Luke meant. I didn't like his tone. He'd gone from neutral to decidedly accusatory, and I didn't feel like I should have to defend myself for making new friends. I dumped fried sausage bits into a pot of gravy, stirring the mixture with a silver whisk as I tried to change the subject.

"Wanna go to the pier after dinner?" I asked.

"What about Travis?" Luke asked. "Do you like him?"

"If I didn't like him, I wouldn't—"

"You know what I mean," Luke interrupted.

I sighed. I didn't want to have a confrontation, but Luke wasn't giving me a choice.

"Luke, I really don't feel like it's any of your business," I said. "And honestly, you seem like you're acting jealous or something. Why?"

Luke was silent. I glanced at him.

"Because," Luke said, looking straight into my eyes. "God showed me you're my future wife."

21

Betrothed

Everything slowed. The light seemed to tunnel out of the kitchen. All I could hear was the whirring of a fan, and only my hand gripping the stove kept me upright.

"Alice?" Luke said.

His voice startled me. He was standing. When did he stand?

"Did you hear me?" he asked.

I felt weighted by numbness.

"God told me you're my future wife."

"You're sure?" I heard myself ask.

Luke smiled and nodded.

"You're *sure*?" I repeated.

"Yes," he said. "I'm a hundred percent sure."

It didn't occur to me to ask Luke how he heard God tell him I was his future wife. I'd never known how God told anyone anything. Neither did I for a split-second think Luke was lying. Luke and I were from the same world. It was a world where people said God showed them life-changing things all the time, a world where it wasn't at all uncommon for God to reveal to men and women who their future spouses were. I'd been primed for that moment my whole life.

But this isn't the way it's supposed to be.

The cry came from deep inside my heart. I silenced it out of sheer terror. God had just revealed who my future husband was. I couldn't go against Him.

Luke stepped toward me. Involuntarily, I stepped back. His hand touched my shoulder and I flinched. Trying to cover emotions I couldn't name, I abandoned the pot on the stove and rushed past Luke to the living room. I felt cold. My hands were trembling. Without thinking, I went to my futon and threw my down comforter over me, holding it tight above my head. When Luke peeled back my covers, he was still smiling.

"I'm just shocked," I stammered.

"I know," he said. "I was, too, when God told me."

It was as though he thought I was happy-shocked. Was I happy-shocked? I didn't know. I didn't know what to feel, what to do, what to say. I wanted to be happy—I should have been happy—but I wasn't. I didn't know what I was. I had to lie. I had to lie because to do otherwise would be to defy God. I forced a smile.

"I just can't believe it's you," I said. "That you're the one I've been waiting for."

Luke stroked my head tenderly. "I know," he said.

It was supposed to be amazing, this moment. It was supposed to be everything I'd dreamed.

"This isn't the way I thought we would have this conversation," Luke continued, taking my hand. "But now you know why it's been so hard for me to watch you go off with these other guys."

"But . . . but I wasn't even—"

"I know," Luke said. "But they were into you."

I was speechless. I needed to be alone to process, to cry. To summon the energy to at least pretend to be happy for now, and not start off my marriage with my future husband knowing I didn't love him. Not in that way.

"I'm just so shocked," I said again.

"It's okay," Luke said. "Take your time."

"I might need a lot of time," I blurted. "Maybe we shouldn't see each other for a few days, or maybe a week." The words tumbled from my lips without forethought. "I'm happy, so happy," I lied. "But I need time to process it. To pray over it."

He couldn't argue with my needing time to pray.

"Okay," Luke said. His eyes danced with joy. "Take a few days. We have the rest of our lives."

The rest of my life. With Luke. I smiled at him, wondering at how my cheeks could do so.

"Thank you," I said.

"And we don't have to get married right away," Luke said. "I thought we could wait a couple years, 'til you're nineteen. Or twenty."

"Okay," I said.

Luke stood. I didn't want to get up. I was afraid he was going to kiss me, so I pulled the comforter close to my face. "I'll call you in a couple days," I said.

He nodded, seeming to accept that we weren't going to hug our usual goodbye. "Okay," he said. He walked out the door, still smiling.

I wanted to cry after Luke left. I couldn't, because crying would be an admission of how devastated I felt. God had promised to fulfill all my heart's desires if I trusted Him to write my love story. He'd promised me a romance beyond my wildest dreams if I waited faithfully for my future husband. That God had just revealed him to be Luke shattered me.

It wasn't Luke's fault. He was a good man, I told myself. Any girl would be lucky to have him. But he was a man for whom I felt nothing more than friendship, a man I cared for, very much, but whom I had never felt attracted to. That was why I never saw it coming. I couldn't cry because I was too afraid of acknowledging God had betrayed me.

That week I stayed busy. I told no one about Luke's revelation, and since my roommates and I were in the process of moving, the mercies of tasks and errands kept my mind occupied. Living with Bella and Juliett in the Santa Monica bungalow had, in many ways, been the most eventful three months of my life, but the lease was up and none of us had the financial stability to renew it. I found my next home through my acting teacher.

A friend of his needed someone to housesit her apartment in Sherman Oaks, and although I never met Nicole, I moved into her home during my week of space from Luke. Nicole's two-bedroom apartment was located on the top floor of a luxury building, with a courtyard view of tropical plants and a swimming pool. Contemporary furnishings in varying shades of olive and beige made up her soothing decor, and her plush cream-colored carpet was spotless. The bedroom where I unpacked my few belongings was almost as large as the entire bungalow I'd left. No one else would be there for the entirety of my stay. Having the place to myself couldn't have come at a more needed time.

My week of space passed. I felt no better about marrying Luke than I had when he first told me I was his future wife. When I couldn't put off seeing him any longer, I called him and asked if he wanted to come see my new home. He said he'd be there in an hour. I forced myself to put on a happy face, hoping real joy would come in time. Maybe if I moved forward in faith, God would reward me with the passion I wanted to feel for Luke.

Luke called letting me know he was downstairs. I felt sick with dread as I walked through the courtyard to let him inside the complex. I was scared he would kiss me, and I didn't feel ready for that. I was ready enough to accept being his future wife, but I wasn't prepared for the physical intimacy that might come with it. We wouldn't have sex until we were married. That went without saying, but I had never asked Luke where his personal boundaries on other forms of intimacy stood. I knew my façade would break if he leaned in for a kiss.

Luke smiled at me through the gated door. I put on my brightest attitude, hoping to hide my nerves.

"Hi!" I said.

"Hey," he said.

I opened the door and reached to hug him quickly, turning my face hard to the side before he could even look at my lips. I didn't know if kissing was on his mind, but I felt certain that if it were on mine, it must be on his. I pulled away and spun on my heel to lead him to the elevator.

"Wow, this place is fancy," Luke said, following me.

"Thanks," I said, forcing a smile.

Luke seemed to be his usual laid-back self. I was even more nervous than I thought. I hoped that once we got inside my apartment, I could try and relax by sitting down. Instead I headed straight for the kitchen cupboard and took out two glasses. Luke wandered into the living room.

"Major step up from the bungalow," he said, appreciating the view from the balcony.

I laughed. "Yeah. It's been lovely having a place all to my own."

"How'd you move here again?"

"Oh, a friend of my acting teacher needed someone to housesit while she's in Dallas. I think she's moving there to get married or something."

Immediately, I regretted bringing up marriage. I knew we'd have to talk about our own marriage plans sooner or later, but for the moment I just wanted to pretend it wasn't happening.

I met Luke in the living room and handed him a glass of water. "Here you go," I said.

He smiled at me. "Thanks."

I wanted him to sit down so I could sit on whatever sofa he wasn't. He lingered by the sliding glass doors as if waiting to see where I would sit. My anxiety wouldn't let me wait, so I walked across the room and sat on the sofa furthest from him, hugging a beaded pillow to my lap. I tried not to look tense.

"How was your week?" Luke asked.

"Good," I said. "Just busy moving. How was yours?"

I barely paid attention to the small talk we made. The awkwardness was too great. It was as though neither of us knew how to transition from friends to lovers. Not even lovers. What were we now? Boyfriend and girlfriend? Was Luke now my fiancé? Were we engaged, or were we just courting? I didn't know. I didn't want to ask. I smiled and nodded as Luke told me about his week—something about how he'd be teaching tennis until he could buy and flip his next house. Then he quieted, staring at me thoughtfully. He seemed to sense I needed some distance between us and sat on the couch opposite me.

"Alice," he said. "I want you to know that I don't plan on kissing you until we're married."

I tried not to show my relief. "Really?" I asked.

"Yeah. I prayed about it, and I told God I want nothing but purity in our relationship."

I smiled at him.

"Of course, I want to kiss you," Luke said, grinning. "I want to kiss you so bad."

I laughed, relieved to let out some of the tension. Luke laughed with me. I hoped he mistook my blush for desire.

"But I want to save our first kiss for our wedding day," he continued.

"Thank you," I said. "I really cherish your respect."

I meant it. Hopefully by the time our wedding day came, I would be as impatient to kiss Luke as he was to kiss me.

"I've also been praying a lot about the next step," Luke said. "I think I need to call your father and ask his permission for your hand."

I blinked. Luke would be the type to call my father, but that would make it real. "When?" I asked.

"Today. I thought we could call him together."

My mind couldn't formulate a way to get out of it. "Okay," I said. "Right now?"

"Might as well." Luke smiled at me nervously. "I've never done this before."

"Me, neither."

My voice sounded far away. It felt like I was underwater as I heard myself take over and speak and move for me. I saw myself get up and move to the couch next to Luke. Our knees bumped when I sat down. I giggled, playing the role of the excited fiancée as though I were in an improv class.

"Shall we call him from your phone or mine?" I heard myself ask.

"I think it would be better if I called him from mine," Luke said, his voice muffled.

"Okay," I said.

The out of body feeling left. My hearing returned to normal, and with it, my anxiety. I felt helpless, like a train was barreling my way with nowhere I could leap for safety. The autopilot version of myself continued performing the way that was expected of her. Wavering between normal and dissociated states was a sensation I would get used to.

Luke dialed Dad's cell number. I watched as he held the phone to his ear and listened to it ring. A few seconds went by. Maybe Dad wouldn't answer.

"Hey, Ted, this is Luke Brenner calling," Luke said. "Good, I'm good. How about yourself? Nice. Well . . ." Luke took my hand. I squeezed it and gave him a forced smile of encouragement. "The reason I'm calling is because Alice and I have something we want to share with you. She's sitting here next to me. But before, I feel it's only fitting if I ask you something first. Sir, I believe that God has shown me that Alice is my future wife. And I wanted to call you because I want to ask for her hand in marriage."

I held my breath. I couldn't imagine what Dad's face looked like just then. He must have been shocked. Was he outraged? Confused? I didn't realize how much I was counting on my father to object until Luke's face broke into a smile. He laughed.

"Really?" Luke said. "No way."

Luke glanced at me, looking relieved and amazed. I watched him, paralyzed.

"Wow," Luke said. "That's just more confirmation. Thank you, sir. I love your daughter, and I promise I will treasure her and take care of her and treat her well. Thank you."

Hearing Luke's words slit me like a knife to the throat. He handed me the phone, beaming.

"Hello," I said.

I heard the smile in Dad's voice. "Hey, missy moppet."

"Hey, Dad."

"I was just telling Luke . . . God showed me this was coming a long time ago."

I was stunned. "What?"

Dad spoke with the authority of the pastor he used to be. "Yep. Years ago, God told me he had a special man for you, and that I would know him when it was time. And I've been wondering when I'd get this call."

I felt I might burst into tears. Dad wasn't even asking me if marrying Luke was something I wanted. But why should he? I asked myself. God's wants had always come before mine.

Despite my intention to marry Luke, I realized a part of me had secretly been hoping he'd been mistaken about hearing God's will. Maybe if my father had denied him permission to marry me, he would have seen that. Maybe if Dad had hesitated, it would have planted doubt in Luke's mind. Not only had Dad not denied him. My father had affirmed Luke's belief with his own confirmation from God. He said he was happy for me and congratulated both of us. I said thanks and then we hung up. It all happened so fast.

Luke couldn't stop smiling. He said we should call his mom next. As though God wanted to make sure that my heart was thoroughly convinced marrying Luke was His will, Luke's mom said that she, too, had heard from God that I would marry her son.

"I knew all along this was going to happen," Donna said. "When God showed me you were the girl who was going to be my future daughter-in-law, I just broke down and gave thanks. You are so sweet, and so special. I couldn't be happier."

Her words wrenched me. It was all happening just like the Christian courtship books said it should. God had revealed to Luke that I was his future wife. He had prayed over it, then asked my father for his blessing. Dad gave his blessing, having heard from God himself that Luke was the man I would marry, then Luke's mother also confirmed God's will for our marriage. I felt as if I were living the ideal of what every Christian dating book I'd read had outlined. To top it all off, Luke had said he wouldn't kiss me until our wedding day.

When the calls were finished, I turned to Luke, forcing another smile I didn't feel. I didn't know how many I had left.

"So, are we engaged now?" I asked.

He grinned at me. "I guess we are."

Engaged. It didn't seem possible. I had never had a boyfriend and now I had a fiancé. I blinked back tears, not knowing why I was so shocked. I had been groomed for that moment my whole life.

When Luke finally left my apartment, I closed the door and collapsed into sobs. One moment I felt hot waves of grief for the love story that would never be mine, the one I had waited so faithfully for. Another moment I felt crushed by shame for not being happier. It didn't matter that God hadn't told me anything about marrying Luke. He never had. My whole life had been ruled by the things God told other people, and it should have been no surprise that my marriage would be any different. People would later ask me why I went along with it. My answer was as simple as it was obvious to me: If I went against God, I risked the eternity of hell. Disobeying God had never been a realistic option for me, no matter what Christians wanted to believe about free will. We all knew God's love wasn't unconditional if hell existed. Jesus was very clear that it did.

My mind saw my situation with grim clarity. It felt like I was entering an arranged marriage, pledged to a man not of my choosing, but of his and our parents' through God. The custom felt ancient. Biblical. I knew arranged marriages still happened in some cultures. I also knew other teenage brides had it far worse than I did, facing husbands they may have never even met. Even so, I suddenly felt a dark kinship with them, the young women in the world who were betrothed to men they didn't love, and with no say in the matter.

Betrothed. That was the word I felt described my status. It implied the sense of helplessness I felt, and it was also the word the Bible used to describe the giving away of a girl from one man to another. She was betrothed. And now, so was I.

22

Not My Will

Those early days of my betrothal passed in a blur. I wept. Every night I wept. I bottled my emotions whenever I saw Luke during the day, but at night, alone in the shelter of my room, I grieved. What I'd always imagined would be the happiest time of my life felt like a period of mourning. Pain poured out of me in the pages of my journal. It was the only safe place I had. Even so, I was quick to follow up any confessions of doubt with hasty and fearful assurances that I would do God's will despite my feelings. There was a spiritual war to be won. I had always been warned my flesh would hate what God called me to.

It would have been easy for someone to tell me it wasn't really God whom Luke, his mother, and my father had heard. Even fellow Christians might have tried to convince me they were mistaken. I would not have believed them. My upbringing taught me that God led my life through my parents. Church taught me that when I met the man I would marry, God would lead my life through him. Every book on dating I had ever read, and every purity retreat I had attended, reinforced the idea that God would confirm who my future spouse was through the Christian elders He placed in my life. If anyone had told me it was not God's will that I marry Luke, I would have been too afraid of demonic influence to listen to them.

My relationship with Luke began to change. I knew it would. We were betrothed now. But our relationship changed abruptly and in ways I never anticipated.

We had our first fight when I went to Luke's apartment in Santa Monica one evening. I hadn't been there since everything had happened. We were planning to go see a movie, but when I knocked on his apartment door, no one answered. The doorknob turned when I tried it.

"Hello," I called out, stepping into the foyer.

Footsteps thumped down the stairs to my right. I looked up and saw Ari, Luke's brother. He smiled widely at me.

"Alice!" Ari said. "Congratulations! I hear you're going to be my sister-in-law."

He enveloped me in a hug, saying how happy he was for Luke and me.

"Thanks," I said. It hit me suddenly that I had a future brother-in-law. Two of them, actually, with a future sister-in-law through marriage.

Luke poked his head out of his bedroom door. "Hey," he said. "Sorry I didn't hear you come in. I just stepped out of the shower. I'll be ready in five."

My fiancé's cheeriness vanished as soon as we sat in his car. "I tried calling you," Luke said. "Where were you all day?"

"Oh, I was hanging out with Miguel," I said.

Luke's fingers gripped the steering wheel. "You were hanging out with Miguel?"

The accusation in his tone caught me off guard. He wouldn't look at me.

"We had lunch."

"Why?"

"I don't know, we just wanted to hang out."

"I don't want you spending time with Miguel anymore," he said. "Or with any other guys. Not unless I'm there."

I started to protest, but Luke cut me off. "You can hang out with your girl friends," he said. "But—"

"I don't have many girl friends, Luke." I fought to keep my voice steady. "I can't help that most of my friends are guys."

"You're my future wife," Luke said. He looked at me and seemed to change his tactic from command to guilt trip. "Every time you hang out with another guy, it feels like you're stabbing me. Do you want to stab me?"

I crumbled. Luke was right. It probably was inappropriate for girls who were betrothed to hang out alone with other guys.

"No," I said quietly. "I don't want to stab you."

"So you won't hang out with guys anymore? Unless I'm there?"

"No, I won't."

"Thank you. Hey, why are you crying?"

Luke reached to touch my face, but I pulled away. He had no idea how much sadness I'd already been holding in, how much sacrifice I felt like I was already making. I had no energy left to pretend I was fine that night. I unbuckled my seat belt and opened the car door.

"Wait, Alice—"

"I need to be alone right now," I said. "I'm sorry. I'll call you tomorrow."

I shut the door and started walking. Luke opened his door.

"Alice," he said.

"Please leave me alone," I said, and I got into my car and left.

~

In submission to Luke, I stopped seeing my guy friends. I didn't want to tell them that I couldn't see them unless my fiancé was there, so I made up excuses to avoid seeing them at all. Things seemed to be okay again for a little while. But Luke's jealousy wouldn't abate. It was as though he could sense my heart wasn't truly his, and so he did everything within his power to try and control it.

We were walking along the Santa Monica pier one night when my cell phone rang. The call was from my manager, Lorenzo.

"Remember that movie you went out for last week?" Lorenzo asked.

My mind scanned through the auditions I'd had. "Which one?" I asked, plugging my ear to block out the noise of carnival rides.

"*Sleepover*," he said.

"Yeah," I said. "That one for the mean high school girl? Did I get another call back?"

"Honey," Lorenzo said, pausing for effect. "You booked the job!"

I stopped in my tracks. *Sleepover* was a big studio film, an MGM movie starring Alexa Vega from the *Spy Kids* trilogy.

"What?" I asked.

Luke gave me a look of concern. I moved to the edge of the pier and rested my elbows on the splintered wood railing.

"You booked it! You got the part. Congratulations, honey."

A slow smile spread across my face. "Really?"

"Honey," Lorenzo said, "I'm not kiddin' you. I just got off the phone with Brady, he says they called him with an offer and they're already getting your Taft-Hartley papers in order."

I couldn't believe it. I was being Taft-Hartleyed. I didn't know where the term came from, but I knew the papers meant that I would be eligible to join the Screen Actors Guild. Once I had my SAG card, I'd be a real actor. It was happening. My career was taking off.

"Are you happy?" Lorenzo asked. "I thought you'd be more excited."

"No, no, I'm very excited," I said. "Just a little surprised."

"Well, I'm not," said Lorenzo. "I told you I have an eye for talent. And you've been working hard, going to class, and I'm proud of you."

Lorenzo told me filming wouldn't start for a few more weeks, but I should expect a call from the wardrobe department wanting to know my sizes. He congratulated me again and we hung up. I turned to Luke, who waited patiently beside me.

"I booked a job," I said to him.

His face broke into a smile. "Yeah, you did!"

I laughed with him. "I can't believe it."

"What's it for?" Luke asked.

"It's for a movie called *Sleepover*. It's not a lead role, just a small supporting. But it's a studio film."

"That's awesome," Luke said. "I'm so happy for you."

He squeezed me into a hug as I ducked from his face. Luke maintained he wouldn't kiss me until our wedding day, and he hadn't tried, but still I felt tense whenever his face came close to mine. I tried not to let the anxiety of his hug ruin my excitement.

My excitement was ruined away. A couple of days later, when I was at Luke's apartment for the afternoon, I told him more about the script.

"It's about this girl who has this last slumber party with her friends before they go off to high school. You won't see my character until they end up at this dance party, where the mean girl, Staci, sees me making out with her boyfriend. So she stomps over to us, and then—"

"Wait," Luke said. "Making out?"

He looked up at me from where he stood at the foot of his bed folding clothes. My smile dropped. I should have known he'd be unhappy about that part. I tried to play it down.

"Yeah," I said. "It's just really quick. She sees us from across the room and then interrupts our kiss, and she's like, 'Why're you dating my boyfriend,' and I'm like, 'What do you mean, he's my boyfriend.' And then we get into a cat fight."

The apartment was silent.

"So you have to make out with a guy?" Luke asked.

"Well, yeah," I said. "It's in the script, and it's kind of the catalyst for the whole cat fight, so . . ."

Luke didn't say anything for a moment. He stared down at a t-shirt in his hands, then looked up at me again. "Have you prayed about whether or not you should do this role?"

A heat ignited in my belly. "What do you mean?" I asked.

"I mean, have you prayed about it? Do you think God wants you to do roles where you have to make out with other guys?"

"Well, He's the one who called me to acting, so I'm sure He knows I'll have to make out with guys."

"No, you don't. You could only do roles where you don't have to kiss anyone."

I didn't think Luke knew what he was asking. I tried to keep my tone patient.

"But I'm a young girl," I said. "I'm going to go out for young girl roles. There's probably going to be a love story involved, where yeah, I'll have to kiss a guy."

"My brother's an actor," Luke said, referring to Ruben. "And when he got married, he said he wouldn't do any roles where he had to kiss anybody. Because he wants to be faithful to his wife."

"And what roles has he booked since then?" I asked.

"The point is," Luke said, growing frustrated, "I can't be married to someone who's going to be making out with other men."

I stared at him, my heart pounding. I couldn't speak.

"It's not fair to me," Luke continued. "I mean, I can't even kiss you yet. And now you're going to go make out with some other guy?"

My words came out slowly. "So, you're basically saying you don't want to be married to an actress."

"No, you can keep acting. Just don't audition for roles where you'd have to kiss someone."

"But that's what actors do. They show stories, and those stories usually include romance. You like watching love stories, you know we all want the kiss at the end."

Luke scoffed. He looked up at the ceiling. "Have you even thought about whether or not God still wants you to act?" he asked.

I glared at him. "No. I haven't thought about it. I haven't needed to, because God's made it crystal clear that L.A. is where I'm supposed to be. I wouldn't have even booked this role if God didn't want me to act anymore."

Luke stood up, shaking his head. "I don't know what to say right now," he said.

I felt like telling him he should think about whether or not God really said I was his future wife. Instead, I sighed. If it was obvious that God had called me to acting, it was even more obvious He'd called me to marry Luke. I needed to be gentle.

"Luke," I said, "if God's called you to marry an actress, then you need to trust that He'll give you the strength to deal with it."

Luke didn't say anything. We both dropped the conversation.

Luke and I fought again the following Sunday. He wanted me to go to church with him and his brother Ruben's family, and I insisted I didn't want to.

"But I can't be married to a woman who doesn't go to church," Luke sputtered.

"Then I guess maybe I'm not your future wife, because I'm not going."

It was the boldest thing I'd ever said to him.

Luke shook his head in disbelief. "But we need to start premarital counseling," he said.

I knew premarital counseling was a standard part of a Christian couple's engagement period. From what I heard, it involved sitting down with a pastor, or an older mentor couple, and going through multi-week sessions of questionnaires and lectures that would prepare us for the joys and challenges of married life. I wasn't ready for that.

"We don't even have a date set," I said. "There's no need to rush."

"But I've already been talking to my pastor about it and he and his wife want to meet with us."

"Well too bad," I said. "I'm not going."

"But—"

"Stop pressuring me!"

My vehemence shocked me. It shocked Luke, too, and I could see him realizing the wife I would be was not the compliant girl he'd known as a friend. It was my duty to submit to him. Luke never said so, but we both knew how a good Christian marriage was supposed to play out. I wanted to prolong the inevitable as much as I could. Everything seemed to be moving too fast.

~

I didn't reach out to Luke anymore. When he initiated spending time with me, I did my best to hide my true feelings, but Luke could sense something wasn't right. He came over to my apartment one afternoon to talk about it.

"I've noticed you don't seem yourself lately," he said.

We were sitting on opposite sides of the living room. I stopped picking at my sweatshirt and looked into his eyes, trying to discern whether he was about to argue with me again. He seemed genuine. I didn't know what to say.

"I was talking with Ruben and my pastor about it," Luke continued. "I know you don't want to feel pressured, but they both think you should come in so we can have premarital counseling."

I shook my head. "I'm not ready," I said.

"My brother thinks you're hiding something," Luke said. "He thinks maybe you don't even want to be in this relationship, or else you'd be willing to go."

I felt stunned by Ruben's perceptiveness. It meant I hadn't been hiding my feelings as well as I thought. I panicked. Luke couldn't know the truth. I couldn't disobey God's plan. I couldn't go to hell. I stood and walked across the living room, sitting beside Luke and taking both his hands in mine. He looked up at me with pained eyes. I spoke as tenderly and sincerely as I could.

"I do want to be in this relationship," I said. "I do want to marry you. I'm sorry I've been acting strange; it's just been a lot to process."

Guilt coursed through me as his face softened. I convinced myself my lies were for his own good.

"Really?" Luke asked.

"Yes, really. I don't want to do premarital counseling yet, but that doesn't mean I don't want to be with you."

"But you've been so different," he said. His sadness broke my heart. I wasn't looking at the Luke who had become possessive and jealous. I was looking at Luke the friend, the one who was gentle and lost and desperate to make me happy in the only ways he knew how. I wanted so badly to be truthful with him. Truth was the only thing I couldn't give.

"I want to show you something," I said. I walked to the bedroom where I kept my journal. I found the page I was looking for and returned to Luke, extending the notebook to him. "Look," I said. "I wrote this for you. Two months ago, before we even knew we were going to get married."

I watched as Luke read a poem I wrote about Travis, the friend of Juliett's I had a crush on. It was a poem no one had seen, one that no one was ever meant to see. In that moment, it was the only thing I had to convince Luke I was his. The poem was about how I wished Travis and I could be more than just friends, though I never mentioned his name. Luke read it in silence. When he finished, he looked up at me, smiling.

"You wrote that about me?" he asked.

"Yes," I said. I flushed, hoping to look embarrassed instead of ashamed. "See? You've been on my heart, too. I just don't always know how to show it."

Luke let out a sigh. His shoulders loosened and his whole demeanor relaxed. "That's encouraging," he said. He chuckled. "For a minute there I thought my brother was right."

I gave him a reassuring smile. "Nope," I said.

Luke reached to give me a hug. Then he pulled me onto his lap and held me close, as though apologizing for his suspicion. Everything in my body wanted to yank away from him, to run out the door and never let him touch me again. I cradled his head to my neck and rocked him soothingly.

That night I cried for God's forgiveness. I told myself I was only trying to survive.

~

For the rest of that month I moved as though in a daze. I went through the motions of life, driving to auditions, hanging out with Luke, and spending more and more time with his family. Things were better between Luke and I since he'd read the poem. It seemed to have given him the reassurance he needed, that I wanted him as much as he wanted me, and we fought less. In fact, we didn't fight at all. There was nothing left to fight for. Something in me had given up the day I shared the poem with Luke, and I resigned myself in full to what I believed God called me to.

I felt like I could see my life before me. Luke and I would go to church every Sunday with the boys he was sure we'd have. I'd dress them up in little khaki pants and button-downs, making sure they stood still through worship. I'd hand them over to the Sunday school teacher, telling them to be good, then I'd make my way back to Luke, who would put his arm around me while we listened to a boring sermon. I'd hate the feeling of his arm on my shoulders, but I'd sit through it anyway. We'd fetch the boys after the service and meet up with his brother's family at their house after church, where the men would watch football while the kids played outside and we wives fake-laughed in the kitchen. Our boys would be grass-stained with messy hair when it was time to go home. We'd send them to a Christian school and take them back to Colorado for Christmases. We'd have to split our time between my parents and Donna, and Luke's dad in Winter Park. I'd never met Luke's dad, but he had generously offered to pay for our engagement party when we had one.

Luke told me he was saving for a ring. I hoped he presented it to me with a real proposal, a down-on-one-knee kind I didn't see coming. I hoped to have at least one girlhood dream of mine come true. But how would I not see it coming? From then on, during every holiday and special occasion, I would be anxiety-ridden with the anticipation of an imminent proposal. We both knew I'd say yes. I could only pray God would give me real joy when that happened.

In early October, I drove to Canada with my family for a Toronto Blessing conference. It had been years since I'd been to the church where the revival was born. Toronto Airport Christian Fellowship felt smaller than I remembered, and the crowd of conference attendees had thinned. I noticed several half-empty rows of seats. When I was a kid, the surplus of conference goers would have been crammed into the aisles dancing.

I went to receive prayer that night, just as I had when I was a little girl. Once more, God gave me no visions when I was prayed over. Yet again, I pretended to be slain by the Spirit and fell backward, eyes closed, into waiting arms. It wasn't so scary this time. Though it had been a few years since I'd faked a Spirit slaying, I'd become used to living Christian lies. A thought came unbidden as I lay on the floor, listening to the laughter and crying of people around me. *Is this how I want to spend the rest of my life?* I wondered. *Pretending to feel God while He keeps speaking to everyone but me?*

My only other choice was to defy God and let Satan bring me to hell.

When the conference ended and we left Toronto, my family drove to Pictured Rocks National Lakeshore in Michigan's Upper Peninsula, camping at the same Twelvemile Beach Campground where I'd nearly attempted suicide. Memories flooded my senses. The scent of campfire smoke brought back the feeling of unshowered grime on my body, and the icy wind gusting from Lake Superior reminded me of my aching loneliness.

One afternoon, Mom sat beside me on a fallen log overlooking the lake.

"How're you doing, girlbug?" she asked.

"Good," I said, scooting to make room for her. We watched the distant froth of whitecaps in silence, basking in the rare sunshine that was a welcome break from the rain clouds.

"Alice," Mom said. "I want to talk with you about this thing with Luke."

I looked at her. She seemed to be treading carefully, and her words came out slow and deliberate.

"I haven't wanted you to think I don't support your decision," Mom continued. "I know this is one of those significant life events that could have lasting ramifications if I don't handle this properly. I don't want you to look back and think I wasn't happy for you. But I want you to know this thing with Luke has been a major point of contention between me and Dad."

She had my full attention. My heart pounded. "What do you mean?" I asked.

"To start with," Mom said, "you're very young. You're still only seventeen. How old is Luke?"

"Twenty."

Mom dipped her head. "That's very young for you two to be thinking about marriage, let alone planning for it."

"Well, not for a couple years. I was thinking it might be nice to legally drink champagne at my own wedding."

I tried to keep the conversation light. Mom wouldn't have it.

"Alice," she said. Her dark eyes bored into me. "Is this what you want?"

"Luke's a good guy. And this is what God planned."

"But is this what you want?"

"Yes."

Mom's stare wouldn't let up. "Are you happy?"

"Yes."

"Because you don't seem happy. You haven't seemed happy this whole trip."

I looked away. She was too close to the truth.

"Alice," Mom said. "You don't have to marry Luke."

I crumpled into tears.

"But God says I have to," I sobbed.

Mom put her arm around my shoulders and pulled me close. "Shh," she soothed. "You don't have to do anything you don't want."

"But He made it so clear." I cried so hard I could barely speak. "He told Luke. And He told Dad. He told Donna."

"Did God tell you?"

"No, but He never tells me anything."

"Alice, God cares about what you want."

"But if I go against His will, He'll allow consequences."

Mom rocked me in silence, her own tears leaking onto my face. It was as though she comprehended for the first time how ruinously Christian teachings had affected me. Mom insisted her version of God cared about what I wanted. At the same time, she couldn't fault me for interpreting how He didn't care. Mom knew the prophetic insights from Luke, Dad, and Donna weighed heavily as evidence of God's will, despite whatever my feelings might be. She couldn't deny the signs. Even so, she tried convincing me that just because God's plan seemed evident, it didn't mean I had to follow through with it.

"God gave us free will," she said, wiping my face with her woolly glove. "That means we don't have to do everything He asks of us."

"But what happens when we don't?"

She couldn't answer that.

"Do you love Luke?" Mom asked.

"No," I said. "Not in that way."

"Do you think God would want you to marry a man you don't love?"

"I don't know. Apparently."

"Well, I disagree. I think God does want you to love the man you'll marry."

"But then why would He do this? Why would He make this happen?"

"I don't know, chickie," Mom said. "But I know God wants you to be happy. He wouldn't force you to marry someone you don't love. That's not His heart."

I didn't say anything. Mom's words resonated too hopefully in me.

"It wouldn't be fair to Luke, either," Mom continued. "I don't think he wants a wife who doesn't love him."

I looked up at Mom and tried to discern if she meant what she said or if she was only trying to make me feel better. Her eyes were solemn. Earnest.

"You don't have to marry Luke," she repeated.

A fresh wave of tears overtook me. I didn't have to marry Luke.

I flew back to L.A. with a joyful heart, firm in my resolve to tell Luke our betrothal was over. Maybe God had only been testing me like He tested Abraham in the Bible. God knew how much Abraham loved his only son, Isaac, so He tested Abraham's devotion by telling him to sacrifice Isaac as a burnt offering. As Isaac carried wood for the fire, he innocently asked his father where the lamb was that they would be sacrificing. Abraham dodged the question by saying God would provide the lamb. When the altar was ready, Abraham abruptly tied up Isaac, who must have felt beyond betrayed, and placed him upon the firewood. I always imagined Isaac screaming as his dad raised the knife. Then, just before Abraham killed the thing he most held dear, God sent an angel to stop him.

"Now I know that you fear God," the angel said.

Maybe now God knew I feared Him. Maybe my willingness to sacrifice what I held dear—the love story I had waited so faithfully for—proved to God that I would obey Him no matter the cost. Maybe Mom had been my angel, sparing me from following through with God's calling because I had passed His test.

Fear engulfed me as soon as the plane landed. What if Mom was wrong? What if her words hadn't been a release from God, but instead, Mom was unwittingly being used by Satan to deter me from God's will? God had told three separate people I was supposed to marry Luke. Mom was the only person saying I wasn't. She was also the only one besides me who didn't go to church anymore. Mom had stopped going to LifeWay shortly before I moved to L.A., saying she no longer wanted to participate in organized religion. Maybe that was why she hadn't heard from God that I was supposed to marry Luke. God might be ignoring her. Could it be that my fleshly heart wanted to be free of Luke so badly that I'd allowed myself to be deceived by the relief of Mom's words? It was possible. Too possible. How could I know which was my true heart, where God resided, and which was my deceitful heart, ruled by my flesh? What made a desire one that God cared about and one that He wanted me to cast aside and repent for?

My head throbbed with questions. Away from the confidence of Mom's assurances, doubt took hold. I didn't know what to do. Marry a man I didn't love, or risk God's judgment and break off the engagement He had divinely appointed? It was a decision I felt paralyzed to make.

My family came to visit me. Mom knew I hadn't ended things with Luke yet because every time we spoke on the phone, she asked me about it. In person with her once more, less than a month after our conversation in Pictured Rocks, she reminded me that God was a God of love and compassion.

"It breaks God's heart to see you so sad," she said. "You're letting yourself be controlled by fear instead of love. God wants you to live in love."

What she said felt true, but it both aligned with and contradicted everything I'd been taught about God. It was as though Mom disregarded the parts of the Bible where it said God was to be feared and focused instead on the better aspects of God's nature and not His wrath. It felt dangerous to cherry-pick faith. The whole Bible was the Word of God, not only the loving parts. All of it demanded belief. Mom had never read the whole Bible, but I had, and I knew better.

I put off calling Luke for days. I told myself I couldn't find the right time, the right words. I was so afraid of hurting him, or possibly even angering him. Sick to my stomach one night, I finally dialed his number. Luke knew right away that something was off.

"What's up?" he asked when I took too long to say anything. "Are you okay?"

"No, actually," I said. "But I need to talk with you about it in person."

I had decided Luke deserved that much. I knew his heart would be broken. I might not have loved him, but I did believe he loved me.

Luke and I made plans to meet at a public park the following Sunday. I didn't see his car when I pulled up. There were no benches, so I sat in the shade of a tree and waited. I felt nauseous. My jaw ached from grinding my teeth, and tree bark jabbed into my bare shoulder blades. I'd worn a lime green halter top that day. Sitting there, I couldn't think why. It seemed inappropriate. Deliberate, even, though I wasn't aware of what my subconscious was trying to prove. Maybe I wanted Luke to see I wasn't sad. Maybe I wanted to flaunt my figure to hurt him, to make him see what would never be his now. But that would mean I was angry with him. I wasn't angry. Was I? I felt sad for Luke. I felt afraid of him, not because I feared he'd physically harm me, but because I feared I could be trapped by his words once more. I was scared that I wasn't strong enough, that I'd cower to what he perceived as God's will even though I wasn't so sure anymore. But was I angry? I didn't think so.

Luke's car made a U-turn in front of me. His eyes locked on mine through the windshield, but he didn't smile. I watched him park, then I stood to greet him with a hug. It felt forced on both our ends.

"Hey," he said.

"Hey," I said.

We sat down on the grass and I pulled my knees to my chest. Neither of us said anything for a moment. I knew he was waiting for me to go first, to say whatever it was I'd asked him to meet me for. Terror left me paralyzed.

"So, what was it you wanted to tell me?" Luke asked.

I would never be able to recall what I said to Luke that day. It was as though my mind blanked, the way I would later learn the minds of trauma victims sometimes did. In that moment, I wasn't just ending my betrothal. I was telling Satan he could have me. It didn't matter what my mother said, or what my heart wanted to believe about God to be true. Too many years of fear-driven programming had convinced me that when we disobeyed God, we stepped outside the umbrella of His protection. What I do remember is that I was shaking. I heard myself at one point, telling Luke never to call me, never to email me, never to contact me in any way again, ever. The anger I didn't know I'd been hiding demanded that I sever our relationship completely. Luke must have said something. Whatever response he gave buried itself into the deepest recesses of my mind. Only an out-of-focus snapshot appears when I try to summon his reaction, his eyes, green and pained. I don't remember how we said goodbye.

~

My faith fell into a crisis. In the year following my breakup with Luke, I waited for God's punishment as though waiting for a death threat to be followed through. It could come at any moment. Maybe an earthquake would swallow me whole in my sleep, or a car crash would leave me disfigured. Maybe God's consequences would come in the form of a life-threatening illness, or, once I did eventually marry, I would discover I was infertile, because I hadn't married the man God wanted me to. I lost sleep imagining all the ways God might allow Satan to destroy me. When weeks passed and bad things didn't happen, I figured Satan was only biding his time.

God, Satan. Satan, God. They were becoming one and the same. If God knew all and created all, and He created Satan knowingly, who was the true evil one? The thought terrified me, yet I couldn't shake it as I imagined Satan's presence lurking in every shadow. God's omniscience meant He knew what He was doing when He created the angel that would become the devil. God knew we would use our free will to disobey Him, and He chose to make us anyway. I didn't know how to reconcile the unspeakable epiphanies that came to my mind unbidden. They made God seem cruel, like He'd given us the illusion of free will just to watch us use it to disobey Him and suffer the consequences. I told myself that perhaps my doubts about His goodness were the very attack from Satan I so feared. I struggled to shake them. Whenever I turned to my Bible hoping to find answers, I only found more questions.

I couldn't remember a time I had ever gone against God's will so deliberately. My disobedience wasn't a simpler sin, like a lustful thought affecting nobody but myself. Refusing God's marital plan for my life meant I had gone against His plan for Luke's life. That made my fear of divine consequences doubly greater. I felt frightened of and furious with God, and because I was too scared to let myself feel either, I simply cried and cried in wordless fear, rocking myself to sleep. My days blurred together, fragmented by crippling bouts of anxiety. I forgot where I was going when I drove. I alternated between binge eating and self-starvation. I drew violent self-portraits. Whenever I saw a tall, light-haired man, I startled, crouching in my seat and ducking behind buildings as I begged him not to be Luke. I knew Luke wouldn't hurt me. God-Satan would.

This intense period of fear scarred me in ways that would have long-lasting ramifications. I never told others how much daily terror I lived in—chronic fear of invisible forces sounded mentally ill. It was. Slowly, my faith began to unravel, and I spiraled recklessly out of control.

PART IV

But I am afraid that just as Eve
was deceived by the serpent's cunning,
so your minds may somehow be led astray
from your sincere and pure devotion to Christ.
2 Corinthians 11:3

But that's no life for you . . . Get rid of it!
And then take on an entirely new way of life.
Ephesians 4:22–24

23

A New Kind of Faith

I took off my shirt. I stood naked except for a black lace thong and jewelry made of bones and feathers. My hair fell long and oiled down my back, and the white of my breasts gleamed against my tan lines in the dark blue light. A makeup artist rubbed her palms together and smoothed a shimmery lotion over my skin as though anointing me. She began at my collarbones, her artful fingers knowing exactly where to highlight. Slowly her hands worked their way down, touching places no one else had seen since I was a child. I kept thinking I should have been self-conscious. I wasn't.

"We're ready for Alice now!"

The production assistant had to shout above the techno music pulsing through the hangar studio. I watched as another model walked off the backdrop curving from the ceiling to the floor. She was topless, too. Several of us had been chosen for an editorial spread in a photography magazine called *Vellum*. It was the first job I'd booked through my new modeling agency, the start of a lucrative side-career to supplement my income between acting jobs. Nearly a year had passed since I ended my betrothal to Luke, and in an act of defiance toward God and the purity culture I'd been raised in, I had accepted the offer of a topless gig with barely a moment's hesitation.

The production assistant led me under blue lights to a spot marked with tape. "Stand here," he said. I aligned my stiletto-heeled toes with the white stripe, thinking of the prayer lines marked by tape in the back of churches I'd been to as a child.

"Gorgeous," said the photographer.

His gaze made me feel safe. His shutter started clicking. I felt a flickering of nervousness, then I took a breath and closed my eyes. When they opened, I made the deliberate decision to let my body move however I wanted.

My arms went up. My back arched. My hips curved. In slow motion, I danced through the fake moonlight as though I was the only person in the room. All I could see was the glint of the camera's lens, and all I could hear was bass vibrating off the walls and through my body. The moment felt raw. Tribal.

"That's it," said the photographer, his camera moving with me. "Now stare straight into the lens. Don't smile. Yes, that's it."

And then something happened. There, in the bluish-black light of the space, I felt overcome by a feeling I couldn't name, a sensation I had never felt. My mind shut down with the awakening of my senses, with the shimmering of my skin and the slipperiness of my hair, with the bold nakedness of my body. I felt beautiful. Vulnerable. Dangerous. Something in my spirit quaked, stirring from a place I had locked, a place I had forgotten existed. In that moment, I felt like divinity itself, woman in all her glory. Bare and fearless in front of everyone in the studio, I felt unleashed. Liberated. The feeling was overwhelming, as fierce as it was delicate, and wholly unrepentant. Then it came to me. I knew what it was I felt. I felt power. And what was power if not an opposite of shame?

I drove home that day exhilarated. My first topless photo shoot had a spiritual quality to it that I didn't understand at the time, a sacredness I never expected that left me tingling with awakening. Something felt different. I felt different. It was as though I had stumbled upon a rebirth, a transformation from a docile maiden to a sacred prostitute. Nothing could have prepared me for the potent medicine of rebellion, or for the healing power of my sensuality that every religion was threatened by. I had discovered something I wanted all women to feel. Freedom. Guiltlessness. Power. No one would take it away from me again. It was as though in that small, significant moment, I forgave myself for being female.

~

My relationship to God and to myself began to change. Simultaneously, my career began to flourish. It was a recurring role on a TV show called *Quintuplets* that led to my big break. Something about my performance in the family sitcom got me noticed by the network executives at FOX and they offered me a holding deal, a purchasing of my time and talent for their exclusive use for up to a year with the goal of putting me on one of their other shows as a series regular. They paid me $75,000. My manager was astounded, saying networks didn't even do things like that anymore. I took it as a sign from God that acting was still my calling, and after a year and a half of couch-surfing, house-sitting, and subletting rooms on a temporary basis, I decided to make L.A. my official residence. I splurged by moving into my very own one-bedroom apartment, a top floor unit in a 1930s four-plex at the base of the Hollywood Hills. Its hardwood floors gleamed when sunlight poured through the floor-to-ceiling windows, and the walls of the bathroom glinted with pink and white Art Deco tiles. I felt like I had finally found a home worthy of replacing the beloved Victorian of my childhood, like God had finally given me a string of pearls in exchange for my plastic beads. My holding deal with FOX resulted in landing me a TV pilot called *Windfall*. The drama about a group of friends winning the lottery went on to be picked up by NBC, and I spent 2005–2006 filming my first show as a series regular, booking more roles in films and other TV shows soon after. Throughout it all, my walk with God evolved.

Ending my betrothal to Luke had also ended my relationship with evangelical Christianity. I had never considered myself evangelical, since my parents remained staunchly nondenominational and I had always attended nondenominational fellowships; but evangelical, I learned, was what the media called our brand of nondenominationalism. Evangelical Christianity thrived on spiritual warfare and sexual purity. It preached free will yet voted pro-life, taught acceptance and rejected the unacceptable. It denied it was legalistic, yet made its rules unquestionably clear, and those who pointed out any inconsistencies were gaslit into believing Satan was either infecting their mind with doubt or they were simply interpreting things incorrectly—and most likely because there was sin in their life. I no longer wanted to practice that kind of Christianity. I was still too afraid of hell to imagine leaving my religion altogether, but if I were to remain a Christian, I knew I needed to reconnect with God on my own terms. It was time for a new kind of faith.

Books played a significant role in my spiritual evolution. One of my favorites was *The Kingdom of God Is Like . . .* by Father Thomas Keating, a monk who took familiar parables in the Bible and presented them with interpretations I'd never heard. Father Keating's version of Jesus was a merciful one. I'd always known Jesus was supposed to be merciful, but I realized my prior teachings of Christ were centered less on His actual words and more on the legacy He'd left behind. My youth groups had focused mainly on the books of the Bible written by the apostle Paul, the ones instructing Christians on how to live. I wondered why my experiences in evangelical Christianity seemed to emphasize living more by Paul's decrees than the words of Christ Himself. Some of Jesus' words still troubled me, especially when He talked about hell, but I allowed myself to become one of the cherry-picking Christians I used to judge. The more I thought about it, the less comfortable I felt even calling myself a Christian. I still believed Jesus was the Son of God, the way, the truth, and the life and all that, but saying I was a Christian felt like saying I was proud to be lumped in with the evangelicals on the news who were picketing the funerals of soldiers with signs that read, "God hates fags." I didn't think Jesus would have done anything like that. I stopped calling myself a Christian and began considering myself a follower-of-Christ.

Another book I purchased was a version of the Bible called *The Message: The Bible in Contemporary Language* by Eugene H. Peterson. Some Christians thought it controversial for its casual, less-holy sounding verbiage. I found it softened my understanding of God's Word. The verses of Ecclesiastes in particular became ones I meditated on during my morning hikes through the hills of Runyon Canyon. The Old Testament book chronicled one man's quest to find the meaning of life, which he deduced was meaningless. "Nothing but smoke—and spitting into the wind." No matter how hard we worked, or how diligently we tried to live from a place of wisdom, we would end up dead just as fools. Therefore, the author of Ecclesiastes said, "The best you can do with your life is have a good time and get by the best you can. The way I see it, that's it—divine fate."

It seemed too good to be true, but I verified Ecclesiastes 2:24 in my New International Version of the Bible. "A person can do nothing better than to eat and drink and find satisfaction in their own toil. This too, I see, is from the hand of God."

Have a good time, God seemed to be saying to me. *Enjoy the life I've given you.*

The book of Ecclesiastes seemed so unorthodox compared to the rest of the Bible. It bordered on dangerous, yet God included it in His Holy Word. If He allowed me to rediscover its verses when I did, maybe it meant He was beckoning me to know a different part of Him, a side that was far more lenient than the Gospels of Jesus' disciples and the strict epistles of Paul. Slowly, as the weeks of my twentieth summer passed, my trust in God began to rebuild. Slowly, my lifestyle started reflecting my broadening faith. I decided to live like the author of Ecclesiastes for a while and deny myself nothing. When I wanted to dance, I let my friends take me to a nightclub. When I wanted lingerie that made me feel fancy, I allowed myself to buy the matching bra and panty set from Victoria's Secret I had always dreamed of. When I wanted to take a puff of marijuana, I let myself, and I discovered what it felt like to exist without anxiety for the first time in my young adult life. Soon, there was only one thing I wanted that I continued to deny myself. I wanted to have sex.

~

The candles were lit. The strums of a gypsy guitar played through my speakers. My kitchen smelled of chocolate and cinnamon, and the night-time fog caressing the Hollywood Hills brought cool air through the screened windows, relieving the day of its heat. The evening couldn't have been more sensuous. I sat on the red silk cushion of my built-in dining booth, breaking open a hunk of homemade bread and watching the steam plume out.

"How was your day?" I asked, reaching for the butter.

He didn't answer.

"Mine was okay," I continued. "I went hiking in the morning."

Only the strains of Django Reinhardt replied to me, cascading their condolence for the silence of the guest at my table.

"I was thinking maybe we'd watch a movie tonight," I said. "I got *Dirty Pretty Things*. Does that sound okay?"

The reassurance I wanted didn't come.

"Or we could watch something else."

I took a bite of my bread and chewed it in silence. The butter knife opposite me remained unused. I wanted him to say something. Anything.

"I wish you could touch me," I whispered.

Tears sprang to my eyes. Embarrassment flushed over my shoulders. The empty space across from me mocked my loneliness. If Jesus was there, He must have been answering me in silence.

It wasn't an erotic fantasy I had about Jesus. It was simply the desire for His company to fill the aching void in my life. All of my friends were coupled up, and I was still saving myself for a man I wasn't sure I could wait for much longer. I kept telling myself that I was never alone because I had Jesus by my side. But Jesus couldn't cuddle me. He couldn't tell me about His day or ask me about mine. He couldn't share a laugh and a bowl of popcorn. I'd felt like a fool setting my table for two when I was the only person in my apartment, but I had hoped Jesus would reward my faith in His company by speaking to me in some way, offering me some small reassurance of His presence. I wiped my tears, imagining neighbors peeking through my windows at the pathetic scene in my dining nook. It looked as if I'd been stood up.

Loneliness wasn't the only thing plaguing me. While I tried to direct my longings for companionship toward Christ, I didn't know what to do when I felt overwhelmed by feelings of lust. I thought about sex all the time. I wanted it. I needed it. I craved it. I thought about it so much that I began to wonder if I was a sex addict in the waiting. Was it normal for a girl to think about sex as often as I did?

I had lost my guilt over masturbating. I couldn't say when exactly, or why, but the shame following orgasm that used to plague me as a teenager had gradually faded until I was convinced masturbation was, in fact, healthy. At least it kept me from crossing the line of actually having sex. Whenever I did feel pangs of guilt, I told myself that God was not a God of shame. He was a God of love and forgiveness. If I was imperfect no matter what I did or didn't do, and if, as Ecclesiastes said, it was all smoke and spitting into the wind anyway, there was no point in heaping shame on myself for a sin I had never been able to stop committing. At least my sin didn't harm anyone else.

I knew I walked a thin line between self-acceptance and taking advantage of God's grace. But my love for Him had only strengthened the more I embraced the sinful nature He allowed me to be born with. I found peace no longer trying so hard to be the perfect Christian girl I thought I had to be. God loved me unconditionally, I told myself, regardless of my actions. So, if I truly believed this, why wasn't I having sex?

It was the most forbidden of sins to me. Sex was the topic I had been most warned about in my youth, the act that seemed to symbolize the ultimate rejection of Christian teachings. Everything in my body told me I should be having sex. Everything in my mind warned against going down the path of no return. Virginity could only be lost once. Part of me wanted to remain a virgin if only to prove naysayers wrong, the ones who said I couldn't possibly wait for my future husband before succumbing to the natural desires of the body. The other part of me wanted to give in and enjoy what everyone else seemed to be enjoying. The concept of virginity as the measure of my worth began sounding even more demented than it had when I attended my first purity conference. Why was a girl's virginity the pinnacle of her purity? Why would God want me to only share my body with one man for all of my life? I had no answers to my questions.

I never consciously decided to lose my virginity. Breaking my vow should have been a bigger deal than it was, something I deliberated over long and hard before going through with it. I would never quite understand how a vow that had carried so much weight for so many years was so easy for me to undo.

～

He was the baddest boy I could have picked. I didn't know until it happened that I didn't want to lose my virginity to a guy I cared about, one who might break my heart and leave me feeling like I'd given him my everything. I had enough girlfriends who'd been through that grief. I chose a guy I felt certain I had no chance of developing real feelings for. He was brash and bold. He had a dancer's body and a reputation for being a player. He certainly wasn't a Christian. His name was James.

I didn't plan on having sex with James, but when the moment came, I went with it. We were friends who knew each other from an acting job, and when he asked if he could crash at my apartment late one night, for some reason, I said yes. When he nuzzled the back of my neck the following morning and crept his hands beneath my sheets, I didn't protest. James was the perfect candidate, I realized. I didn't tell him I was a virgin.

It didn't hurt. Neither did I bleed. I was self-educated enough to know that my lack of blood was normal, and I wondered at how differently I might feel about its absence had I waited until my wedding night. Would my husband have accused me of not waiting for him? I'd never know. I expected my first time to be at least uncomfortable, but to my surprise, it felt good. What surprised me more was how I felt after James left. I felt absolutely fine, as if nothing had happened at all.

The normalcy with which I resumed my day almost troubled me. I should be feeling massive amounts of guilt, I thought. I should be feeling regret, shame, and loss. Grief, for giving away something I could never get back. I ought to be feeling some supernatural connection to James now that he'd been inside me, or at least as though he'd taken a piece of my heart with him when he drove off. That was what all the Christian courtship books warned I'd feel if I gave myself away. I felt none of those. If I felt anything, it was a mild sense of relief. My virginity was gone. The embarrassment I felt over being the only person I knew who hadn't had sex would never have to be felt again. The final taboo had been crossed; my last act of freedom claimed. I smiled with comfortable amusement that, at last, something that had had so much build-up around it was finally done with.

Weeks passed. James and I continued sleeping together, and I continued feeling zero guilt about it. I also started hooking up with another guy. Nothing bad happened. Satan didn't smite me. I didn't break out in STDs or get pregnant. I didn't lose my self-esteem or develop a sex addiction. I wondered if God was saving His consequences for later, perhaps by making me unable to have orgasms with my husband when I did marry. I recognized that God as the God of my youth, the one to be feared and obeyed. The God I wanted to worship was a God of love and freedom. He didn't care if consenting adults enjoyed each other's bodies. I wasn't pledged to anyone else and I wasn't hurting anybody. I just liked having sex. Casual, meaningless sex.

When I eventually confessed to my non-Christian friends that I wasn't a virgin anymore, nothing could have prepared me for their reactions.

"I'm so glad to hear that," said my friend Andy. "Sex is a big part of being human, I think."

"Yes!" gasped my friend Doug. "Finally. I was worried about you."

My friend Lyndsy had smiled, saying, "I'm so glad we can talk about our sex lives now."

I didn't know why I feared my friends in L.A. would judge me—maybe because they might perceive me as someone who didn't have the backbone to stand by her beliefs, even if mine weren't beliefs they shared. But instead of condemnation, I found encouragement. Where I feared I'd lose respect, I gained support. I wasn't used to such acceptance.

My friend Johnny's reaction moved me the most. When I told him I'd been hooking up with our mutual friend James, his mouth dropped open in playful awe.

"It's like you're like a real person," he said.

I chuckled, uncertain what he meant. "How?" I asked.

"I always used to feel so bad around you."

"Why? Because I didn't have sex?"

"Because you were so good. Yeah, you didn't have sex, but you also didn't swear, you didn't drink, you didn't smoke. It made me feel horrible about myself sometimes. Like you must think I'm this terrible person."

His words broke my heart. Johnny was quick to clarify he still thought I was a good person. "You're just more relatable now," he said. "Like, there's still all the Alice-goodness, but without the side of you that was so strict."

"Did I ever say anything that made you feel judged?" I asked.

"No," he assured me. "It was never anything you said. It was more just in how you lived."

I was stunned. Youth pastors had told me to live a life worthy of imitation. They said that others would be drawn to my light, and that if my lifestyle reflected obedience to God, others would feel His love emanating through me. The opposite had happened. I didn't make people feel loved by holding myself to some standard of Christian purity written nearly 2,000 years ago. I had made them feel ashamed.

Part of me knew I wasn't to blame for however my friends felt around me. Yet it assured me that I was on the right path if embracing my humanness made people feel more loved than rejecting my humanness did. Johnny's words were echoed by other friends of mine. Most of them expressed that, at some point, they had felt a divide between us because of the way I lived out my faith. It amazed me how my simple act of having sex brought my friendships closer in ways abiding by Christian teachings never could. I had always been told that love was God and God was love. What I experienced was that love was found in humanity.

It was love that changed my faith the most. Real, human love. With the exception of my family, I never felt more loved than by people who weren't Christians. I didn't know what to make of this unexpected grace. The paradox of moving further away from Christ to become more Christlike baffled me, yet it was my truth. Slowly walking away from Christianity allowed me to discover in myself the Christian traits I'd worked so hard to cultivate throughout my teen years, traits like humility, honesty, and compassion. By having sex, I hadn't only broken the last of my fear-driven shackles. I had joined my fellow humans. I had removed myself from the pedestal of purity and immersed myself in the messy, broken, beautiful world of my peers.

The concept of hell began to trouble me in ways it never had. What was this place Jesus sent people to who didn't believe in Him? How could sweet Lyndsy, who was Jewish, burn for eternity, or Johnny, a kind-hearted Scientologist, be damned to everlasting torture? How could Markus, openly gay and deeply spiritual, or Doug and Andy, two of the most accepting people I knew, be cast into a blazing furnace with weeping and the gnashing of teeth? As I pondered how kind my friends were, and how dear they'd become to me, I realized I couldn't picture any of them ending up in hell. It felt wrong to imagine, cruel even. There was too much goodness in them. Yet Jesus Himself said hell was real and that He would cast everyone who didn't accept Him as their Savior into a lake of fire on Judgment Day. It frightened me to realize that I could no longer find the love in my beliefs. I didn't know what do with the implications of this realization. So, I did my best to simply ignore it.

~

For all of my efforts to lose my virginity to a man I thought I had no chance of developing feelings for, James and I began dating shortly before my twenty-first birthday. The hazel-eyed dancer had been slowly stealing my heart for six months before we made our relationship official. His brutal honesty made me feel safe, his flippant sense of humor made me laugh, and his goofy handsomeness reminded me of a young Jim Carrey. James was five years older than me and brilliantly smart. He had a genius-level IQ and could debate viciously, and I enjoyed the intellectual challenge. Irreverent and combative, charming and oh so sure of himself, James was the total opposite of everything I was supposed to want in a man. Maybe that was why the rebel lurking in my heart eventually fell for him. His thoughtfulness made me feel guilty for writing him off as the kind of guy I could never fall in love with. I had judged James as a bad boy, and I thought I would only ever date good guys. But with good guys, I'd learned, bad things lurked beneath a chivalrous surface. With bad boys, there were only good things left to discover. I couldn't be disappointed by what was shown to me up front.

James and I had been officially together for a couple of months when he said something that offended me for reasons I didn't immediately understand.

"I've always dated sweet girls," James said as we drove to an awards ceremony.

I glanced at him from the passenger seat.

"Girls like you," he continued. "Girls who are sweet, kind, giving. My mom and sisters always said I should date a Christian girl, because she'll be looking to God to fill her needs instead of me."

While I knew James meant to be complimentary, his words struck a nerve. James wasn't a Christian himself, though he'd been raised by church-going parents in the Bible Belt. One of the things we'd bonded over was our disturbed nostalgia for children's worship songs. What bothered me about James's statement was threefold: that he'd called me sweet, which I felt meant boring; that he seemed to be implying he wouldn't be there for me if I needed him; and that he thought of me as a Christian girl.

"You know," I said, smoothing the hem of my cocktail dress. "I don't really consider myself a Christian anymore."

James looked sideways at me. "What? I thought you were all Father-God and all that."

"I am," I said, struggling to express my changing views out loud. "I was. But I find the more I know about Christianity and Christians, the less I feel like being identified with them."

I couldn't tell if James was turned on or disappointed. I got the feeling he thought of faith as a crutch for the stupid, yet it was also the crutch that might keep him in the clear of winding up with a needy girlfriend.

"So you're not a Christian anymore?" he asked me.

"No," I said. "I don't think I am. I still believe in God, but I haven't said I'm a Christian for a while now."

"Why do you still believe in God?"

His words stumped me. "I don't know," I said. "I just do."

I fell silent. Something about the starkness of James's question elicited an equally stark response from within me. Why _did_ I still believe in God? That I couldn't think of a single answer horrified me. Where was my faith? Had it suddenly vanished in the blink of an eye? I tried to ignore my growing anxiety as James and I arrived at the event. My smile felt stiff as I walked the red carpet, hoping the flash of cameras wouldn't reveal my inner turmoil. Surely I was only having a moment of doubt, a panicked floundering from being put on the spot. I absolutely believed in God. Didn't I? I fought the possibility of the alternative. It was too frightening for me to consider.

In all of the spiritual questing I'd done, asking myself whether I still believed in God had never come up. I must have always assumed that I did. The God I believed in was different from the one I had tried to obey growing up, but it was still a God I worshipped and whose exis-tence I didn't question. It was still the God of the Bible, albeit more the

Ecclesiastes version and less the apostle Paul's. I knew my beliefs had been changing, but they couldn't have changed that much.

I flashed the paparazzi my fakest smile.

24

The Test

James's question burned a hole in my heart. Why did I still believe in God? The more I thought about it, the more I struggled to find an answer. Any answer.

I told myself I believed in God because I couldn't explain the existence of the universe any other way. It felt trite as soon as I thought it. There were probably a million different theories of how the universe came to exist that had nothing to do with faith. I told myself I believed in God because hadn't He provided for my family all those years that my parents were unemployed? That answer, too, was inadequate, ripped apart the more I acknowledged human kindness. God had not taken care of us when we were homeless and broke. It had been the generosity of people that sustained my family. They could call it God moving through them or putting it on their hearts or whatever. I thought it was their own compassion that had led them to give us money, or a place to sleep and shower for a few days, or a few weeks, or even months. It had been nothing more than the innate goodness of people that compelled them to leave groceries on our steps or anonymous envelopes of cash taped to our trailer door or shopping sprees to outfit my siblings and me when we outgrew our clothes. I thought of the time when one of Mom's sisters, my Auntie Gail, gave me a brand-new pea coat from The Gap when I was twelve.

"That's so awesome!" I'd exclaimed, trying it on and modeling it for her. "God knew I wanted this pea coat when I saw it at the mall the other day, and He provided it for me through you!"

I gave Auntie Gail a hug. She squeezed me back, but when she pulled away, she'd held my hands tightly.

"Alice," she said, her eyes commanding mine. "I gave you this coat. Not God."

The seriousness in her voice sobered my excitement. I knew my aunt wasn't a Christian—no one on Mom's side of the family was—but I was so used to praising God for the things I believed He gave me through other people that I didn't realize how my words might have hurt my aunt's feelings. My faith had diminished mere human generosity when I failed to thank the people who had given to me from the kindness of their hearts, and not from the faith their humility compelled them to hide behind.

So why did I believe in God? Why did I even want to? Why was I standing up for God when God had never stood up for me? It was humans who had stood up for me. Humans who had housed me when I needed shelter, humans who had fed me when I was hungry. Humans who had clothed me, loved me, and comforted me. The only thing God had ever given me was silence.

I was reminded of God's silence when James and I hung out one morning in early summer. We were snuggling in his bed when he put on a documentary he'd been wanting to see. It was called *Jesus Camp*. I watched, my heart up to my throat, as a children's pastor named Becky Fischer led a group of children in prayer. They echoed her chants, voicing their willingness to obey God, to do what He wanted them to do and say what He wanted them to say. When the pastor concluded, a large crowd of kids stood in the church auditorium with their eyes closed and arms outstretched, rocking side to side the way I used to when I mimicked how I'd seen adults pray.

"If you don't open your mouth," Becky Fischer went on, "the Holy Spirit can't talk. Now I want everybody to raise your hands and we're gonna pray in tongues! Hallelujah, let's do it! Oh we love you, Jesus, okoho rashadeh kahah . . ."

An icy hot pain crept through my chest. Images of little boys and girls no older than ten or eleven filled the screen. They cried, shouting out to God as the hands of grown-ups pressed against their foreheads. I wanted to smash the television.

"I can't take this," I said.

James looked at me quizzically. We weren't even ten minutes into the film.

"I can't watch this," I said, struggling to hide my shaking hands. "I'm sorry."

I grabbed the remote from him and powered off the TV. My breath came in shallow, uneven huffs. My eyes blinked back tears.

"You okay?" asked James.

I nodded, even though I wasn't. James didn't know what to do. I didn't know what to say. I wanted to tell James there were too many flashbacks assaulting my memory. I wanted to tell him that Becky Fischer reminded me of every pastor I knew as a child, and that I used to fake praying in tongues to make adults like her leave me alone. I wanted to tell James about the boiling hatred toward every children's pastor that had ever existed that suddenly seized me. Instead I sat on his bed in silence until I decided to go home.

I couldn't tell James the extent of my childhood baggage that day because I didn't want to acknowledge it myself. It was too confusing. Too painful. If I had kept watching *Jesus Camp*, I would have felt a solidarity with the homeschooled kids whose science books taught them Creationism. I would have empathized with the young girl who felt called to be an evangelist. I would have recognized Lou Engle, the pastor who had visited my youth group in Kansas City and invited us to TheCall in Washington, DC. I would have scanned for my face in the crowd he spoke to, relieved not to see myself on-screen among the modestly dressed teens. Watching echoes of my childhood from a film's distance would have allowed me to see how indoctrinated I was, allowing me to weep with validation and catharsis. I wouldn't finish watching *Jesus Camp* until years later.

I wanted to block out the memories that flooded me in the weeks after I left James's apartment. I couldn't get the images from the documentary out of my head. They brought back all the pain of being rejected by God, all the times I'd begged Him to slay me with the Spirit and He hadn't, all the times I'd faked praying in tongues and the shame I'd heaped on myself afterward, and all the times I'd thrown myself to the floor in an effort to escape the hands of adults who wouldn't go away until I fell. I thought I'd made peace with the fact that God had never touched me. It was only a lie I had grown accustomed to in order to replace the pain of feeling unloved.

How many other children were out there pretending to feel God's love? How many of them were faking manifestations of the Holy Spirit because they could no longer endure being told there was a sin in their life that left them unworthy of truly experiencing God? How many others were feeling left out? Alone? Ignored? Abandoned? If God loved me, why had He never touched me? Why wasn't I worth it? How could I still, after all this time, believe in a God who had never believed in me?

My anger would not be ignored. My pain would not be suppressed. An urgency that would not be quieted kept me awake at night, clenching my jaw and thrashing my sheets. I wanted answers. I needed them. The doubts I'd so skillfully pushed aside ever since I was a child would be smothered no more. I needed to know if God was real. There was too much at stake. My entire life had revolved around what I believed God wanted, and what if it was all for nothing? What if God wasn't even there?

A solution wavered in the corners of my mind begging to come forward. I could hardly consider it. Every trained voice in my head warned I would be committing a cardinal sin if I tested God. I didn't know what else to do.

~

It was a hot September afternoon when I realized I couldn't wait any longer. There was nothing in particular that happened that day. I was washing dishes at my kitchen sink, my growing doubts about God's existence gnawing at me like an infected wound, and I simply couldn't wonder one moment more. I set down the kitchen sponge and turned off the faucet. Fear made my mouth dry. I didn't know if I was more afraid that God wouldn't be real or that He would be. The mental reflexes I'd spent a lifetime honing screamed at me to stop, to turn back in faith before I risked losing it forever. Deuteronomy 6:16 warned, "Do not put the Lord your God to the test." If God was real, surely He would allow punishment for my faithlessness. I tried to tell myself He would understand—God had to understand that I tested Him not because I didn't want to believe in Him, but because I wanted to believe so badly. The meaning of my life depended on it. I couldn't begin to imagine what the point of living was without God. I stared out my open window as sunlight gleamed off treetops. I felt the urge to hesitate, to make more of a ceremony out of my test. Something as momentous as this deserved some sort of formality. But why?

I didn't have a plan. All I knew was that I had to be specific about how I needed God to show me He was real. I didn't want to suddenly hear a bird coo and be tempted to think it was Him answering me through one of the doves inhabiting my neighbors' roof. Neither did I have the faith to think God would answer me with an audible voice. I couldn't let God decide how He would prove His existence to me, it had to be something I decided. If God was capable of anything, truly all-powerful and omnipotent, and if He truly loved me and wanted me to believe in Him, He would understand and answer any test I set up. It had to be something concrete. Something obvious. Something that left me no way of fooling myself. If God was real, I never wanted to doubt Him again.

I glanced at the spice rack built into the wall on my right. The small cabinet door was open, displaying shelves of dried herbs, ground seeds, and flavored extracts. I knew then what my test had to be. It was arbitrary and physically impossible enough for me to be convinced of God's existence if He passed it. I gripped the edge of the sink.

"If you're real, God," I said. "Knock that jar of cinnamon off the spice rack."

My eyes grew dry without blinking. The jar of cinnamon didn't budge. A silent scream rose within me, pleading for acknowledgment. I told God it was okay if He knocked off another spice instead—cumin, nutmeg, anything. If He'd parted seas and turned people into pillars of salt to make His existence known before, surely He'd trouble Himself to bring back a prodigal daughter by doing something as simple as knocking over a plastic cylinder. I begged. I cried. Every jar remained still and upright.

I stared at my spice cabinet for over thirty minutes. I knew because the clock on my microwave told me. The understanding sank in slowly. God wasn't real. My faith was over. I could hardly imagine what that meant. In that moment, standing there on my kitchen mat only a few feet away from the jar of cinnamon that had unwittingly stolen the very meaning from my life, I didn't know how I felt. Somewhere between stupefied and betrayed, between relieved and heartbroken. Was that really it? I wondered. How quickly it had all ended, something that had taken me a lifetime to cultivate. A lifetime wasted, I realized. How many times had I beaten myself up with shame for being rejected by someone who was never there? How many opportunities for love had I missed? For friendship, for joy, for pleasure, for peace?

A calm numbness settled over me. There was no cry that could escape my lips, no tear that could offer relief. There was nothing. So nothing was what I felt.

The next couple of days passed in muffled serenity, as though walking through a reality I was completely removed from. I felt no emotion. Sometimes I wondered why. Unable to feel troubled, I simply observed my thoughts from the safety of a detachment I didn't know I was experiencing.

It was an audition that shattered my calm. I was driving to the casting office running lines in my head. Satisfied I had the scene memorized, I began to pray out of habit.

"Please let me do well on this audition," I said under my breath. "I've always wanted to do a movie like this. If it's not your will I book it, I know you'll have something better for me, but—"

My breath stopped as though guillotined. My mouth hung open mid-sentence, and my eyes widened in shock. There was no one listening. God wasn't there. I was only talking out loud, the way a child would to an imaginary friend. God didn't care whether or not I booked that audition. There was no being who looked out for my financial security or cared about the desires of my heart. I was alone.

It felt as though my soul had slipped on ice and found itself falling, falling, falling. Like someone had yanked a rug out from under me, only there was no floor to land on, just spiraling free fall. My heavenly father had died.

~

That afternoon in my car wasn't the only time I caught myself praying. Over the next several days, I froze each time words formed in my mouth that were meant for God. It felt like a slap every time I remembered no one was listening. No one ever had been. I was stripped of all comfort, all safety, and all understanding. No one loved me unconditionally. There were no angels guarding me from harm. There was no reason for why bad things happened. I felt four years old again. If there was no God, what created the universe? What happened when we died? How did you know what to do without God to guide you? I had been told for twenty-one years that the purpose of my life was to glorify God. If he didn't exist, why did I? Why did anything?

I cried tearlessly. I felt too spooked to allow my vision to blur. My senses became acute, as though I needed to learn how to survive for the first time. My ears picked up sounds I'd never noticed. My eyes saw danger everywhere, the way the eyes of a new parent scanned every setting for opportunities for death. I took no joy in eating. The act of putting food into my mouth just for it to become garbage seemed stupid. Everything seemed absurdly stupid. My sense of smell was the only faculty that didn't seem affected, and at night, the familiar scent of orange blossoms wafting through my bedroom window soothed me. The smell of my neighbor's morning coffee made daylight seem normal. Even the fumes of L.A. smog were a comforting reminder that although everything in my life seemed different, the world was still the same.

I didn't tell anyone that I suddenly stopped believing in God. Not my family, my friends, or even James. I knew it would only bring up questions I didn't want to answer, like why hadn't I thought of giving God a test sooner? Why had I chosen the test that I did? What would my parents say? When would I tell them? What did I think my life's purpose was now? I didn't have answers to these questions. I hadn't liked talking about my faith when I was a Christian and I didn't want to talk about my non-faith now that I wasn't. I told myself it was nobody's business.

In truth, I was too afraid. The world no longer looked the same to me and I was insecure about my place in it. Being answerless to important questions made me feel like I had no footholds in life, like I was falling into a void I didn't know I could find my way out of. Talking about how my faith had come to an end might leave me vulnerable to unkind remarks I wasn't strong enough to bear yet. It might expose me to ridicule in support of or against my decision. It might make me second-guess myself. It also would prompt a more thorough retelling of my childhood.

My friends knew I'd moved around a lot as a kid. They knew I'd been homeschooled and sheltered from most of American pop culture. My friends did not know about the more traumatic experiences of my past. They didn't know about the pastor who pushed me on a flight of stairs, or about the time my mission trip leaders staged a mock persecution at gunpoint. Few knew about the betrothal I'd broken off, and I had never told anyone about the terror I'd experienced afterward for disobeying God. I didn't like to talk about these things for the same reason I hadn't been able to finish watching *Jesus Camp*. I didn't want to remember the confusion and pain that had been the majority of my faith. I didn't want to remember how rejected I felt by God when he touched everyone but me, or how devastated and angry I felt every time my parents told me God said we had to move again. I didn't want to have to explain why my parents had chosen the life they did. I didn't fully know myself, except to acknowledge they were following their hearts. It wasn't that I wanted to keep my past a secret. I just wasn't ready to face it. I wanted to move on, to put faith as far behind me as I could.

Deciding not to tell anyone about my deconversion wasn't only because I wanted to avoid painful memories. In the more honest parts of my heart, the parts I kept hidden even from myself, I also wanted to avoid shame. Only once I left Christianity did I fully see how unkind it had made me. I felt embarrassed for the times my faith made others feel judged, like the time I asked friends to turn off a radio song they loved because it fueled lust. I cringed at how self-righteous I must have sounded when I told people I didn't smoke, drink, or have sex. The inaccurate things I'd proclaimed, like saying the world was only 6,000 years old and being gay was a sin, made me want to go back in time and gag myself. I was mortified by some of the things I'd believed, things I'd professed to other people in the name of love but had really been in ignorance. I didn't want my friends to know I'd prayed in our nation's capital for George Bush to win the 2000 election so America could be brought back to God. I didn't want anyone to know I'd once aspired to be a missionary, to have the gall to tell people their faith was wrong and mine was the only one that was right. I wanted to cry whenever I remembered how prejudiced I was, overwhelmed by how much programming needed to be undone. I was grateful to feel remorse for the ways my former faith had harmed others, and myself, but I didn't want to feel shame. Shame was in my past. It was a state of being I wanted to have no place in my new life.

~

Freedom.

That was what I began to feel after my first week without God. Abruptly, my grief gave way to a lightness I'd never known. If God wasn't real, neither was Satan. If Jesus wasn't real, neither was hell. I realized I was free from rules. Free from guilt for breaking the rules. Free from the agony of never being certain what the rules were. I was free from fear and free from submission. Free from worrying whether I was obeying God enough and free from the anxiety of committing sins I wasn't even conscious of. I was free to be myself, in whatever ways felt most true.

Weeks passed. Freedom kept rushing at me like an unstoppable wind. I walked into a Barnes & Noble elated that I could read a book from any section in the store. I turned on the radio and guiltlessly sang along to lyrics that glorified the human body. I shopped on Melrose Avenue and purchased every piece of clothing I wanted without justifying its skimpiness as useful for a prostitute audition God might bring my way. I no longer had to justify these things. I could simply do them if I wanted to, as much as I wanted to, and in whatever form they took.

The only time I wavered in relishing my newfound freedom was when it came to sex. I didn't tell James about the intense bouts of fear I sometimes experienced after we slept together. There were moments after he left my apartment or I left his that I panicked, afraid maybe God was real, and I'd burn in hell for forsaking him and becoming a fornicator. In an irony lost to me at the time, I could only calm down by reading my Bible. I read it to remind myself its authors never fully explained what fornication was. Most Biblical scholars thought the word *fornicate* was translated from the Greek word *porneia*, which some said meant harlotry and others said meant incest. For every definition I found, a new definition was needed. If one online article claimed the apostle Paul was talking about sexual immorality when he wrote about fornication, I had to look up sexual immorality, which led to adultery, which led to illicit intercourse, which led to sexual impurity, which led back to fornication. All of the terms were frustratingly vague.

I couldn't find a single verse in the Bible where Jesus said in explicit terms that an unmarried man and an unmarried woman were forbidden from having consensual sex with each other. Almost everything in the New Testament on the topic of sexual purity had been written by the apostle Paul. He was also the one who wrote that women should be quiet, dress modestly, and never instruct men. Jesus never personally said anything about premarital sex. He spoke against lust, infamously saying we were to gouge out our eyes and chop off our hands if they caused us to lust, but Jesus didn't specify if we were to self-mutilate when we lusted over our spouses or only if we lusted over those we weren't married to. Surely he didn't mean for humans to stop procreating. Although I didn't believe in Jesus anymore, rereading what little he had to say about sex brought me peace.

Another epiphany of freedom came when I realized I didn't have to get married. I didn't even have to have children. I could still do those things if I wanted to, but the looming obligation of committing my life to one man and producing his offspring fell from my sense of purpose like shackles. Christianity taught me that my role as a woman was to be a helpmate to a man, to give him sole custody of my sexuality, and produce his heirs for the glory of God. I no longer had to abide by the curse of Eve. The impact of the realization was so meaningful to me that it became the last time I ever wrote about God in my journal.

I don't know if I want to get married, I wrote. *I don't like a lot of the associations attached to the word "married" or "marriage," or "husband" or "wife." There's a lot of obligation attached with those words, and it's not all pleasant. When I hear "husband," in my head I see someone who's bored. When I hear "wife," I think of myself as being submissive and really good at housework and babies. I feel like this whole marriage thing is related to my changing views on God. The word God has some negative associations with it. To me, it's contaminated.*

With that, God vanished from the entries of my journal without so much as a postscript.

25

Aftermath

I celebrated my first Halloween that October. My parents had never let my siblings and me celebrate Halloween, taking us instead to church Harvest Parties and Neewollah's, which was Halloween spelled backward. None of the Halloween-alternative parties I'd gone to would have allowed me through the church door in my Nancy Callahan costume. The proverbial stripper with a heart of gold from the film *Sin City* wore black chaps, a push-up bra, and a bandolier of bullets across her chest in her sexiest dance scene. I didn't have Jessica Alba's curves, and my waist-length hair was dark brown instead of blond, but my skintight leather chaps showed off my ass like I'd never seen it before. I stared at my reflection in the mirror of my bedroom, remembering reading somewhere that Jessica Alba had been accused by her youth pastor of being too distracting to her brothers in Christ. She'd left the church because of it. I wondered if I would ever get to meet her and discuss what we might have in common.

My friends Johnny and Brian had invited me to their joint house party. They lived with several other guys in two old houses side-by-side on Wilton Place, and collectively the homes were called the Wilton Hilton, an in-the-know party spot for the burgeoning stars of young Hollywood.

Amanda Seyfried, Evan Peters, and Brittany Snow all came through the Wilton Hilton's heavy oak doors. The cast of *The O.C.* made headlines for pranking the Wilton Hilton's rooftops with a covering of toilet paper. Katy Perry was dating my friend Johnny. The singer wasn't famous yet, but the tremulous rasp of her voice stopped everybody's conversations when she sang at the open mic gatherings called Acoustic Night. Friends said Katy and I were raised very similarly—pastors' daughters who grew up in evangelical-leaning churches. I sometimes longed to talk with her about it, lonely for someone who understood the world I came from, but my reluctance to divulge the crises of my faith inhibited me from asking Katy about hers. I also felt gripped by shyness whenever I went to the Wilton Hilton. It was like being in a fantasy come true. The group of friends I'd once yearned for, the ones I'd imagined laughing and flirting with over pizza and music, had materialized in my life with the gloss of celebrity. I felt like an imposter at every one of their parties. I still hadn't gotten used to the sheer secularity of the Wilton Hilton's hedonism.

My boyfriend James must have had to work that Halloween, because I went to the party without him. Adrenaline raced through me as I walked up the pathway to Johnny's house. The cold night air seeped through my black lace panties, reminding me of how much skin my outfit revealed. I thought about going back home then rebelled against the thought. I deserved this night. A zombie bride answered my knock, throwing open the front door with a gravelly, "Welcome!" Her fake wounds glistened with gruesome realism, indicating she was probably friends with a talented makeup artist. I stepped into the grand foyer of the cobweb-strewn house. Two Obi-Wan Kenobis clashed lasers in the dining room, and a couple dressed as Mr. & Mrs. Smith made out against the stairway banister. I found my friend Brian in the crowded kitchen. His mouth fell open when he saw me.

"You look so hot!" he said.

I laughed and gave him a hug.

"What do you want to drink?" he asked.

"Do you have OJ and rum?" I asked.

Brian pointed with both hands to the abundance of beverages covering the counter. I downed a cocktail with him there in the kitchen, then found myself finishing another. I did a shot of tequila with everybody and accepted yet another glass of something, gulping my drinks too quickly to feel their effects. I rarely drank alcohol. I didn't like the taste or the sadness it put me in touch with whenever I had more than a few sips. Maybe it was the high of celebrating my first Halloween, or maybe I wanted to relieve the social anxiety urging me to run and hide in the bathroom. I don't know why I decided to get drunk that night.

I didn't realize how dizzy I was until I found myself leaning against Elijah Wood's deejay booth. Brian's friend had set up his music station in the living room corner, and alcohol gave me the courage to stumble my way over to make a song request.

"Do you have any salsa?" I shouted.

Elijah's orb-like eyes looked up at me, even bluer in person. I thought of a sermon I once heard a pastor give on how Frodo from *The Lord of the Rings* represented us, burdened with the ring of God's calling, aided by Gandalf's representation of Jesus, who even died in the shape of a cross before coming back to life.

Elijah smiled and shouted back at me above the noise. "Sorry, what?" he asked.

"Do you have any salsa?" I repeated. "Salsa music, for dancing!"

My hips shimmied all on their own. When I started to tip over, I reached out and grabbed the edge of the deejay booth. Elijah's brow furrowed with the regret of disappointing someone.

"No, I'm so sorry, I don't!"

I gave him my biggest smile. "It's okay!" I shouted.

I made my way back to the kitchen and grabbed another glass of orange juice with Captain Morgan. I'd chugged it by the time I returned to the living room, leaving my glass on an entry table in the foyer. I had decided to look for my friend Johnny when the sensation of being watched drew my eyes to the living room archway.

Two girls stared at me with what could only be lust in their eyes. They wore almost nothing, grinding against each other as their heavily lined eyes flitted up and down. I had never been so blatantly checked out by a girl before. To have two of them looking like they wanted to devour me nearly stopped me in my tracks, but the momentum of my drunkenness propelled me forward. The girls moved toward me with the liquid grace of mermaids. Wordless, I let them slither their arms around me and pull me in between them as a slow, heavy beat played from the speakers. The girl wearing a cowboy hat pressed her boobs against mine, squeezing my exposed ass with her hand as she smiled at me seductively. I found myself smiling back. The girl behind me, whose intoxicating fragrance reminded me of juicy pears and heady gardenias, slid her warm hands over my bare waist. I melted into the rhythm of them, dipping with their hips and marveling at the softness of their bodies. The girl in front leaned in as though she would kiss me. I tilted my face so that her lips met the side of my neck. I didn't push her away. Lost in the sensuality of the moment, I closed my eyes and nearly quivered when her tongue glided up to my ear.

The hooting of deep voices let me know we were being watched. The girls sandwiching me laughed, pushing their pelvises even harder into mine. A dark feeling came over me. What was I doing? My head spun as I untangled myself from the girls' erotic embrace. I staggered to a corner and bumped into a piece of furniture. Was it a piano? An antique bar table? I didn't know. I rested my elbows on its surface and let my head fall to my forearms. Nausea spun me every time I shut my eyes, so I left them open, gazing out the blurry glass of a window. Moths beat themselves against porch lights as beautiful girls and boys smoked outside. I stood there, slumped over, as my breathing steadied.

"Whoooooooaaaa!"

The exclamation came from directly behind me. I managed to look over a shoulder and saw a guy dressed as a medieval knight standing with his eyes on my backside, his arms raised as though he'd scored a victory. His friends, drunk as myself, joined his vocal appreciation of their view.

Too dizzy to straighten up and not as bothered as I knew I ought to be, I smiled. The knight held up his plastic sword and lightly swatted my butt with an oafish grunt. I laughed. One of his friends grabbed the toy weapon and took his turn, slapping my bare bottom with a strike that made it jiggle. Each of the other boys followed suit. Their faces were bare of masks and makeup, but I didn't recognize them. I arched my back further to give them better aim. One by one they took turns slapping my ass with the plastic sword. I felt naked. Debased. Ashamed. Turned on by how I turned them on. I wallowed in shame's heat, giving in to the dark turn my drunkenness always took. I didn't understand how self-loathing could feel so good. Maybe I was punishing myself. I'd been a bad girl. What happened to naughty little girls, my mother used to ask me. They got spanked.

I wouldn't connect my Halloween debauchery to the grief of losing God until years later. All I could see when I closed my eyes was my children's ministry teacher Miss Valerie talking about the Sword of the Spirit.

~

I wasn't conscious of any deeper motive when I decided to move. I thought it was only for practical reasons, like getting away from the noisy construction that had been going on next door for over a year. Looking back, I would see that I wanted—indeed, needed—my outer life to reflect my inner change. Nothing started a fresh chapter for me like a move.

It was early November when I signed the lease on a one-bedroom loft in downtown L.A. Once again, I had chosen an old dwelling to make my home, an eighth-floor corner unit of the historic Higgins Building built in 1910. Floor-to-ceiling windows, polished concrete floors, and exposed ventilation ducts gave my loft an Edwardian-industrial feel. It was a colder look than the golden hardwoods I was used to. I couldn't wait to warm it up with my Oriental rugs and velvet furnishings.

My family came to L.A. to help me move. I cried after we picked up the last load from my old apartment, my emotions unearthed by memories of all the times I'd moved before. I knew this move was different. It was on my terms and to a place I chose and loved, but saying goodbye to my Art Deco apartment on Gardner Street left me sadder than I'd anticipated. The three years I'd spent there had been the most transformative of my life. The eighteen-year-old girl who moved in during the summer of 2004 was not the twenty-one-year-old woman moving out in the fall of 2007.

My family drove back to Colorado the Sunday after Thanksgiving. I reentered my new loft after seeing everyone off, and felt acutely aware of my aloneness. It was a time I would have turned to God for comfort. I would have pretended in faith that I felt God comforting me, holding me in phantom arms as I summoned the energy to unpack the rest of my moving boxes. Instead, I felt the echoey silence of a glass and cement space.

Something in me snapped. At the time, I blamed it on the stress of moving, the fear of being alone in a strange apartment, and being overwhelmed by having to settle into a new place. The only thing I didn't attribute it to was the loss of my faith. It would be so clear to me years later, so obvious. No one ever told me that when I left the only framework for existence I had ever known, a psychological shattering was almost bound to happen.

26

Panic Attacks

I t was as though I couldn't get comfortable. I tried rearranging the pillow behind my back, then plumping the cushion of the sofa. I sat cross-legged instead of knees tucked and moved to another couch altogether. Nothing helped to alleviate the squirming discomfort inside me. I couldn't shake the feeling that something was wrong, terribly wrong, though I had no idea what. It was my first night alone in my new loft. Was I scared? Not really. My building felt very secure, especially being high up on the eighth floor with a 24-hour doorman below. Was there something I had forgotten to do, something important? Everything in my loft was unpacked. A disassembled stack of boxes lay against the wall of my dining corner. Being settled in so quickly made me feel accomplished. So why did I have a nagging sensation in my gut?

I tossed and turned through the early hours of morning. I must have fallen asleep at some point, because when I woke up, sunshine poured into my living area. I felt fine that next day. Sleepy with little appetite, but the uneasy sensation had left. Then the sun went down. As darkness fell, a nameless fear writhed in my gut, sending surges of heat through my body with a warning I couldn't discern. Whenever I sat and tried to calm myself, the feeling grew worse. Constant movement seemed to help, so I marched aimlessly through my loft, rehanging pictures and moving decorations from one shelf to another as I tried distracting myself from whatever propelled me. The helplessness of being unable to identify why I felt afraid made my anxiety worse. Only when cracks of deep orange split the eastern horizon did my body feel like it had permission to rest, and I collapsed into my blankets, grateful just to be limp.

Each night it got worse. Days were fine, and I fought to keep my routine as normal as possible. But with every sundown, something took over my mind and body that I had no name for. It drove me to pace in circles for hours. It made me clutch at my stomach and cry without provocation. It terrified me.

I was on the phone with my sister Madeleine after a week of barely sleeping. She was telling me about a new trick she learned on her snowboard when I realized it was getting dark out. Dread clawed at me. It was coming. I tried to ignore it. *Stay calm*, I told myself. *Just keep talking. Maybe it won't come tonight. Maybe you're just freaking yourself out.*

"Alice?" Madeleine said.

"Huh?"

"I said, have you been getting more auditions?"

"Yeah. I mean a few. Actually no, none this week. Um, I don't know. I just . . ."

"Are you in the middle of something?"

"No, it's just . . . I can't . . . I . . ."

My voice broke. I couldn't fight it; I had to stand up.

"What's wrong?" Madeleine asked. "Are you crying?"

"Yeah," I said, unable to pretend I wasn't. "Sorry. I'm okay, it's just, every night since you guys left, around this time of day, I get these weird breakdowns."

"Breakdowns?"

"Yeah. I don't know, I'm not sure what it is. I just haven't been able to sleep and I don't know why."

I knew the breakdown was only going to get worse. I didn't want Madeleine to worry, so I told her I had to go.

"You sure you're okay?" she asked.

"Yeah, I'll be fine, I just have to take a hot bath or something."

Almost as soon as we hung up, panic consumed me. It was as though talking about it out loud gave it all the permission it needed to go full-blown. My hands shook. I gasped as though I couldn't get enough oxygen. I staggered to the bathroom where I turned on the faucet of my tub, thinking maybe a bath would help. The thunderousness of the water only made my panic worse.

My body writhed as I forced myself to lie in bed. My jaw clenched and unclenched while my hands pulled at my hair. Blankets felt too smothering. I threw them off and paced once more, anger flashing through my anxiety like bursts of sanity. What the fuck was happening? Why couldn't I hold still? My muscles ached with tension. My eyes felt raw and grainy from sleepless nights. Sleep. That was all I wanted. If only I could sleep. As if to smite me, the panic surged through my body in another intense wave, causing me to double over shaking. Stillness. I needed to force myself to be still. I collapsed to the floor and curled into a ball. The polished cement felt cold on my ribs through the thinness of my shirt. I wrapped my arms around me, hoping to hold myself still. It didn't work. I rocked back and forth in the fetal position until the rhythm of my movement scooted my body against the wall, and when the back of my head hit the floor molding, I remembered how I sometimes soothed myself to sleep as a child.

I sat up and slammed my head backward. My skull hit the rough texture of cement with a solid thud. Everything buzzed numb, and for a moment, my whole body felt limp. There was quiet. Calm, dark quiet. Minutes passed, and when the stirrings of panic threatened to overwhelm me again, I threw my head backward once more. Calmness came over me like a weighted blanket. As long as there was physical pain to distract me, I could be still.

Maybe this is why people cut themselves, I thought. I got up and went to my knife set hanging from a magnetic strip in the kitchen. I picked one up, thumbing its blade to test for sharpness. It made a quiet scraping noise against the ridges of my thumbprint. But where would I cut myself? Not my wrists. Too exposed. Not the insides of my thighs, either. No, cutting wasn't an option. I couldn't think where to hide the scars it would leave. I was working on a TV series called *Lincoln Heights* that got picked up for another season. My character was always dressed in skimpy outfits and I never knew when I might have to be in a bikini. Scars from cutting would be too noticeable. Banging my head against the wall would have to do.

The panic worsened every night. When head banging started losing its effectiveness, I discovered that slapping my face until it went numb and biting my hands until they were raw also offered brief moments of relief. Then the auditory hallucinations began. I searched my cabinets in vain for a baby that cried. My consciousness took turns splitting back and forth between lucidity and psychosis, and in the afternoon golden hour that became my dawn, my thoughts drifted to suicide. There were no screens on the double-hung windows of my loft. I sat in my open windowsill for hours, imagining what it would be like to tip over into the parking lot eight floors below. I played a game with myself where I took deep, repetitive breaths, as though stretching my lungs in preparation of a dive to the bottom of a swimming pool. When I made my final exhale, I held it until my body forced me not to black out. Inhaling meant life. I didn't want to inhale anymore.

One night in mid-December, I called James for help. My boyfriend knew I'd been having a difficult time, but he didn't know the extent of it. We'd hit a rough patch when I moved downtown because James hated making the thirty-minute drive from his place to see me. When I finally told him what was happening to me every night, he came over and held me as I cried. James felt helpless, and, I could tell, worried. He tried spending the night with me, but my full-size bed was too small for his six-foot-two frame. After tossing restlessly on the couch, I saw James's silhouette approach me in bed. The backpack slung over his shoulder told me he was leaving before his words could.

"I can't sleep here," James said. "It's just too uncomfortable. I'm gonna go."

Panic exploded within me. I felt too hurt to speak, too devastated to move. He was leaving me when he knew I needed him most. I could barely nod my head in acknowledgment.

As soon as I heard the door shut, I sprang from my bed. I fought the urge to run into the hallway and beg James to come back. I was too afraid he wouldn't. I ran to the window overlooking the parking lot next to my building, watching as James got into his Jeep. I scrambled from window to window as he made his way into the street, willing him to stop, to turn around and come back and say he was sorry and that he'd never leave me like that again. His taillights disappeared behind a tall building.

I bit my hand until I heard the crackling of tendons. I smashed my head against the wall until I saw stars. I slapped myself harder than ever. Nothing helped. Shaking, I crawled toward the cordless phone on my nightstand. The only person I could think to call was Mom. It was almost six in the morning where she was. I heard the concern in her voice right away.

"Alice?" she answered.

I was crying too hard to speak.

"Alice, where are you?"

I tried to tell her I was in my bedroom, but my voice came out like a silent scream.

"Alice, you need to take deep breaths," Mom said, her voice full of authority. "Breathe in and out."

I forced myself to inhale, then I forced myself to exhale. My breaths were too quick, shuddering into the speaker of my phone. Mom heard when I stopped breathing altogether. My body went completely still, empty of fight and dizzy from hyperventilating. A drowsy peace came over me.

"You have to breathe in, Alice," Mom said to me. "Take a breath, Alice, please."

But I was immobilized. My crumpled form lay on polished cement, my eyes half-open and staring beneath my bed at nothing.

"I'm going to call an ambulance if I don't hear a sound from you," Mom said. My body gasped and I heard Mom fighting tears. I hadn't meant to scare her on purpose.

"I'm flying out," Mom said. I heard her speak to my dad. "Ted, hand me my laptop. Are you still there, chickie?"

"Yeah." My voice sounded hollow.

"I'm coming today, okay? I'm going to help you find a therapist. You need help, Alice. It doesn't sound like you're capable of caring for yourself right now."

I wanted to protest, to reassure her that she needn't go through the expense and trouble because I was perfectly capable of taking care of myself. But I wasn't. I hadn't showered or eaten in days. The wardrobe mirror in front of me reflected the back of my ribs through my shirt. My hip bones jutted out sharply from the sweatpants I hadn't changed. My face, swollen from crying, appeared distorted in contrast to the rest of me that was gaunt.

Mom's voice guided me into bed. She told me to stay on the phone with her, even though I couldn't say much. Mom was the lifeline reminding me to breathe. We breathed together until the first cracks of sunlight hit the industrial pipes along my ceiling.

If Mom was shocked by my paleness and frailty when I met her at the airport, she didn't show it. She smiled and pulled me into a tight hug.

"What's wrong, baby?" she asked as she drove us back to my loft. She held my hand. I hoped she didn't notice the tiny scabs from where my teeth had broken skin. I slumped in the passenger seat, my knees cradled to my chest.

"I don't know," I said. "It just started happening."

Mom listened as I tried to describe the past two and a half weeks.

"Can you think of anything that might be triggering this?" she asked.

I felt so tired, I could barely shake my head. "No," I said. "That's the scariest part. There's no reason I can think of." My health was good, aside from my present state. I had money with job opportunities on the horizon. I had friends and a family who loved me. A boyfriend. I didn't tell Mom how James had left me the night before.

My thinness wasn't lost on Mom. As soon as we settled into my loft, she ordered me soup from a nearby restaurant and watched me until I ate at least half a bowl. She made me pinky promise to keep eating at mealtimes, even if I wasn't hungry. I also showered. Having Mom in my home made me feel like I could go into the dark, loud space of the tub without panicking.

Mom had several therapists pulled up on my computer when I awoke the next day. I decided to try out a woman named Wendy who specialized in anxiety. The first thing I noticed about Wendy was her voice, loud and grating on my ears. I felt horrible for thinking so and tried to overcome my shallowness in favor of the help she could give me. It soon became apparent she couldn't give me much. When I finished describing my nightly breakdowns, Wendy squinted her eyes and looked at me with what felt like professional sympathy.

"Have you tried lighting candles and listening to some music?" she asked.

I knew then that Wendy was not the therapist for me.

The next therapist I saw was just as unhelpful. A third suggested I might be experiencing panic attacks when I spoke with him over the phone, and when he explained what a panic attack was, it was the first time someone told me something that made sense. Then his office assistant sent me to the wrong address when I tried to meet with him. It would be two days before they could reschedule me, so I told them to forget it. They were fallible humans just like myself, but I didn't have time or energy to waste. Even though Mom was staying with me, I still had a breakdown every night. They weren't as bad as when I was alone. Mom held me as I cried, letting me rock into her instead of against the wall. She prayed over me, thinking maybe I was under a demonic attack. I didn't have the courage to tell Mom I didn't believe in demons anymore, or God. I didn't understand what was happening to me, but I felt certain there was a rational explanation. I just needed a therapist who could help me find it.

~

"What brings you to therapy today?" he asked. His voice was soft. It didn't seem to match the striking blue of his eyes, or the slick black of his hair.

"I've been having panic attacks," I said. "I mean, I think I've been having them. I don't know."

"Can you describe them to me?"

"They always start at night. I can't breathe, I can't sleep. I . . ."

I stopped. I didn't know if I had the energy to explain all of the symptoms yet again. Dr. Bennett Williamson—Bennett, as I would come to call him—was the fourth or fifth therapist I'd seen. I couldn't remember. They all blurred into the same middle-aged pair of spectacles telling me I should try meditating the next time I felt like I was suffocating. The advice I'd been given thus far felt trite and useless.

Bennett was different. He didn't have a notepad in front of him, nor did he wear spectacles. I had nothing against glasses, but I guessed it was Bennett's relatively youthful appearance that made me feel like he might be able to offer something the others couldn't. Something that would help me understand why I was having the breakdowns and what I could do to stop them.

"When did they start?" Bennett asked, his voice bringing me back into the sky-lit room.

I struggled to focus. My exhaustion had turned everything into a haloed fog. "Right after Thanksgiving," I said. "Nothing specific triggered it. Just out of the blue, for no reason, I started feeling like I couldn't breathe, like I was going crazy."

Bennett listened as I did my best to describe why I thought I needed therapy. Paranoia. Terror. Rage. Fantasies of suicide. Self-destruction.

Self-starvation. Auditory hallucinations. Relentless pacing driven by an unknown fear that wrung my arms, slapped my face, and made me march in circles until the sun came up.

"Then I sleep most of the day," I said. "When I wake up, I'm fine, until the sun sets. Then it starts all over again, and it's been getting worse and worse."

Bennett agreed I might be having panic attacks, although why, we had yet to determine. He didn't tell me to light candles or to take a bath with New Age music playing. His first piece of advice was to let the panic attacks happen.

"Let them take over," he said. "Don't fight them. Trying to stop a panic attack will usually make it worse, and there's little you can do when one is happening."

Finally, I thought. *A therapist who knew.*

"The next time you feel a panic attack coming on," Bennett continued, "I want you to try and lie down if you can. Let your body do whatever it feels like doing. Don't try to control the panic, because that might be why you're pacing and hurting yourself. Instead, try lying down and pay attention to where in your body the panic moves. See if you can notice where it starts and where it ends."

"But what if I can't lay down?" I asked.

"That's okay. Just try. I know panic attacks are frightening but remind yourself that it will pass. Do your best not to fight it. You might find that letting them run their course shortens their duration."

Bennett also gave me a referral to a psychiatrist. I protested, saying I didn't want to have to take medication regularly.

"There are other medications you can take as-needed," said Bennett. "You don't have to, but sometimes people feel more in control knowing there's something they can take if they feel like the panic and anxiety get to be too much. Does that sound like something you might want?"

It was. I accepted Bennett's referral and agreed to meet with him again the following week.

That night, like every night I'd lost count of by then, I felt the familiar creeping of fear into my nervous system. As usual, I couldn't name what I was afraid of. I only knew that it was coming. It was seething. It wanted to destroy me, and I wanted to destroy it. So, I did as Bennett suggested and forced myself to lie on the cold cement of my floor. I couldn't make it to my bed in time. Knowing the advice Bennett had given me, Mom stayed back and let me ride it out.

The panic seized me and I let it. I managed to do as Bennett suggested and observed that the fear began in my stomach. My belly quivered, clenching and unclenching. Soon I felt like I couldn't breathe. The panic writhed its way through my chest and lodged in my throat, contorting the left side of my neck. I felt tears streaming from my eyes and heard myself crying. Then, almost as soon as I registered the thought that at least I knew the panic's course, it began to ebb. Maybe only a few minutes had passed. My head rolled back. My lungs released me into limpness. The stiffness in my joints loosened.

Bennett was right. In not fighting my panic, its normal duration had shortened.

A couple of days later, I met with a psychiatrist who prescribed me Klonopin, a medication for seizure, panic, and anxiety disorders. He said half a pill would make me sleepy and therefore help prevent the onset of my panic attacks. I took my first dose of Klonopin that night. It made me feel calm and heavy. While I was aware of the panic that wanted to slither its way in, it was never able to fully take hold. It moved forward and away again, hitting against my heart like a snake who hadn't yet realized it had been put in a glass cage. I fell asleep without tears in my eyes.

27

Repercussions

I t looks like you have a hard time trusting people," Bennett said.

"What?" I asked. "How did the test get that?"

"Well, you answered a few of the questions with what would be considered asocial choices. See, right here you checked that you don't trust people."

My therapist held out the sheet of paper to me. Question 73 read, "Do you trust people?" I had shaded in the "No" with my hardest pencil pressure.

"Oh," I said. I had barely registered the question when I was filling out the form. Seeing the stark response that came out of me made me feel exposed. "Yeah, it's true," I admitted. "I don't trust people."

"Why do you think that is?"

I blinked at Bennett. He stared back at me patiently.

"Because," I said, "people aren't trustworthy."

It was a month or two after my twenty-second birthday. My panic attacks had lessened, thanks to Klonopin and therapy, and soon I was only having one a month. I still wanted to know why they had started. Bennett and I would never find out together, but even so, he was able to help me. I never knew what to talk about in therapy, so Bennett had given me a test measuring my propensity for personality disorders. He didn't think I had one, and normally, he said, he wouldn't have given me such a test. It was only when I told him how much I enjoyed psychology quizzes that he suggested I might take one of the evaluations he offered. He thought the results might shed light on areas we could work on together. He was right. Bennett did not give me a diagnosis, but so far, my high scores in excessive anxiety and emotional alienation indicated a slight leaning toward schizoid personality disorder. I was wary of people, indifferent to how they felt about me, and willfully isolated. I had a few friends, but I was the occasional responder, rarely initiating get-togethers myself. Therapy would remind me of how my unstable childhood had led to an avoidance of intimacy. I felt ambivalent about investing in relationships too deeply, and my skills at remaining pleasantly engaged but emotionally detached were finely honed.

"What makes you feel people aren't trustworthy?" Bennett asked.

"I just don't think people should be trusted," I said.

I knew I wasn't being a very cooperative patient. One hour wasn't enough time to get into the depth of my answer, and I didn't know where to begin. The question was too vague. It hadn't asked if I thought my loved ones were trustworthy, it had only said "people." People were not to be trusted. Not even my loved ones, as I thought about it more. I felt guilty, like I was wrong to feel that way. Yet my gut reaction, which I'd been retraining myself to think of as a response based on the accumulated data of my experiences, and not as a voice from God or Satan, told me I was right. People were not to be trusted.

Later, it would be perfectly clear to me why I didn't trust people. I thought of when my parents told me we were going on a road trip to California, and how the vacation had turned into a year of living in people's driveways. I remembered how my youth pastors had tricked me into believing I was being held at gunpoint as a martyr. My trust issues made sense when I recalled how much I had trusted Luke as a friend, and how betrayed I'd felt by him and God when he announced I was his future wife. More keenly, I remembered the jars of spices remaining still on their shelves as I begged God to knock one over. Trust had been the cornerstone of my faith, the foundation of nearly every facet of my life. It felt like the gravest mistake I'd ever made.

I didn't share those memories with Bennett that day, nor did I share them the following week. Only a few of those recollections ever made it into his office. They still felt too painful, too fresh to bring up. Perhaps the biggest reason I did not want to talk about God in therapy was because I didn't want to give him any more power over my life. Acknowledging the ways my former faith still affected me would do that.

As it turned out, I didn't have a choice about the ways my former faith affected me. Although my panic attacks continued to lessen, I began noticing when certain things seemed to trigger them. If I could trace the panic's cause, I decided, it was no longer a panic attack. It was an anxiety attack. Panic attacks came from nowhere, sourceless and harrowing. Anxiety attacks were more understandable, and therefore felt less threatening, because they came with clear provocation. Like the time I went to my friend Caitlin's home for what she called Philosophy Night.

When Caitlin said her friend leading the philosophical debate night was a priest, alarm bells went off in my head. I tried to ignore them, sitting warily on a floor cushion as I eyed the priest talking with some people in a corner. He looked young. Probably fresh out of seminary school, or wherever priests went to train. He opened the evening with a bit about his background and said to feel free to ask him any question at any time. One girl raised her hand.

"I'm sorry," the girl said. "But . . . are you a virgin?"

The whole room laughed. So did the priest, whose name I could never remember.

"Yes," he said. "Yes, I am. And I bet you weren't the only one wondering, so don't feel bad."

My skin crawled with the urge to flee. Only one type of person made it to their late twenties without having sex, especially if they appeared physically able, mentally sound, and reasonably attractive. That type of person believed premarital sex was wrong. I couldn't trust anything more the man had to say. As I forced myself to sit there listening to him, uncertain how to leave without being rude, I couldn't help feeling like the philosopher had blown his cover. I knew a religious agenda when I smelled one. My suspicions were confirmed when the priest repeatedly argued for the existence of the Christian God. That he was a virgin because of his beliefs had jumped the discussion straight to the religious end of philosophical discourse. I felt swindled. My throat began to tighten. My hands began to shake so I sat on them, begging myself not to have an anxiety attack. An impromptu snack break finally gave me the opportunity to leave. I thanked Caitlin as profusely as I could, explaining that I didn't feel well. I drove home with a sweaty back and a pounding heart. It was the first time I became aware of the spiritual triggers I now had.

As the year wore on, I discovered more. A trip to a museum ended when a docent shushed me in a room full of religious artwork, eliciting a flashback of being in church that sent me running out the exit door in tears. Street evangelists on Hollywood Boulevard, a yoga class that ended with chanting, and even secular concerts, where people raised their hands to the music, all made my heart pound with fear. I felt guilty for my intolerance of the slightest hint of faith, judging myself for being judgmental. My anger at my reactiveness, especially when it seeped out in front of friends, pushed me to overcome my anxiety by deliberately subjecting myself to things that were spiritual. My self-induced exposure therapy didn't work. Trendy enlightenment books like *The Power of Now* made my hands shake. Meditation made me want to break things. A New Age documentary called *The Secret* tipped me over the edge with its so-called Law of Attraction, which was just another way of saying your faith or lack thereof determined your lot in life. Millennial spirituality seemed to teach that your success in work, health, and love was given to you by the capital-U Universe if you *believed* in it. When things didn't turn out the way you manifested, or when tragedy struck, it was your fault. Your "vibration" must have manifested the wrong things, consciously or not. The similarities to faith healing and other divine mind games were too familiar to me. So was the reincarnation theory of karmic debt. I thought "bad karma" was just another way of saying "original sin," and I found belief systems like astrology and numerology to be no less superstitious than religion. I decided I was done viewing life through the disempowering lens of magical thinking.

~

It was a sunny day near the end of 2008 when I found the courage to tell Mom I no longer believed in God. The dread had been eating at me, and I knew I had to come clean to my family sooner or later. When Mom visited me in L.A., an opportunity presented itself as we sat at a picnic table overlooking the Pacific Ocean. I can't remember what prompted it. Something Mom said compelled me to be honest with her, and it was as good a time as it was ever going to be.

"Mom," I said. "I don't believe in God anymore."

She blinked at me from across the table. "What do you mean?" she asked.

"I just don't think God's real."

I explained to her how I'd never felt touched by God, how he'd never given me visions, and how I'd made them up and faked praying in tongues.

"But don't you think it's possible that maybe you just weren't hearing God the way you expected to?" Mom asked.

I fought a sudden flash of anger. Not at Mom, but at the familiar cop-out I'd told myself for so long.

"Yeah," I said. "It's possible. But I kept asking God to speak to me in a way I would understand, and he never did." Tears threatened to choke me. "So I gave him a last chance. I told him that if he was there, he had to let me know. And it had to be in a way I couldn't trick myself into believing. But nothing happened."

I didn't want to tell Mom the specifics of the test I'd given God. I feared she might tell me it had only been my lack of faith that made no jars fall off my spice rack, and part of me feared she would have been right. Jesus said, "According to your faith let it be done to you." I didn't want to admit it then, but I still felt shaky in the godless new world in which I found myself. I wasn't ready to hear anything that might scare me into being trapped by faith again. If there was a God, and if he was the God of love I'd believed in, he would have cared about me enough to make himself known. The reminder gave me strength whenever my programming tried to tell me I was going to hell.

Mom was staring at me. I half-expected her to burst into tears. Instead, she shook her head and said something along the lines of how I was just in a season of doubt. Her confidence angered me.

"No," I said. "It's not like I've just fallen off the wagon for a little bit. I'm not a Christian anymore. I don't think I ever will be again—I don't ever *want* to be again."

It was as though Mom couldn't compute how I'd gone from being such a devout follower of Christ to an adamant nonbeliever. She didn't seem ready to accept that I truly didn't believe in God anymore, and I supposed I couldn't fault her for thinking I might only be having a temporary lapse of faith. We ended our conversation on an unsettled note. As the afternoon wore on and we meandered through a garden path, Mom eventually put her arm through mine. She looked like she was trying not to cry.

"I want to respect where you're at," she said. "Does this mean I shouldn't tell you what God's doing in my heart anymore?"

We'd always spoken freely about our walks with God. Whether we debated the paradoxes in Jesus' teachings or simply shared what we prayed for during our quiet times, the adult relationship I'd developed with Mom had been largely based on our shared faith. I could tell Mom would miss those conversations.

"You can still tell me what God's doing in your heart," I said. "I just don't want to mislead you into thinking I still believe in him."

It felt patronizing to say out loud. Like I was the parent, telling my child they could still write a wish list for Santa, as long as they knew he wasn't real. Mom only nodded her head.

~

The next several years took a fragile young woman and turned her into a hardened skeptic. It was a slow morphing from credulity to cynicism, hope to doubt, and fear to reason. Learning to heal from the more harmful parts of my faith meant allowing myself to undergo deep transformations that felt like deaths. They were changes I never anticipated, changes the old me, the faithful me, would never have chosen. Sometimes it felt like the changes I went through were healthy. Other times I questioned if they were reactionary. It didn't matter. All I cared about was if they felt true. Discovering who I was and not who I wanted to be was a necessary part of my healing.

It was social interactions that challenged me to know and accept my changing self the most. Leaving Christianity had released me from the Christ-like obligation of forcing niceness, and with nothing left but habit and observation to guide me, I found I couldn't help questioning social customs and their integrity. My desire to know which parts of me were authentic, and which were only the results of Christian programming, left me with a wariness of being fake that made me feel ten years old again. I struggled to understand and play along with certain rituals, like asking someone, "How are you," especially if I'd just met them. It felt like lying. Why did I care how they were? I felt uncomfortable when strangers asked me the same question. Pretending we cared about each other's days felt insulting. It also reminded me of church, when the pastor would ask the congregation to exchange greetings. Forced niceties felt suspicious.

Small talk was a landmine of triggers and challenges. Sometimes my nomadic childhood leaked out in conversation, never failing to elicit questions when it did.

Were you an Army brat? people wondered. *Why did your parents move so much?*

They just felt God called them to, I'd say if I was feeling honest.

Oh. Were you a missionary kid?

Something like that.

More curiosity usually followed—*what religion were you, where did you go to school, why were you homeschooled, what did your parents do for work*—and eventually led to the part I always dreaded.

So, what are your views on faith now?

Every time this question came up, I froze, torn between glossing over reality for pleasantries' sake and being truthful at the risk of causing offense. It was tempting to give people the happy ending I felt they wanted to hear—that I had turned out fine and totally had my shit together. That I now considered myself spiritual but not religious. The truth was that I was an atheist with more anger than I knew what to do with. I didn't want to alienate anyone or make them feel judged. Neither did I want to risk their judgment. Yet I also wanted to let others who might be struggling through their own loss of faith know that they were not alone. That urge compelled me to err on the side of honesty rather than refrain.

I don't believe in God anymore, I'd say.

Sometimes people were polite. Most raised a curious eyebrow and changed the subject. Others, however, took it upon themselves to tell me in varying ways that I grew up believing in the wrong God. The God they believed in would never have put me through what my parents and youth pastors did.

You know, that wasn't really God, they'd say.

How do you know? I'd ask. *What makes you think your idea of God is any more true?*

Because God is love. I know because I've experienced it.

I always felt stabbed. Their words were exactly what my parents and youth pastors used to say.

My distrust of people wasn't something I felt eager to change. Most people I met had faith of some sort, and people of faith terrified me. *They are dangerous,* my mind would tell me. *They cannot be trusted.* I was incapable of discerning what people called healthy faith from the unhealthy. It was all toxic to me. Faith was dangerous because when people were convinced of things invisible, there was no limit to what they might justify in the name of their unprovable conviction. I knew most people were kind, helpful, and good-intentioned. So were the conmen of my childhood. Wolves were disguised not as sheep, but as shepherds. I could no longer trust my instincts. Only time revealed true character, and I was a patient woman.

As I came into my mid-twenties and friends started getting married, I uncovered a new layer of social hurdles to get through. Milestones like getting married and having children baffled me. I smiled and congratulated friends on their engagements and pregnancy announcements, but inside I felt deeply troubled. Could we not care for one another without signing contracts? Were there not millions orphaned who were already here? I was only half-blind to how Christianity had poisoned my outlook on marriage and childbearing. That women existed to submit themselves to husbands and produce heirs, preferably male, left me with little regard for the patriarchal institution of matrimony, holy or not. The only way I could rationalize those apparent rites of passage was by chalking them up to our instinct to breed and attain an artificial sense of security.

The inability to trust love was perhaps the deepest wound faith left me with. I didn't know how to trust a human emotion that had the same name as a being whose supposed existence caused me nothing but confusion and shame. God was love, I'd been taught by the church. Love was marriage, I'd been taught by society. It would never surprise me that when I stopped believing in God, I stopped believing in marriage. My arranged betrothal at seventeen had left a dark stain on the once-romantic idea.

The reason I didn't want to have children was less clear-cut. Most people assumed my reluctance to have biological children stemmed from vanity, or fear of pregnancy and childbirth. The truth was too vulnerable and in need of elaboration to explain: I didn't know the meaning of life. I felt like I had no right to make someone else have to live until I did. There was too much suffering and too little point to it all, and it would sound banal to say that out loud. It was my deepest sincerity. Adoption appealed to me, but not procreation, and I acknowledged that I might feel differently one day. I gave myself full permission to change my mind. For the time being, I could not justify bringing someone else into existence to wonder why they were here. What answer could I give them?

People told me I was cynical, an anti-humanist, and a nihilist. I preferred pragmatic to cynical, and I didn't so much feel *anti*-humanist as I felt merely skeptical of the goodness of the human species. My views might have been unconventional, but I didn't feel they were tinged with the hatefulness others seemed to assume. Regarding nihilism, I had to agree that I thought life was inherently meaningless, and I did resonate with what philosophers called ". . . extreme skepticism maintaining that nothing in the world has a real existence." How did one measure reality? I once believed things were real that, as far as I could tell, weren't. My own self-deception had caused me to fear believing in anything ever again, including what we called reality. The physical world we knew might only be a cosmic dream, or a hologram among parallel universes, or simply a fart of elements. Science discovered new breakthroughs about the nature of perceived reality all the time. I didn't want to feel secure in a truth that might only be shattered with the next discovery. It was preferable to live in a suspended state of non-belief.

By the time I reached my late twenties, I was still getting used to the woman I'd become. I loved her, but I wasn't sure I liked her. She was so different from anyone I thought I'd be. My own mother said it was as though I'd undergone a personality change, and maybe I had. I didn't mind too much. A shift in personality reflected the truth of an inner transformation. Yet some of my changes were tinged with a fear or anger that, while true, I hoped might fade. I treasured how far I'd come from the misleading world of faith and hope, but it was dismaying to be written off as bitter. I didn't want to be naive, but I didn't want to be a cynic. There had to be a way I could be skeptical without being snide. Critical without being combative. I wanted to find a way to work on my social graces without fearing it meant

I was reverting to some sort of fakeness that felt forced like Christianity. It had been an arduous undertaking to find out who I was without God and learn how to love myself. I wanted to like myself, too.

It wasn't that I was entirely unlikeable. My friend circle had changed over the years, but I knew the people in my life loved and appreciated me. Some of my older friendships had drifted apart. It had only made room for new ones. Trusting people was still something I struggled with, but the test of time left me grateful to be mistaken for my wariness more often than not. I could still count on one hand how many people I felt close to. We still preferred hikes and dinner parties to bars and nightclubs. Coffee shop people, as James had called us.

James and I broke up for good after five years of off-and-on dating. Nothing bad had happened and we remained on friendly terms. We simply reached our maximum point of incompatibility. Losing my faith left me a different person than the girl he'd fallen for. James had changed a lot, too. He'd gotten calmer and more self-reflective as he got older, and he expressed how awful he sometimes felt over the ways he hadn't been there for me. I forgave him. I knew it couldn't have been easy trying to help a girl who was falling apart.

After James and I broke up, something in me shifted. Maybe it was the reassessment of life that seemed to occur when anyone was newly single. Maybe it was the culmination of everything I'd learned in therapy. Whatever sparked it, the shift following my break-up with James allowed me to view my life as if for the first time, taking in with grateful eyes how fortunate I was. I had a thriving career. I had time to travel. I had good friends and a loving family. And, for the first time ever, I realized I was free of both God and man. The future had never felt so exciting, so brimming with possibility and without the paralyzing fear of consequence.

I made a sacred commitment to myself one night: that I would live in my humanity in any way I desired. I had health, money, and the knowledge I would only be young once. So, I made a conscious decision in the sparkling quiet of my heart. I gifted myself with a delayed adolescence. I let myself do whatever, whenever, and whoever I wanted. It was my own private recompense for all those years of being obedient and responsible. I traveled, I danced, I drank, I fucked, I did drugs, and I relished every single moment of it. My only regret was not letting myself live in such freedom sooner. I was filled with gratitude for leaving faith when I did, for not having a husband I might need to divorce or children I needed to be responsible for, or a community of only church friends that I needed to leave. I knew how differently my life could have panned out. Despite what others called a nihilistic outlook, I felt pretty damn lucky.

28

Rebuilding

I was twenty-eight when I learned there was a clinical term for what I'd been struggling with throughout my adult life. It was the winter of 2014, and I had recently returned to L.A. from filming a TV series in Texas called *The Lying Game*. Acting had continued to be a lucrative career for me. I enjoyed being back in my woodsy canyon home above Beverly Hills, sipping my morning tea on the balcony and skimming through social media to the songs of birds. I would never be able to remember how I found the post. Whatever compelled me to click on the page I stared at didn't matter. All sounds faded away as I sat forward in my chair, my eyes glued to the screen.

Religious Trauma Syndrome is the condition experienced by people who are struggling with leaving an authoritarian, dogmatic religion and coping with the damage of indoctrination.

The muscles of my throat constricted.

RTS is a function of both the chronic abuses of harmful religion and the impact of severing one's connection with one's faith. It can be compared to a combination of PTSD and Complex PTSD . . . Not as extreme but also tragic, are all the people who are struggling to make sense of life after losing their whole basis of reality. None of the previously named diagnoses quite tells the story, and many who try to get help from the mental health profession cannot find a therapist who understands.

Tears leaked from my eyes. Someone understood.

The article's author, psychologist Dr. Marlene Winell, had been the one to originate the term Religious Trauma Syndrome (RTS). I spent the rest of my morning learning everything I could about it.

Therapists, like others, Dr. Winell wrote on her website, *expect that if you stop believing, you just quit going to church, putting it in the same category as not believing in Santa Claus. Some people also consider religious beliefs childish, so you just grow out of them, simple as that. Therapists often don't understand the fundamentalism, and they even recommend spiritual practices as part of therapy. In general, people who have not survived an authoritarian fundamentalist indoctrination do not realize what a complete mind-rape it really is.*

I wanted to scream with recognition. To laugh with relief. To cry with remembrance.

Dr. Winell had written a book called *Leaving the Fold: A Guide for Former Fundamentalists and Others Leaving Their Religion.* I downloaded it to my iPad and read it in one sitting. All throughout, I sobbed, my heart split open by a validation I'd given up hope of finding. There was a reason for my panic attacks. There was a reason for my spiritual triggers. There was a reason for the wariness that made it hard for me to make friends. And I was not alone.

I saw myself in every page that described the symptoms of Religious Trauma Syndrome. There were the cognitive symptoms, which manifested in me as crippling bouts of confusion, negative beliefs about self-worth, and poor critical thinking ability. Then there were the emotional symptoms, such as depression, loss of meaning, anger, and anxiety. Dr. Winell even included what she called social and cultural symptoms, including learning gaps, feeling unable to make sense of the secular world, and struggling to relate with peers on topics of pop culture.

I also recognized every phase of leaving faith that Dr. Winell wrote of. First came what she called Separation—when questions and doubts could be silenced no more. My separation began when I broke off my betrothal to Luke. Then came the period of Confusion, which led to the crisis of faith I'd experienced in the year following my broken betrothal. A second wave of Confusion slammed me when I could no longer sustain my beliefs at all, leading to the psychological breakdown that sent me to therapy. I realized my panic attacks had started only two months after God failed my test. Of course I had been gripped by fear. I'd been instilled with that fear all my life, warned of what would happen if I ever turned my back on God. Just because I no longer believed in hell didn't mean the fear of it simply left my nervous system. After Confusion came the phase of Avoidance. Avoidance was the phase that made me realize I wanted nothing more to do with anything that reminded me of faith, the phase that left me unable to hear the word "God" without flinching inside. I was still in the phase of Avoidance. I also recognized myself to be in the midst of the fourth stage, which Dr. Winell called Feeling. Feeling explained the rage I'd learned to bury and the dark spirals of depression that came from nowhere, leaving me wavering between a nameless grief and a reckless apathy. I called them my existential mindfucks.

There was one more phase that lie ahead: Rebuilding.

In the rebuilding phase, Dr. Winell wrote, *people rediscover their self-worth . . . Perceptions and beliefs are reconstructed. You too can find new principles to live by and new meaning for your life.*

I finished *Leaving the Fold* with a tear-splotched face and a flickering of hope. I would rebuild, goddammit. It was time.

⁓

My determination to heal from what I now knew to be Religious Trauma Syndrome drove me to find closure for the parts of my past holding me back from living fully in my present. Using *Leaving the Fold* as a guide, I made my way through the remaining steps of the Rebuilding phase. I felt like I had already rediscovered my self-worth, appreciating the time I'd taken to know myself and my willingness to love but not always like what I found.

Self-love was an ongoing journey I felt grateful to have undertaken. That left Operation One of Mission Rebuild: Reconstruct Perceptions and Beliefs.

I knew right away what perceptions and beliefs most needed reconstructing. If there was one piece of my Christian past that kept me from being able to leave it behind, it was the signs and wonders of the Toronto Blessing. As an adult, I had tried to block out the memories I had of Spirit-slayings and revivals. I had tried to forget the cacophony of tongues, the fear of watching my parents tremble and seize, and the shame of feeling rejected by God time and again. The supernatural aspects of my former faith still haunted me, making me feel shackled by anger and doubt. The Toronto Blessing had led to some of the most formative moments of my childhood. The touch of God had transformed my parents' faith and therefore our lives. I needed to know what the manifestations of the Holy Spirit were if not what people claimed them to be.

It was a YouTube video that compelled me to find out. One day, shortly after learning about Religious Trauma Syndrome, someone who knew nothing of my Spirit-filled background laughed as they tilted the screen of their phone toward me, saying I had to see what they were watching. The throaty screech of a singer screamed, "Let the bodies hit the floor," as I watched evangelist Benny Hinn send crowds of people flying backward with the wave of his hand. The editor had timed the falls to the music perfectly, like a parody music video of Hinn's revivals set to the heavy metal soundtrack of a song called "Bodies" by Drowning Pool. The video was meant to be comedic. Chills ran through me. Women lay on their backs, limbs twitching like fresh roadkill. Men stood rigid, their bodies convulsing as though electrocuted. Some would have visions and others would receive healings. All would attribute their experiences to God.

I hadn't been a Christian in almost eight years. Even so, my fear of God and Satan came rushing back at the sight of spellbound worshippers. It was my fear that told me there was an opportunity to heal. I didn't want religion to have any more power over me. I didn't want to be triggered by symptoms of religious trauma all my life. That day, instead of pushing aside the anxiety that came from watching the video, I let myself feel it. My emotions went from fear to anger to tenacity.

I immersed myself in research over the next several months. The spiritual revival that began in Toronto, Canada, did not go unnoticed by the media, and journalists and historians gave many names to the movement that spread across the globe throughout the 1990s. Some referred to it as the Laughing Revival, due to the Holy Laughter spells prevalent in its wake. Others, especially critics of a more conservative Christian faith, called it the Counterfeit Revival. Regardless of the movement's name, by the year 2000, 2.5 million people from over thirty countries had walked through the doors of Toronto Airport Christian Fellowship. It amazed me that what had been normal to me as a child had gotten such worldwide press. Critics both secular and religious compared the sight of the revival gatherings to a madhouse, or to a spiritual possession that was demonic instead of holy.

Leslie Scrivener of the *Toronto Star* wrote, "From room to room come barnyard cries, calls heard only in the wild, grunts so deep women recalled the sounds of childbirth, while some men and women adopted the very position of childbirth. Men did chicken walks. Women jabbed their fingers as if afflicted with nervous disorders. And around these scenes of bedlam, were loving arms to catch the falling, smiling faces, whispered prayers of encouragement, instructions to release, to let go."

In a *Time* magazine article titled "Laughing for the Lord," journalist Richard N. Ostling described the Toronto Blessing as a "frenzied display."

"A young worshipper falls to the floor, hands twitching," he wrote. "Another falls, then another and another. Within half an hour there are bodies everywhere as supplicants sob, shake, roar like lions and strangest of all, laugh uncontrollably."

Dr. Cathy Burns, a Christian theologian, called these manifestations of the Spirit blasphemous in her article titled "Unholy Laughter."

"Obviously," Dr. Burns wrote, "laughing during a communion service or during a sermon on hell can hardly be called the 'leading of the Spirit of God,' yet we are being told this movement is of God . . . Do the above disturbances and commotions sound like something that is Scriptural? Hardly! First Corinthians 14:40 clearly states: 'Let all things be done decently and in order.'"

I knew there were dozens of other verses Toronto Blessing devotees would have used to dispute Dr. Burns. Like First Corinthians 2:14 which read, "The person without the Spirit does not accept the things that come from the Spirit of God but considers them foolishness, and cannot understand them because they are discerned only through the Spirit." Or Romans 8:26, "The Spirit himself intercedes for us through wordless groans." I knew how the Bible could be used to justify nearly any stance a person took.

The biggest revelation I uncovered during my research took the very air out of me. My eyes widened as his meaty, clean-shaven face stared at me from the front page. His name shouted at me from the headline of the *Media Spotlight* article titled, "Holy Laughter: Rodney Howard-Browne and the Toronto Blessing." My heart thumped between my ears as I read the piece Albert James Dager had written about the Christian pastor who had pushed me on a flight of stairs.

"On several occasions," Dager wrote, "I've witnessed [Rodney Howard-Browne] 'slay people in the Spirit,' and, if they didn't begin to laugh, he would place his foot on their stomach and tell them to laugh. Some he would kick as they lay there, and accuse them of not yielding to the Holy Spirit. He would keep at it until they would obviously begin to force some kind of laugh out of themselves."

My eyes burned with vindication. I wasn't the only recipient of Rodney Howard-Browne's spiritual abuse. I trembled at the memory of his hand gripping my head, of its weight I tried not to buckle under until my neck gave way with his force. I remembered the warning I felt emanating from his eyes, saying not to tell anybody what he'd done.

"This is intimidation at the basic level," Dager's article continued. "While everyone around you is losing their minds, you feel out of place—conspicuous, unholy, unrighteous, guilty—because you don't feel the bubbling up of holy laughter."

Dager had described me.

Reading articles critiquing the revival that shaped my childhood brought a sense of relief I didn't expect. Watching video clips of the bizarre symptoms I'd had to normalize as a kid affirmed the Toronto Blessing had indeed been just as surreal as I remembered, if not more so. Strange as it now seemed to me, and how it had appeared to critics, I still thought something genuine had to have taken place for at least some people. Something real had to have been occurring for the movement to have gained such a following. No matter what the external symptoms looked like, my parents and others maintained there was nothing mad or unholy about the intense love they felt when they were being touched by God. Their lives had indeed been changed. How?

The methods I discovered stunned me.

I was at my computer one morning, researching how pastors performed miracles such as prophecies and faith healings, when I came across a radio interview explaining the process in detail. An ex-Pentecostal pastor named Mark Haville wanted to come clean about his past tactics and expose some of the ways pastors continued their fraud to this day. Todd Friel, one of the Christian broadcasters for *Way of the Master Radio*, asked Haville how it was that so many job-holding, tax-paying, average citizens—*citizens like my parents*, I thought—let themselves be knocked to the floor and allegedly healed of illnesses at mass spiritual revivals. Haville's answer was simple: hypnosis.

"The reason they're falling down," said the British ex-pastor, "is because people are suggestible. By getting a person into a suggestible state—or what we call an altered state of consciousness—it means that they are effectively in a state of hypnosis."

Haville explained that hypnosis was largely misunderstood—a person could be hypnotized and still fully aware. Haville said the best way to hypnotize a crowd at a spiritual revival was to first have a long period of praise and worship. Ideally, the music would mirror the functions of the cardiovascular system, when the rhythm pulsed at the speed of a nice, relaxed heartbeat. I thought back to the pulsating drums and melodic bursts of piano at Toronto Blessing conferences. Another integral part to hypnosis, Haville went on, was the repetition of certain words and phrases by the worship leader or pastor. Biblical references to the Holy Spirit, fire, and revival worked well.

"I'm not saying that [pastors] are deliberately doing that," Haville clarified. "But there are definitely certain patterns and tone within the way that we speak that will affect people and put them into a hypnosis state. That repeating [of] the same sentences and phrases, of course, is integral to the whole thing."

I remembered how Rodney Howard-Browne repeated phrases like, "The fire of God," and, "More wine," as he knocked people over. It seemed so obvious now. So blatant.

Medical experts seemed to agree with Haville's claims. In an HBO documentary called *A Question of Miracles*, Dr. Michael Persinger, a neuroscientist, explained the effects of hypnosis on the brains of revival-goers. To start with, Dr. Persinger said, the people drawn to those kinds of meetings were ". . . usually mildly depressed. They usually feel as if there's something missing in their lives."

Dr. Persinger went on to explain the group dynamic effect of hypnotizing a crowd. When thousands of people were gathered, he said, particularly in a large space where they were made to feel diminutive, such as a cathedral, their close proximity produced a special kind of physiological arousal. That arousal was what gave people a sense of wholeness. "Then," Dr. Persinger said, "the music will rise and fall every four to five seconds and produce this kind of wave of experience that elevates this special kind of arousal and releases the opiates, which we know experimentally increases hypnotizability."

I remembered how every adult around me stood with their eyes closed and faces tilted upward, their arms outstretched as their bodies rocked gently side-to-side. Dr. Persinger explained that once a crowd was in that kind of ecstatic, expectant state, the speaker or evangelist could come out and orchestrate cognitive experiences. That individual would usually make gestural movements that allowed a sense of power and control. "And then as the person begins to give the message," Dr. Persinger said, "they're full of emotion. They're full of imagery. These images take on tremendous personal value because of the elevation of the opiates, because of the group state of ecstasy. And then you see all the features of an opiate release. You get the smiles, a very mild glow, very much like a drunken state."

That, I realized, was how people became drunk in the Spirit. Everything Dr. Persinger said described a Toronto Blessing conference so well that he could have been there himself.

A Question of Miracles showed another component that often left people convinced of God's power. While the documentary focused on faith healings, of which there were many in the Toronto Blessing, I saw how everything explaining faith healings also applied to Spirit slayings. I was always told being slain by the Spirit was indicative of psychological healing, if not bodily healing as well. I learned the same principles applied. The film showed Dr. Neil Abbot, a researcher, conducting a study on volunteers suffering from chronic pain. He told them to lie in a room for half an hour while an energy healer worked on them from a nearby enclosed cubicle. Filmmaker and narrator Antony Thomas said, "Those who believed in the power of healers reported clinically significant reduction in pain and also described balls of light and powerful physical sensations to Abbot's researchers. But here was the catch. In half of these cases, the healer was present performing the full ritual; for the rest, the box was empty. And the results were the same, with or without a healer in the box. This is known as the placebo effect, where patients get better because they believe they'll get better."

Dr. Persinger added that the charismatic leader of revival gatherings was simply the catalyst that started the person's ability to heal themselves. "[Healing] doesn't come from the healer," he said. "It comes from the person's own brain and their own expectations, and their own changes in brain chemistry and brain electricity that produce changes in their own body."

Perhaps the explanations of hypnosis and placebo effect were obvious to some. For me, they were revelatory.

It both mystified and comforted me to learn that what I'd called being slain by the Spirit was called numerous names by other religions and ideologies. Practices based on Indian philosophies such as Hinduism and yoga called it Kundalini awakening. Chinese practitioners of Qigong called it Qigong deviation syndrome. An Indonesian Muslim who founded a spiritual movement called Subud called it the latihan kejiwaan, the !Kung people of southern Africa called it n/um, and the Quakers and Shakers in England and colonial America were known to call it ecstatic worship. No matter what it was called, or where and when, every culture described strikingly similar symptoms: involuntary shaking, spontaneous laughter and crying, feelings of bliss, seeing visions, speaking in tongues, and, notably, often having the ability to pass along the trance state to another, especially through touch on the forehead, or what some called the third eye. Learning how universal the experience was affirmed the Christian version wasn't literally the Holy Spirit. I didn't think it was anything supernatural. I figured we just hadn't found a way to effectively measure the abilities of consciousness yet.

Satisfied that I had reconstructed the perceptions and beliefs that had most troubled me, I turned my attention to Operation Two of Mission Rebuild: Find New Principles to Live By. This felt like a tricky one at first. Something about finding new principles felt inauthentic to me, as though I needed to trade one code of ethics—religion—for another. Why did I need any principles? Why couldn't I just live? As I mulled it over, I realized a simple rewording would allow me to accomplish the task without feeling dishonest. Instead of looking for new principles, what principles was I already living by? That felt safer. Principles, I decided, could not come from outside myself. They needed to come from within.

The first and only principle that came to mind was as cliché as it felt stark solid: to always be true to myself. I'd spent far too many years being true to other people, following their true selves at the cost of my own. I had stopped doing that, so there was a principle I already lived by. More would come to mind eventually. For the time being, and with the discoveries of neuroscience still fresh in my mind, I became fixated on knowing why faith had never been true to me. And there was another principle I already lived by, I realized: science. There were no greater principles than those that adapted with rigorous inquiry and the humility of allowing new evidence to change them.

To understand why faith wasn't true to me, I found it helpful to first learn how it was true to others. Dr. Michael Persinger's work inspired me to learn more about the field of neurotheology, or what some called the neuroscience of spirituality, where I found numerous studies attempting to explain what were collectively called mystical experiences. More than mere belief, these were the experiences that left people convinced of the supernatural. Brain scan images of tongues-speaking churchgoers showed places in the cerebrum that changed when participants engaged in glosso-lalia. The scans of meditating Buddhist monks showed the same changes. Articles abounded on spiritual websites interpreting fMRI images and EEG readings as evidence of everything from astral travel to spinal serpent awakening, and one website called The Christian Post saw the decrease in frontal lobe activity when people prayed in tongues as proof that the Holy Spirit was moving their speech patterns. Evidently, something could happen in the brain as the result of inducing a spiritual trance state, affirming that not everybody like myself had faked it.

I learned that mystical experiences activated the same reward circuits in the brain as drugs, sex, and love. The neurological cocktail I'd called being slain by the Spirit was likely a combination of feel-good serotonin, thrilling dopamine, and blissful hits of oxytocin, a meld that left people feeling transcended from themselves and lost in the infinite love of God. That opiate release was also what kept them coming back for more. One really could get high on Jesus or drunk in the Spirit. Neurologically, revivals were not unlike a mass drug outpouring, and there could be good trips and bad trips. All were considered healing journeys. These findings overwhelmed me with a new perspective of my parents. Being able to see what had happened in their brains made their experiences real to me in a way faith couldn't, deepening my understanding of the people who raised me.

As I had hoped, neuroscience also helped to explain why I never felt the love my parents and so many others did. Maybe my brain had a harder time letting go of its frontal lobe activity. The frontal lobe was the section of the brain responsible for staying in control, and while some people had the ability to melt right into the bliss of the nucleus accumbens, the region for processing reward, others like myself appeared to be more inhibited in those neural capacities. Brain scans of people deep in prayer showed decreased activity in the parietal lobes, where our brains oriented our sense of space and time. Maybe brains like mine were more reluctant to decrease their activity there. Indeed, there did appear to be a genetic component to whether or not a person was wired toward spirituality. One geneticist, Dean H. Hamer, even went so far as to propose that a single gene, VMAT2, was responsible for our inclination toward faith or not. He wrote a book about it called *The God Gene*.

I felt liberated. No wonder faith had never been true to me. The realness of faith wasn't a choice. I chose and chose and chose. No amount of choosing, no amount of praying, no amount of hoping and trying and declaring by faith to have faith, had made God any more real to me. I realized people who did experience what they called God probably didn't choose that, either. Maybe some people could choose what they believed, and maybe that choice made it real to them on an experiential, undeniable level. But I certainly had never been able to accomplish such a feat. I came to see that I wasn't left out by God at all, or any other entity. There was never a sin in my life that kept God at bay, and it wasn't because I hadn't had enough faith that God never touched me. Maybe my assortment of genes simply wired me to be less inclined toward mystical experiences. The findings of neurotheology soothed the ten-year-old girl still beating herself up for being a faithless, lying poser.

As the calm reassurance of science helped mitigate doubts that had plagued me, slowly releasing Christianity of its lingering hold, I felt hopeful about life for the first time in a long time. I knew I might never be completely free of spiritual triggers. Even so, I appreciated what releases I found. Understanding how revival trances were debunked by the effects of hypnosis and placebo removed the sting of feeling ignored by God. Learning that the manifestations I'd called being slain in the Spirit were found elsewhere nullified their testament to the Christian faith. Discovering the choicelessness of faith left me overwhelmed with compassion for myself and others. We might never know what mystical experiences were, or why humans were capable of having them, but I had encountered enough broad evidence that put to rest any wariness of paranormal claims. That left Operation Three of Mission Rebuild: Find New Meaning for My Life.

For twenty-one years, my life's purpose had been to die to my flesh, advancing God's kingdom through spiritual warfare and womanly submission. Losing that purpose, however harmful it now seemed, had left a gaping void where there had once been meaning. Sometimes I missed it. I missed the security of believing in a master plan. I missed the assurance I would see deceased loved ones again. I missed the greater sense of mission I had been a part of. Believing there was a reason for my existence and a justification for not just my own suffering, but that of every being's, provided a framework that gave me the will to live. I never could have estimated how hard it would be to want to exist without the belief that there was something more.

I was in the midst of a heavy depression when I learned about Religious Trauma Syndrome. Creating new meaning for my life felt like an impossible task. Mine was the kind of depression that couldn't be named, an untraceable and immovable fury that made me feel there was no point to life. I couldn't just make up some arbitrary sense of meaning, like a quote stuck to a refrigerator. So, I decided to make a deal with myself. No declarations of meaning would be made, but whenever I felt my depression get near its breaking point, I would remind myself of something: Every day I did not commit suicide was a day I chose to be here. To be born might not have been a choice, but to die was, as long as there was no physical restraint holding me back. I knew some might find it a bleak perspective.

To me, it felt true, and therefore trustworthy. It proved far more effective than trying not to be depressed and creating meaning out of nothing. From then on, whenever my thoughts drifted toward taking my own life, I gave myself full permission to do so. I didn't fight the darkness of my mind. I thanked it, and doing so allowed me to see the brightness in the happenstance of my existence.

It wasn't instant. Finding meaning would be ongoing, I discovered, like learning self-love. But slowly, over the next several months as symptoms of religious trauma began to lessen, and everything I'd learned helped release me of lingering anger and confusion, my depression began to lift. I knew it might come back. It may always. Yet I dove into its depths and found myself floating. It felt like the ultimate mind game of reverse psychology, and for reasons I didn't know, it worked. Nihilism never felt so full of meaning. Pessimism never felt more bursting with optimism. Hope and faith had no place in my new worldview. I couldn't be shattered by what I never hoped for, and I couldn't be disappointed by what I was already skeptical of. Assuming the worst allowed me to appreciate all of life's bests, and there were many. Positive thinking had never worked for me, for it felt dangerously close to denial. Diving into the negative made everything sparkle with awe. Surrendering to the maddening pointlessness of existence made every beautiful accident in the universe seem utterly, profoundly magical. For me, the key to happiness lay in wonder. Instead of sending my mind into answerless spirals trying to find the meaning *of* life, maybe I needed to rephrase my quest as that of looking for meaning *in* life.

It was in the humbling awe of stars. The elating numbness of standing under a waterfall. The sun-drenched scent of a pine forest. It was in the purr of my cat and the laughter of my family. The friend-bonding closeness of firesides and wine. The sensuality of making love. It was in the elegance of ancient civilizations carved into limestone cliffs. The conversations relished while getting lost in a medieval city. The taste of raspberry ice cream on a hot summer day. These were where I found meaning in life.

In the years following my discovery of Religious Trauma Syndrome, I made a conscious effort to notice where I found wonder, for where I found wonder, I found meaning. I learned that my life's purpose was up to me and me alone. Because I no longer believed in a mystical reason for existence, I discovered my own reasons with what I could see, hear, feel, taste, and touch. I was taught to deny pleasures of the flesh. I came to realize the physical, material world I was told to fear and abstain from was the very thing that made me want to live. Sex, food, drink, and nature. Music, dance, books, and kisses. Family, friends, animals, cuddles, and the belief-shattering salve of science. These were where I found peace and awe. These were where I found fulfillment and love. In an irony I adored, it was the proverbial seven deadly sins that embodied these to me.

Gluttony, the enjoyment of food, was once denied in the form of spiritual fasting. Depriving myself of sustenance was supposed to drive me closer to God. I now savored food as one of life's daily delights and took joy in nourishing my body.

Vanity, the nurture of one's beauty, was especially condemned for me as a woman. I now embraced the freedom to beautify myself however I wished, whether with makeup or my wardrobe.

Envy, the desire to attain what others have, used to be considered toxic. Now I found breaking the tenth commandment and coveting my neighbor inspired me to take responsibility for myself, motivating me to create the life I wanted to live.

Sloth, perceived as laziness, used to spurn me to always be working for the Lord in all I did, to have a servant's heart, and put others before myself. I came to see that I was of no use to others if I didn't put myself first and take care of my needs, which included indulgent relaxation.

Lust once seemed the deadliest sin of all. It was my responsibility to guard the eyes of men by dressing modestly so I wasn't a pitfall of distraction. Yet I'd discovered healing in the power of my sensuality, and I found that sex and other forms of physical touch were among the most meaning-ful parts of being human.

Greed, the desire for money and material wealth, used to be shallow and selfish. The fear of being greedy coupled with my family's self-imposed poverty once instilled guilt around the money I made. I now saw nothing wrong with wanting a life of abundance, for it afforded me the ability to travel, to donate to causes I found worthwhile, and helped facilitate mak-ing the dreams of loved ones and myself come true.

Pride, thinking I was enough without God, was another of the most wicked of sins. I was taught that I was born with something wrong with me, that we all were, and that this deformity was called original sin. I came to develop a self-esteem that no longer doubted myself or my accom-plishments. I didn't think there was anything wrong with taking pride in one's work, and I finally believed there was nothing wrong with me. I was enough. I was worthy because I chose to exist and for no other reason.

The seven deadly sins became in many ways my seven saving graces.

Epilogue

"Who are you today?" a woman in my memoir group asked me.

I was twenty-seven and in the throes of writing this book. The pages I had submitted for that week's critique were from the panic attacks in my loft, followed by my reflections that I no longer trusted faith, hope, or love. It was the end of my book as I knew it. I had not yet learned about Religious Trauma Syndrome, and all I knew was that I needed to tell my story. I blinked at the women staring at me from across the table.

"We don't want to feel . . ." another woman said, trying to find the right words. "We don't want to think little Alice became bitter."

"But I am bitter," I said, mincing not a second owning up to their fear. "This is what happened."

Silence filled the room. Disappointment flickered through their eyes, but only for a brief moment, their gentle nods and downturned gazes eliciting the warmth of a sad understanding. If I was bitter, I was bitter, and they knew why. I wondered if I'd make a horrible memoir writer.

I am now thirty-three years old at the time of this writing, dear reader. I'm near the end of my Jesus year, as Christians in the know might say. Jesus died at age thirty-three. Supposedly that was when he also rose again. If Religious Trauma Syndrome was a death, I am happy to tell you, I have risen. I am not bitter. Life has only gotten more meaningful, and Mission Rebuild was a smashing success. Even though there will always be hardships, struggles, and tragedies, I know I'll be okay.

Since I know you're probably wondering how the rest of my family ended up, I thought I'd give you a recap on where they are all at today. This story is (almost) as much theirs as it is mine. Let's start with my siblings.

Teddy, now thirty-one, has never settled down from the momentum that began when we were children. The places he's lived as an adult include Southeast Asia, Spain, and presently Northern California. The job titles he's held include painter, tattooist, stage designer, ranch hand, and farmer. He is always an artist.

Madeleine, thirty, lived in Alaska as an ice climbing guide after graduating from college. She now lives in Kauai, Hawaii, where she got her captain's license and gives boat tours of the breathtaking Na Pali coast. She spearfishes in her spare time and loves taking home medals from Brazilian jiu-jitsu tournaments.

Bryant, twenty-eight, finds structure and sense of purpose through his service work as a wildland firefighter. Spring through fall, he travels by bus and helicopter to forest fires throughout the American wilderness, and in the winter, he enjoys the nightlife of Denver. Tinkering on his truck and dirt bikes keep his free time occupied.

Kate, twenty-six, ended up joining me in Hollywood. She landed her dream job right out of college as an art director of TV and movie posters at one of the industry's top marketing agencies. When she's not working, she loves playing video games, hanging out with her cats, and joining me on day trips to Malibu for hiking and Thai food.

My siblings are the greatest gift my parents gave me. Our unusual childhood, limbs tangled in cars by day and sleeping bags overlapped in tents by night, gave us the bond of a uniquely shared experience, a closeness that has lasted well into adulthood. We understand the world we came from. We now play together in the worlds we have chosen, traveling together, partying together, and always being there for one another. Far-flung we may be, but we make conscious efforts to stay in touch and visit each other often. None of us are married or have children yet. All of us are agnostics or atheists. For Teddy, it was coming out as bisexual that led to his abandonment of Christianity, following a brief and failed attempt at conversion therapy. For Madeleine, it was God's refusal to end her recurring nightmares, accompanied by feeling like there were too many rules to follow. Bryant tells me he never really believed in God and that church was always more of a social outlet for him. When I asked Kate what changed her faith, her answer was blunt. "My period," she said. "No God could make girls have to have cramps for most of their lives."

Each of my family members could write their own memoir, and each would have a different version of our story. Teddy remembers our childhood as a wilderness adventure interspersed by church. Madeleine would tell you she doesn't know what the fuck church was all about, but she liked traveling. Bryant and Kate, the youngest two, don't remember as much from our nomadic years, and both consider themselves having grown up in Colorado with relative stability. None of my brothers or sisters took faith as seriously as I did. Why, we don't know, and I'm content to chalk it up to personality differences. I was the one who got the figurine of a child kneeling in prayer the year Nannie's annual tradition of sending us personalized Christmas ornaments came from the porcelain Snowbabies collection. Everyone else's figurine was engaged in some other, more fun activity, like throwing snowballs or shoveling stars. Maybe it was because I was the oldest. Maybe I simply took things too literally and to heart, including the Bible. I still don't understand how some people can read certain verses as metaphor and others as factual truth, but my parents say I was always a deep-thinking kid who asked endless questions.

My parents. Yes, I know you're wondering about them. Where are they now? Are we close?

Mom and Dad are still married. They still travel the great outdoors. They are not still entrenched in Christianity. That my parents are different from the people who raised me is an understatement, and whenever anyone asks me how our relationship is, especially after hearing I'm no longer a Christian, I take delight in surprising them with the answer.

"My parents aren't Christians anymore," I say. "They're still pretty spiritual, but one of the things I admire most about them is their willingness to grow. So we're very close."

It's the truth.

Dad still considers himself a Christian "foundationally," but admits he's "a bit further out there than most." He still uses the language of Christianity to describe his relationship with God, but it's a different relationship than the one he had when I was growing up. My father no longer believes accepting Jesus into one's heart is the only way to heaven. He isn't even sure there is a heaven. He wants there to be a joyous afterlife of sorts where loved ones will see each other again, but he admits he just doesn't know what's waiting for us. He still believes in God because the profoundness of his conversion still rings with truth to him. When the fracture in his leg healed overnight from the motorcycle accident that caused it, Dad was convinced it was his renewed faith that allowed such a miracle. I once asked him what he thought of the possibility that maybe his bone fracture simply happened to fuse into invisibility that evening. He shrugged.

"Yeah, maybe," he said with a smile. "But I think it was God."

Dad and I are now comfortable talking about the faith we used to share. I barely spoke to him in the year following my betrothal to Luke, because although I loved my dad and knew without a doubt that he loved me, I hadn't trusted my own ability not to see him as a godly authority I had disobeyed. Dad has apologized more than once for giving Luke his blessing to marry me. At the time, Dad says, he thought I must have wanted it. We've reached a place where we can laugh about it now, in a rueful sort of way. I've forgiven his misinterpretation of God's guidance.

Mom remains very private and prefers not to share any of her life publicly. Expressly stated, my mother would have chosen not to be a part of this story at all. Her acknowledgment of how difficult it would be to cut her out of it completely, as well as her unwavering support of me being true to myself, are acts of grace few memoir writers may be lucky to receive. Despite the differences of our recollections, both Mom and Dad are very supportive of me and we have retained a close relationship.

Many kids who leave their parents' faith or write a book about their upbringing cannot say the same. I know how deeply fortunate I am to have parents committed to never letting our differences come between our love for one another.

Mom and Dad had no idea how damaging certain aspects of Christianity were to my siblings and me. I was shocked when Mom told me she never believed in hell. Dad had believed in hell but said that for him it was more symbolic. Mom insisted she hadn't believed in hell at all.

"What?" I asked her, incredulous. "Even as a Christian?"

Mom shook her head. "No, I never did. I believed in God, but whenever pastors would start talking about Satan and all that spiritual warfare stuff, I just tuned out." Her tone turned somber. "I might have paid more attention to what you were absorbing had I known what they were teaching you."

Mom wishes she had been more vigilant about what my siblings and I were being taught in the many children's ministries we attended. While she and Dad were being slain by the Spirit, which they came to think of as working through their childhood wounds in a mass spiritual setting, they thought their kids were merely being babysat by people who sent us home with crayoned drawings of Bible stories. They didn't know we were also being force-fed ideology in preparation for an imminent spiritual war. They didn't know the fear that was instilled in us. If they had, they said, they would have made more of an effort to shield us from it.

I didn't know how I felt when they expressed this. I recognized a flicker of anger—what the fuck, guys, you never believed in actual hell?!—followed by the tempering admission of retrospect. Although spiritual warfare had been the driving force behind many a children's sermon and youth group meeting, beating Satan and his army hadn't been much of a conversation at home. My parents' faith had always been more focused on the faithfulness of God than the fear of hell. Even so, they didn't fault me for taking literally as a child what they as adults saw as metaphor. They only wished they had thought to explain their interpretation of the demonic more clearly to us.

I once asked them what their interpretation was.

"Hell is right here on earth," my father had said. Mom had spoken of demons as symbolic of what God didn't want for us, believing the God of love she knew wouldn't send anyone into a lake of fire. She saw those parts of the Bible as pure allegory.

How my parents, siblings, and I went to the same churches and came away with completely different experiences is just one more testament to the diversity of neurological makeup. It is also indicative of the difference between being born into a belief system, where your brain develops in that framework, and choosing it as a fully developed adult like my parents had, better equipped to discard any aspects that don't ring true. When I was a child, everything rang true to me. Why would people be saying things they didn't mean? Jesus said to let your yes be a yes and your no be a no.

That my parents and I can talk about our spiritual differences with respect is something I don't take for granted. Sometimes our reminisces are filled with laughter as we swap memories of our travels. Other times they're trickled with tears of fresh understanding and forgiveness. I have come to see them not just as my parents, the pastor and homeschool teacher who raised my siblings and me on the road. They are also Ted and Jane, an attractive couple who have led an unconventional life from the suburbs to the mission field to the inner cities and the backwoods. Viewing them as I imagine strangers might gives me a broader perspective of them. They were two average Americans, a police officer and a piano teacher, who fell in love, had a family, and got heavily involved in a spiritual revival for a while. It happened.

～

As for me? I still live in Los Angeles. I still act, though work has gotten sparser, but no one said making art would make a steady living. The meaning of my life continues to be found in wonder. Nature, science, and love are where I most find awe. My circle of friends amazes me. They're like a second family, and I'm so glad I overcame my fear of intimacy and decided to let people in. I cherish deeply the individuals who have enriched my life in ways I can't put to words. In romance, I have also been lucky, sharing my heart—and yes, my body, free of shame—with men who have shown me it is okay to be vulnerable. It is okay to challenge them and be challenged. It is okay to form bonds and healthy emotional attachments. Who knows, I may even get married and have a family one day.

Though I feel happier than I've ever been, there are still times I wrestle with the aftereffects of religious trauma. I suspect I always may. Triggers reveal themselves at unsuspecting moments—a friend talking about their kundalini yoga practice, a live band asking an audience to throw their hands in the air, a game of Dungeons & Dragons where fickle gods betray loyal followers. I've learned to thank my body for sending me signals of alarm. I've learned to breathe through the discomfort and to run my hands under cold water when breathing isn't enough.

I've also learned that words like "trigger" and "trauma" sound harsh to those who still find comfort in religion, or to people who think those like myself were merely brought up on Bible stories. Our childhoods were so much more than that. Trauma, I've learned, is not an event itself, but the internalization of an event. Religious Trauma Syndrome's comparison to complex post-traumatic stress disorder (C-PTSD) is an accurate one. PTSD is usually the result of one major event, such as a sexual assault, a military battle, or a car accident. C-PTSD occurs as the result of many events happening over a prolonged period of time. Certainly not all former Christians feel traumatized, and not all who leave their faith experience symptoms of Religious Trauma Syndrome. For those of us who do internalize the more harmful aspects of religion, the shattering of faith can be difficult to overcome. Yet experience tells me it can get easier.

My recovery from religion has been a slow but steady journey. It took years for me to come to terms with my past and create a desirable future for myself. With the help of mental health professionals, family, and friends, I am still healing. People are my healers. Not gods. I define my purpose.

Not faith. The fleshly world I once feared and condemned is now where I rejoice with my fellow humans as we navigate, mourn, and celebrate this gift-burden we call life. And though I still find comfort in philosophical nihilism and pessimism, life does feel more like a gift. No one can answer my deepest question for me. The meaning of life is whatever I can make it.

Dare to Doubt

dare • *verb*
> 1. to have sufficient courage
> 2. to confront boldly

doubt • *verb*
> 1. to call into question the truth of
> 2. to lack confidence in

—Dictionary by Merriam-Webster

If there is one thing, dear reader, that I hope you might take with you when you put down this book, it is this: Dare to doubt. Dare to ask questions. Dare to seek answers. If it doesn't feel true to you, don't waste your precious time trying to make it so.

Helping others leave belief systems they come to find harmful is where I find my greatest sense of purpose. In March of 2019, I founded DaretoDoubt.org, a resource site for people healing from the damage of indoctrination. Dare to Doubt exists to connect those recovering from religion-gone-wrong with mental health professionals, aid organizations, and peer support groups who can help. If you've ever struggled with the ramifications of questioning or leaving your faith, this site is for you.

I didn't intend to start a not-for-profit. I knew I wanted to help other ex-believers reorient themselves during or after a spiritual transition, but I had imagined supporting an existing organization; never starting one myself. As I found myself unable to narrow my passion for one singular group or nonprofit, it became clear to me: I wanted to shed light on the many organizations offering support for people like my twenty-one-year-old self. People who were shattered, overwhelmed, and in need of help. People who didn't know where to turn, because the kind of help we need is taboo in a society that glorifies God in everything from our currency to our national anthem. People who mustered the courage to think for themselves and found they could no longer belong to a belief system that went against their conscience.

From Christianity to Islam, Mormonism to Scientology, more people are leaving religion than ever before. These former believers cite many reasons for why they left their faith—the inexplicable death of a loved one, the realization they weren't heterosexual, the betrayal of a trusted spiritual leader. Often, it is the slow unraveling of numerous events and secretly banished thoughts that, at some tipping point, can no longer be ignored. A furtive internet search punctures the notion of Earth's age. The taste of a forbidden food brings no consequence. A sweetheart's kiss defies the warnings of purity culture. Global connectivity through web browsers and airplanes sows seeds of doubt at a rate our species may have never encountered before. These encounters are upsetting the status quo that has governed humanity for millennia.

Today, the fastest-growing religious group in the United States is the religiously unaffiliated. Seventy-eight percent of those who identify as "none" were raised in a religion, and six in ten Millennials leave the faith of their childhoods. I was merely one of them. This scattered demographic is scarred and estranged. They flood online message boards with stories of abuse, betrayal, and shame. They connect on Twitter through sweeping hashtags like #ExMuslimBecause and #Exvangelical. They bond in anonymous Facebook groups wondering how to come out as nonbelievers to their families.

Yet this demographic is also resilient. We are as brave as the martyrs we were raised to be. We are battling the spiritual war we were trained to fight. We're just not on the side of religion, and believe us—no one is more surprised by this than ourselves. We are condemned, prayed for, and loathed as much as we are feared. But persecution was once our fuel. Our skin is thick with the courage to fight for truth as we see it, and where we once saw through dogma-colored glasses, we now see through the lenses of relativity, reason, and the validity of our own experiences. It is easy to dismiss us as bitter. It is understandable to write off our deconversions as desperate attempts at individuation and rebellion. It is compassionate to ask us why we left, instead of praying for us to rejoin.

Maybe your faith is more solid than ever. Maybe you have nagging questions you can no longer push aside. Maybe you've been a closeted atheist for decades. No matter where you are in your spiritual journey or lack thereof, it is my sincerest wish that you are simply living in your truth. My observation tells me truth evolves. Sometimes this is because we let it, while other times truth changes because life changes, and what we once held dear as fact is no longer supported by the evidence of our experiences. True humility, I think, is giving ourselves permission to question, and to face the answers we find with brave vulnerability.

The shattering of a belief system can be one of life's greatest blows. If you could use the guidance of a professional therapist, secular or faith-friendly; if you could use the safety of an LGBTQ-affirming domestic shelter, whether for a couple of nights or a couple of months; if you could just use someone to talk to, someone who gets the world you came from, there are people waiting to help. Numerous free hotlines and places of refuge exist solely to offer you support. Visit www.DaretoDoubt.org, where you can find resources based on your immediate needs or your spiritual background. You are not alone.

If God is real to you, I am not trying to take away your faith. Neither do I mean you any disrespect. In fact, I am deeply honored that you even picked up this book, especially if you believe it might be spiritually dangerous. Thank you for being willing to hear my story. Thank you for listening. As one of many voices, I am humbled to contribute to our growing conversation about the unintended consequences of spiritual belief.

As I hope I've made clear, I think the experience of God can be viscerally real to many people. I only hope you might be able to accept that he, she, them, or it is not real to everyone, and it is not their fault. It is not even necessarily their choice. It is their truth. May we all have the courage to find and live in our own.

Acknowledgments

To my family . . .

Mom and Dad, words aren't enough to express the gratitude I hold for your love, provision, and support. You always encouraged us, your children, to follow our hearts. You lived and continue to live that example. Thank you infinitely for your ongoing commitment to me.

Teddy, thank you for always expanding my mind and never letting shame hide your truth. You inspire me to grow in ways I wouldn't have allowed myself without the example of your courage. You're my first sibling and my longest friend, and this book wouldn't exist without your generous investment in its making.

Madeleine, your boldness and strength leave me in awe. Thank you for always being there for me with sound advice, staunch support, and plans for fun at the ready. Life without a Madeleine is a life without adventure, and I'm so damn grateful I get to call you my sister.

Bryant, my pride knows no bounds when I speak of you. Your rigorous self-discipline motivates me to always do more than I think I can, and your reliability and humor make you a gift to all lucky enough to know you. Thank you for sharing your quiet wisdom with me.

Kate, you might be my baby sister, but you're one of my greatest teachers. I'm stunned by your tenacity and your talent. Your honesty and drive remind me never to underestimate the power of self-commitment. Thank you for your constancy through thick and thin.

I love you all. Thank you for letting me tell my version of our story.

To my friends . . .

Brigida Santos D'Agostino, if it wasn't for you, I never would have signed up for the fateful writing class that inspired this memoir. Thank you for being my other set of eyes and my sister from another mister. The pages of my life would be empty without you in them.

Devon Graye, for the countless drafts of this book you read, the opinions you never made me feel like I was imposing upon, and your endless praise, truly, I thank you. Your feedback validated why I needed to write this book. Your friendship enriches my life beyond measure.

Taryn Southern, thank you for always cheering me on this journey with a gleeful fist pump and the exhortation to ruthlessly tell my truth! Your advice throughout this process was invaluable. You inspire me in everything you do and I'm so grateful for your magic in my world.

I'd also like to thank Grey Damon, whose supportiveness kept me from giving up and whose generosity made moving forward possible; Carolyn Dennis-Willingham, whose feedback on early drafts I can't express my gratitude for; Christian Ivanov, who patiently listened to long sections read out loud while keeping me fed; Jeff D'Agostino, Caitlin Campbell, Derick James, Diane Gaeta, Jordan Gavaris, Robert Adamson, and Adria Olaiz, all of whom nurtured my story and offered the respite of their friendship when I needed a break; and Butters, whose purrs and biscuits comforted me through my hardest pages.

To my creative team . . .

For their pivotal contributions to the making of this book, I'd like to extend my deepest thanks to Leslie Schwartz, the writing teacher who convinced me my story was more than an anecdotal cookbook; the ladies of Leslie's writing group (you know who you are!), whose gracious critiques shaped some of my most important pages; Adam Griffin, Ryan Bundra, and Cindy Collins, the reps who believed in my memoir from day one; Laurie Chittenden, whose editorial guidance made a far-too-long manuscript readable; Melissa Nasson, my brilliant attorney who introduced me to the relief of "transformative use"; and photographer and friend Randall Slavin, who persuaded me to give hybrid publishing a second look. Thank you, all.

To my incredible team at River Grove Books and Greenleaf Book Group, thank you for taking a chance on an unknown author. You have far exceeded my hopes and expectations in every way. I'd especially like to thank Kesley Smith, who first reached out to me on Twitter; Danny Sandoval, who patiently walked me through the publishing process; Jen Glynn, whose supportive diligence as project manager kept everything on track; Lindsey Clark, my lead editor who eased my anxieties with her understanding and supportiveness; Ava Coibion, whose editorial prowess whittled my pages into a real book; Stephanie Bouchard, whose helpful proofread went above and beyond correcting typos; Cameron Stein, who designed a cover more gorgeous and laced with impact than I ever dreamed, and an interior to match; Stephanie Smylnarski, Tyler LeBleu, Sujan Trivedi, and Tiffany Barrientos who each contributed to making my first publishing experience an utter joy; and Greenleaf Book Group CEO Tanya Hall, for building a publishing model that aligned with my conscience. I'm so proud to see my first book alongside your titles.

Lastly . . .

To every single person who fed me, clothed me, or sheltered me, thank you. To the friends who offered me companionship in the many new places I arrived, thank you. To my beloved chosen family, you hedonistic heathens who give my life meaning every day, thank you. To my former boyfriends and lovers, for your patience and your passion, thank you. To the multi-faceted ex-religious community of Twitter and Instagram; to the skeptics, neuroscientists, and evolutionary psychologists demystifying what we call faith; and to the doctors and counselors working to validate religious trauma, thank you. You have impacted me.

And to my partner, Ryan Essmaker, who has ruined my life by making it too good to be true . . . Thank you. Your advice throughout this experience gave me confidence. Your understanding and adoration give me wings. You make existence seem short and love seem eternal.

Finally, I'd like to thank me. Yes, me. Thank you, Little Me, for letting Older Me revisit you. Thank you for letting her pry open trunks you wanted to keep shut, pick away scabs you had almost turned to scars, and listen to you the way you always wanted to be heard. You were enough the whole time and there was never anything wrong with you.

About the Author

ALICE GRECZYN is an actress, writer, and the founder of Dare to Doubt. Born in Walnut Creek, California, Alice's nomadic childhood moved her around the United States until her modeling career as a teenager led to an acting career in Hollywood. Alice is fascinated by the subjective experience of life which she explores through acting and storytelling. Her own story includes a painful yet rewarding transition from Christianity to atheism, a journey that inspired her to found DaretoDoubt.org, a resource site for people detaching from belief systems they come to find harmful. Encouraging people to trust themselves and live courageously in their own truth is what gives Alice a sense of purpose. She lives in Los Angeles and loves hiking, traveling, and the relentless pursuit of knowledge.